Groupwork

Perspectives and Practice

Groupwork
Perspectives and Practice

Harry Wright
RMN
Cassel Hospital Cert in Psychodynamic and Family Centred Nursing,
ENB Cert in Psychodynamic Techniques
Clinical Nurse Specialist in Psychotherapy
Powys Health Authority

SCUTARI PRESS

All rights reserved. No part of this publication may
be reproduced, stored in a retrieval system or
transmitted, in any form or by any means, electronic,
mechanical, photocopying or otherwise, without the
prior permission of Scutari Press, Viking House,
17–19 Peterborough Road, Harrow, Middlesex, HA1 2AX,
England

First published 1989

British Library Cataloguing in Publication Data
Wright, Harry
  Groupwork.
  1. Medicine. Group therapy
  I. Title
  616.89'152

ISBN 1-871364-03-5

Typeset by MC Typeset Limited, Gillingham, Kent
Printed and bound in Great Britain by The Alden Press, Oxford

Contents

Foreword

Psychiatric nurses are becoming increasingly concerned to improve the quality of the treatment they provide for their patients whether it be in individual psychotherapy and counselling, in group and family therapy or in institutions, notably therapeutic communities. At first it was by no means easy for nurses to get appropriate training for such work although much more is now available. The author has been in the forefront of these developments. As a teacher now himself he came to the conclusion that there was no suitable comprehensive textbook available for his students, so he decided to write one – the book, as he says, that he would have liked to have had when he was beginning his own work in this field.

The book represents the distillation of years of hard and thoughtful work, in clinical practice, in absorbing, understanding and extending theory, and in teaching, and it is indeed comprehensive. It begins with a review of the development of the individual from birth, with his mother, in his family and so out into the wider world around him. Links are made between developmental experiences and psychopathology and so to the impact that psychotherapy has on the individual. He next goes on to consider extensively the theory and practice of groups and the nature of their potential therapeutic effect. He provides a practical guide for people who conduct groups. Throughout he stresses the importance of being in touch with the latent content of the group processes if one is to understand and further the progress of group members. Finally, he extends his perspective to include the interaction between groups and the functioning of institutions particularly, but not only, therapeutic communities.

The author set himself a very ambitious objective involving an enormous amount of work. He has gone a very long way in achieving that objective. His wide reading and knowledge of relevant theories are apparent. The clinical examples from situations as diverse as the mother–child relationship and social institutions are vivid and appropriate; his concern for people, be they patient, student or others is very apparent. He has made good use of his own training experiences to guide him towards providing a significant textbook for his successors. His devotion to and enthusiasm for his work, particularly writing this book, are very clear.

I have enjoyed the book and am sure that others, not only nurses, will enjoy it and find it useful.

Isabel Menzies Lyth

Preface

This book grew out of a one-year course in Group Work and Family Therapy that I had been running for some years, and from my own abiding fascination with human behaviour and relationships. Whilst there is a wealth of material written about groups, there did not seem to be one single text which explained their functions and processes, nor the origins of group dynamics, in any cogent form. There did not appear to be a text which took the reader from the beginning in the maternal relationship, through the family, to the outside world. I wanted to provide my students with a book which would help them make sense of their experiences on the course, and which would deepen the understanding that they gained from the lectures. In many ways, it is the book which I wanted for myself when I was setting out on my career as a group worker.

The aim of this book is to follow the individual from birth through to adulthood so that we can identify important formative influences and psychological processes as they occur. As we witness these developmental milestones we can examine their relevance to groups. Later, when we focus upon groups more closely, we shall see how many of the psychological and developmental processes which we identified in the life of the individual are re-enacted in the life of the group, thus making it possible for all the group's members to rework and come to terms with earlier, unsatisfactory experiences.

There are many useful texts in the field of group work, and many models which help us to understand groups, so that there is a varied body of opinion which can seem bewildering. I have tried to draw the most important and helpful ideas from the main texts and place them in context so that the reader can readily see the similarities or differences between them. However, these ideas are presented in an introductory form, and, whilst this provides a solid and substantial background, it cannot replace the original works. A list of references is given at the end of each chapter to encourage the reader to explore some of these exciting and informative texts.

Some people maintain that group work can only take place within therapeutic groups, that is, in meetings which have been set up to work through the emotional problems of its members. I have tried to establish that all who work with gatherings of people are working with groups, and consequently that a knowledge of group structures and dynamics is essential to all managers, whether they work primarily in the administrative or the clinical arena.

I hope that I have fulfilled my aim to instil as basic to our thinking the notion that society is a relevant field of study and one does not have to be a 'therapist' to work with groups therapeutically. The role of the conductor, for instance, is applicable to the nurse in charge of the ward; and the informal gatherings of people which assemble throughout the day are groups which can be managed in a way that promotes health. The work of the conductor-as-therapist is examined in the book and the tremendous value to be gained from therapy groups is acknowledged and explained.

The final part explores the application of theories of groups to management systems and therapeutic communities. The intention is to show how a good grounding in group work practice can help us to manage the ward, unit, hostel, etc. more effectively and more therapeutically for all involved with them. It is interesting to note that there is an obvious correlation between what is humane and what is most effective in the long run, and that a *laissez-faire* attitude is often confused with being humane. These and other misperceptions are acknowledged and investigated so that we can see more clearly what is helpful and what is not.

If there is one basic viewpoint, or set of values, which I would wish the reader to take from this text it is that all who work in the field of human relationships should adhere to the principles of constancy and continuity of care within a predictable relationship. A continuing relationship with someone who is valued is tremendously helpful to those with emotional problems. Through this continuing and predictable relationship it becomes possible to work through and overcome many difficulties. In other words, if we arrange to see someone at a certain time, then we should be there. If we say we shall do something, then we should do it.

I have a debt of gratitude to the many teachers who have helped me along the way. In particular I would wish to thank Doreen Clifford (*née* Martin) formerly Matron of the Cassel Hospital, Dr Tom Main who was Medical Director of the Cassel during my time there, Beau Stevenson who introduced me to the work of S H Foulkes and has become a good friend, Danny Fourdwour who had the thankless task of being my supervisor, and Isabel Menzies Lyth who has contributed so much to our understanding of society's role in human development.

This book would not have been written without the help of Mrs Friedl Brown, who knows how much I learned from her.

Lastly, my thanks are due to my family for their tolerant responses to my many intolerant requests for quiet.

Harry Wright

Introduction

Over the past few years colleagues in a variety of professions, and especially in nursing, have been aware of an increasing interest in work which includes an understanding of the emotional life of the patient, his relationships and their role in the problems that beset him. In recent years we have seen the establishment of several new organisations for those interested in psychodynamic work. These include the Association for Psychodynamic Psychotherapy within the NHS and two new bodies within nursing – the Nurses Association for Psychodynamic Psychotherapy and the Psychodynamic Interest Group which has been set up within the Royal College of Nursing. The syllabus for psychiatric nurse training now requires students to be introduced to family, counselling and group work skills in greater depth than ever before. There is a more profound awareness of the need for nurses to view their patients as 'whole' people whose emotional life is as important as any physical ailment.

This book has been written with these concerns in mind and, it is hoped, to fulfil the need in nursing for a sound introduction to group work and the theories of development which underpin it. However, this book is not designed to be used solely by nurses; each chapter is relevant to *all* who wish to develop their skill in working with and understanding groups.

A background to practical group work is given in case studies with a number of groups at different stages during their lives. Our knowledge of why work is undertaken in groups and why it is productive is furthered by illustrating the links between psychodynamic theories of human emotional development and therapeutic practice.

Psychodynamic theories are firmly rooted in the solid ground of observed human experience from birth onwards, as will be shown by the accounts given of the relationship that grew between an ordinary mother and her baby. The word 'ordinary' is used to acknowledge that the mother and her child were just like the rest of us, they were not selected because of any particular qualities that the mother was known to possess. However, the observer became aware of the very special nature of the relationship as it changed and developed throughout the year of his observations. He regards himself as being very fortunate to have witnessed the unfolding of this ordinary miracle of life.

THE BOOK PLAN

The book has been written in four parts which are designed to be read consecutively. They trace the development of the individual from the early maternal relationship, through his widening relationships with his family and thence into the world outside the home. Having established this we move on to examine group development, phenomena and process and to consider some practical matters such as selection, the role of the conductor, and so on. The four parts are delineated as follows:

Part I

In this part particular attention is paid to individual and family development and to the family as a group. The theories that we consider here are supported by case material and observations from clinical work with families and others. By observing the ordinary we can see how the unusual occurs – how unsatisfactory experiences in childhood produce emotional debility in later years. From this we can understand why therapeutic methods which acknowledge the importance of developmental issues are effective.

Part II

Here we follow on from Part I by showing how the forms of relationship established in the family are repeated in groups. The similarities between individual, family and group development are examined and relationship patterns which were founded in family life are identified as observable group phenomena and group processes.

   The reader will benefit if the book and particularly this part is read with his or her own family of origin in mind, as many of the processes described apply to all families and their individual members. This part closes with an examination of the role of the group conductor, his responsibilities and his relationship to the group. The meaning of the title 'conductor' is examined and clarified.

Part III

Having looked at how individuals and groups develop, we move on to think about the practical considerations which are an integral part of group work. We explore the importance of the setting in which groups are held, how to assess for admission to groups, and how to understand the various levels of communication, including the symbolic. We consider what facilities and opportunities might help us in our work.

   The importance of training and clinical supervision to those who want to work in groups is considered, and the question of whether or not some personal experience of therapy is necessary to all those who work with groups is examined.

Part IV

In this part the practical issues which face group workers are developed further by looking at everyday, informal, fluid groups and at productive styles of management and therapeutic communities. It includes a final chapter on beginning as a group worker to encourage the novice to recognise and accept his own anxieties and to value them as clues to what other people in the group may be feeling.

THE FUNCTION OF THE BOOK

This book may be used as an introductory text which provides useful guidelines that may be followed safely if they are used sensibly, thoughtfully and appropriately. It is not intended to be used as an instruction manual or a step-by-step guide on how to 'do' groups. Successful work in the field of human relationships begins with the recognition that everyone is an individual and there is no easily applied formula which can be followed. Skill in this field is gained through maturity, a sound knowledge of one's own feelings, strengths, abilities and shortcomings; it is gained through being able to approach each person with integrity, an openness of purpose and a willingness to *listen*.

Whilst this book is not intended to replace training courses – and indeed emphasises the importance of training – it may be used as a resource by those in training, or by established practitioners, to help them think about, identify and understand group behaviour. It can be read from cover to cover, and has been written sequentially so that to do so makes sense, or it may be 'dipped into' to help the group worker identify a particular phenomenon or process.

It has been written in the knowledge that, as we all work with a great variety of groups every day, an understanding of the dynamics of group life is of tremendous value to anyone who is in charge of a ward, unit, hostel or home. It is intended to help those who work with groups as managers, as well as those who wish to work as group conductors in therapy groups.

Throughout the book I have tried to acknowledge the contributions of women in the professions, in society and in the family. Many of the case presentations which are used to illustrate the theoretical part of the text come from the work of women colleagues and have been chosen because they are particularly clear and helpful. However throughout the text I have stayed with the convention of using 'he' as the generic pronoun unless it is apparent that the subject is female. This is simply a matter of convenience and does not reflect any particular attitude of mine.

PART I
From the Family to the Group

1

The Child and the Mother

We all, individually and as groups, contrive to employ processes and mechanisms which we first learned in infancy. We also tend to respond to and deal with others in the same way that we learned to deal with members of our family. This relating to others 'as if' they were members of our own family, or other important figures from the past, need not create problems. Where relationships were satisfactory in the past then present and future relationships will most likely be so too. But where they were unsatisfactory, then it is probable that all future relationships will be tainted with dissatisfaction and difficulty. Consequently it is necessary to understand the origin of these processes and mechanisms, what functions they serve, and how they operate if we are to make sense of the working of groups. We also need to discover how families grow and develop if we wish to make sense of the changing patterns in the life of the group.

THE FIRST MONTHS OF LIFE

The newly-born baby begins life with a hazy sense of self, or 'rudimentary ego' (Klein, 1952). This dawning self-awareness is established in the womb as the baby becomes aware of a variety of sensations. He can feel with all of his skin, but he has no corresponding feeling from the surfaces he touches. In this way he can build up a dreamy picture of what is me and not me (in French the ego is called 'le moi'; simply, 'the me'), and so begin to form a notion of himself as both separate from and part of something else. This sense of self is incipient at first, so that there is muddle and confusion between me and not me, inside and outside, fantasy and reality. The newly-born baby has spent nine months within the vessel of his mother's womb. In consequence it would be hard for him to have a firmly established view of himself as both separate and independent. His sense of touch has informed him of the limit of his own envelope, but he was held within the enveloping womb. The womb was outside of him, yet he was inside it as well as inside his own skin. Furthermore, he was suspended within the warmly surrounding sea of amniotic fluid, and in foetal respiration (the process by which the foetus inspirates amniotic fluid to further the development of the lungs) he inhaled it, and in this way he surrounded it. It is difficult for the baby to achieve anything more than a vague self-awareness and perhaps a sense of himself as being interconnected with . . . something.

Alongside this growing sense of self other views and notions, or indistinct dream-thoughts (Bion, 1962), occur. The baby has a sense of being within himself, within a container, of the boundaries between himself and the container being indistinct (through foetal respiration), yet also definite (through the contact between himself and the wall of the womb). This rich confusion of experiences makes it possible for the baby to believe that he can separate a part of himself from the rest and then push out that part of himself into a receptive vessel. This is where the defence mechanisms of *splitting* and *projection* begin. When the baby is born he brings to his world a wealth of instinctual drives and impulses which are necessary to his survival and include drives towards the gratification of his need for food, physical and emotional warmth, and the mitigation of anxiety. Anxiety is a product of the tension which results from internal conflicts and the welter of new experiences which the baby faces when he is born into our world of sound, sight and sensation.

Let us think a little about these internal conflicts. Each of us is aware of having loving, kind, generous, warm, helpful, hopeful, joyous thoughts, wishes and feelings. Most of us would prefer to see ourselves in this positive light. Yet we know that we also give way to envy, jealousy, anger, spite and aggressive and destructive feelings which we would prefer to deny or conceal from ourselves and from others. We do not like to see or show ourselves in this negative light. As adults we have learned to integrate both of these aspects (the positive and the negative) of ourselves into a reasonably well-balanced whole. In the infant they exist as a sort of primal swamp which heaves with good and bad feelings, often in opposition one to the other. The bad feelings – that is, the aggressive and destructive impulses – are perceived as a threat to the continuing survival of the infant. The baby fears that they may overwhelm him and his good feelings, and so he feels anxious and afraid. Klein (1946) called this state the 'paranoid schizoid position'.

The baby deals with anxiety in a number of ways. First, there is a fantasy that the bad feelings can be split off from the good feelings. This develops into a consequent fantasy that the unwanted feelings can be expelled into a container. Usually the infant will imaginatively dispose of bad feelings in this way, although at times he may do the same with good feelings in order to protect them from the awesome force of his infantile rage.

It is the mother who rescues him from the ravages of his aggressive drives and it is she who becomes the container of his unwanted feelings. Through her constancy and her consistency, and via the medium of her love, she becomes a faithful, helpful, external presence. She comforts her baby during his worst moments, holds him safe, is not destroyed by his destructive outbursts and feeds him with milk from her own breasts so that his sense of inner goodness is replenished and strengthened. In consequence her predictability gives the baby a sense of inner certainty, of his own ability to continue and survive. Gradually, as he is able to relinquish his desperate need to control access to his mother, he is able to see her as separate and distinct from himself. As his inner certainty of his mother's continuing presence outside develops, so the baby is able to tolerate intervals of increasing length without her. He is able to call upon the memory of a helpful mother, a mummy inside, to help him deal with frustration and anxiety. He learns also, through his mother's survival as well as his own, that his destructive impulses are not necessarily as overwhelming as he had feared.

The mother also has another function here. By allowing her child to experience anxiety and frustration for just enough time she encourages in him the realisation that all his anxieties do not need a mother's presence to make them safe.

Here is an account taken from two sessions of baby observations, which show how one mother managed to help her baby to begin to cope with frustration.

Baby Kay

This observation was made when Kay was eight weeks old.

● . . . Mum said that Kay probably wanted feeding, having only taken half of that morning's feed. She placed Kay in her cot on her back and went to make up the bottle. Kay sucked hungrily at her thumb, forcing her head forward to fit her mouth around it. She made grunting sounds and her movements became more rapid, the sucking deeper until she began to cry. Several times she regained her thumb and the process was repeated with her apparently becoming very frustrated with it. After a time she seemed to look into the middle distance and looked ready for sleep.

Mum returned with the bottle and lifted Kay from the cot. Kay quietened at once and seemed to be looking at some ornaments. Mum gave her the bottle at which she sucked steadily and with great concentration until it was nearly finished. When Kay stopped sucking Mum sat her up and she released quite a lot of wind without further help.

There followed a period of play lasting about 20 minutes until: 'After this time she made some crying noises and Mum picked her up saying that she expected Kay was tired. Mum returned her to her cot where she quickly fell asleep.'

Here is the second example, from an observation which took place a week later when Kay was nine weeks old.

● Twenty minutes before I left she made a face again, this time she opened her eyes. They looked glazed. Mum and J. moved to the cotside and talked to her. She seemed still to be asleep. Several times she pulled a face, moving her head to one side then the other. She pulled her legs up to her chest and moved her arms about, making crying noises. Mum continued to talk to her, saying 'Come on, give us a smile'. Kay smiled at Mum, at the same time seeming to struggle with something inside. She grunted, windmilled her arms and pushed her legs down. Mum made sympathetic sounds throughout, but left her in the cot. It seemed to me that Kay tried hard to smile throughout, even though other things were happening to her. It came out as a cross between a smile and a grimace. After a short time she found her thumb and, sucking it, she began to settle to sleep.

We can see from these two observations that Kay's mother was able to respond to her by ensuring that her needs were met and not just her wants. Kay needed to experience some frustration in order to learn that she could tolerate it, that she could find ways of dealing with it for herself. Instead of rushing in and picking Kay up when she cried, her mother left her in her cot for a time. In the first observation Kay managed, by sucking her thumb, to remind herself of good experiences she had gained in her mother's arms. This memory was sufficient for her to be able to tolerate the discomfort of hunger and the delayed arrival of her bottle.

In the second example Kay was able, without direct physical contact, to use her mother's voice and her nearness to stop her feeling overwhelmed by uncomfortable griping pains. She smiled at her mother, even when grimacing with discomfort. In this way Kay was able to begin to believe that loving and painful feelings could coexist without one being overwhelmed by the other. She also began to learn that she need not be overcome by the tension produced in the conflict between apparently incompatible feelings. It is through these sorts of very ordinary, well-timed and constantly repeated good experiences that each of us achieves emotional integration. It is upon these early experiences that our ability to make mature and lasting adult relationships is based. The mother enables her child increasingly to tolerate disappointment and anxiety by controlling her own need to give immediate comfort to the child.

We are all too aware of how emotional deprivation, loss, separation and poor contact between the mother and her baby can produce disturbance in later life. The overconcerned mother may also unwittingly produce the distress that she works so hard to avoid. The following is an account taken from the personal history of a young woman who was being treated for a profound anxiety state.

Carol

Carol was a young woman in her late twenties. She complained of such severe anxiety that she found it difficult to leave her flat. She could not travel on trains, buses or cars. She found shopping a terrifying experience; even walking down an empty street left her feeling weak and drained. She could not stay in her flat, the loneliness frightened her, and when she was driven out of it she found that her fears travelled with her. If she sought company she felt suspicious of her companions and worried that they wanted something from her. When friends visited her she felt torn between her pleasure at seeing them and her feeling that they intruded too much upon her or took control of her flat. She felt at these times that her life was not her own. She felt taken over and taken for granted. She could not say 'no' to any request and she slept poorly for only a few hours each night.

Although she was still married, she had lived separately from her husband since shortly after her mother's death some years before. She still saw her husband and was fond of him. She was comfortable with him but regarded this as too easy a solution to her anxiety. She saw that she gained security only through the sacrifice of her independence. She was strongly determined to stand unsupported.

Carol was an only child. She loved both her parents and had felt loved by them. Her mother worked but always made sure that she was at home when Carol returned home from school. She cooked wonderful meals with love and care. Carol explained that she would often eat them, although she was not hungry. She knew that her mother would be disappointed if she did not clear her plate. Even when she was a teenager and her classmates nicknamed her 'Tubs' because she was overweight, she continued to eat all her mother put before her. Despite feeling hurt by her nickname, she never complained, and never said 'no' to Mum.

Carol explained that she could not understand why she should feel so frightened all the time, since her mother had never once abandoned her. She could not even remember being left with a babysitter whilst her parents had an evening out. She was not left alone in the dark – her mother was too kind and thoughtful to leave Carol to face night-time fears on her own. Her mother, out of love and commitment to Carol, would lie down beside her on the bed and hold her until Carol fell asleep. She did this until Carol was married at 17 years of age.

This was a very sad story. If we contrast it with the way in which Kay's mother cared for her we can see that the determination with which Carol's mother worked to disallow frustration and avoid anxiety ultimately left her child unable to tolerate any anxiety at all.

Through her mother being ever-providing, always there before she was needed, Carol was prevented from learning the lessons which Kay had begun to learn at two months old. In other words, she had not learned that it is possible for opposing wishes and feelings to coexist safely. She learned from her mother, who never said 'no', never to say 'no' herself. Although she lived apart from her husband she had not said 'no' to him either, as she still saw him regularly. She did not learn that her destructive impulses were not overwhelming. She learned to deny them, to channel them into areas of apparent caring as her mother had done with her.

When her mother died Carol felt that she had somehow killed her by leaving her. She felt empty inside, that she had no continuing mother in her mind's eye. It was as if her mother's inescapable and very physical presence had said to her: 'You need me always by your side, your anxieties are real and you cannot survive them without me. Any mental image you have of me is not sufficient; you need me to protect you.'

In the very early weeks and months of the baby's life the mother cares for her child by helping him to experience just enough frustration and anxiety to learn that he can survive it. As the baby grows older he grows in awareness and is able to understand that this mother, who has been the recipient of his aggressive attacks and his pushed-out, unwanted bad feelings, is also the good mother who cares for him, clothes him and feeds him. There is a sense of regret which is accompanied by feelings of guilt and a wish to make up for the damage he feels he has done.

We are all familiar with these feelings. Which of us, after a row with a loved one, has not experienced something similar? The growing, depressing realisation that the person upon whom we have so recently poured scorn and venom is the same person we have loved and still love. Following this, do we not wish to make amends and do we not sometimes find that the depth of loving feelings is so great as to become akin to adoration? Klein (1946) called this state the 'depressive position'.

These feelings first find expression early in infancy as do the rages and anxieties that provoke them. They are positions which we can move into and out of throughout our lives. We can become as wary and overwhelmed as a newborn baby and respond with suspicion and elaborate caution to new people, places and experiences, and we do sometimes unfairly view our loved ones through the darkest of lenses, projecting them in our minds as thoughtless, cruel or malicious and treating them malevolently and with disdain. Regret, sadness and self-reproach follow in the wake of such storms of temperament, and most, but not all, of us learn a little more each time so that increasingly we become more tolerant, understanding and loving. As a result, the older we get the more mature we become, the more satisfying our relationships are, and the time that we spend in either of these two extremes diminishes. The product of this oral stage of development is the establishment of a sense of basic trust (Erikson, 1965).

This sense of basic trust is important to the next stage of development as it is necessary for the child to have some sense of good things lasting if he is to have the wherewithal to deal further with the conflicts which continue to battle within him.

THE AGE OF AMBIVALENCE AND
WILFUL SELF-DETERMINATION

This age coincides with the maturation of the sphincter muscles, which allows the child increasing control of his bowel and bladder. This is important as it is upon these new physical developments that the child builds new emotional structures. His ability to retain or eliminate bodily products facilitates the notion of control of his own person. There is a dawning realisation that he can be less dependent on his mother for feeding and for personal motivation. Congruent with this realisation his sense of independence increases. This stage, which lasts until the child is two or three years old, is characterised by many battles, particularly around feeding and toileting.

Just as the child holds on to or pushes out bodily products, so in feeding he experiments with admitting or excluding food into or from his mouth, that is, accepting it and spitting it out. This behaviour indicates something of the nature of the internal conflicts which the child is experiencing. When playing with his food or experimenting with managing his excreta and laying claim to a right to evacuate when he will, where he will and on his own terms, the child is also establishing his right to hold on to or get rid of feelings as he chooses.

It is a time of experimentation with relationships too. The child attempts to control his parents, by refusing to comply with their wishes, by demanding that they give in to him and let him have his own way. This is when the child is most likely to give vent to the wildest of temper tantrums if his wishes are not instantly acceded to. The child screaming with rage at the supermarket cashpoint because his mother will not let him have these sweets, that toy, these crisps, is likely to be around this age.

It is a confused, angry and difficult time. Because the child is himself unreasonably attempting to bend others to his will, there is a concomitant anxiety that others want to do the same to him. This leads to further entrenchment and renewed resistance. With fair parenting the child learns to be less demanding and achieves a more acceptable balance between his wishes and the constraints of the world outside him. He is helped in this by the satisfactory experiences he enjoyed during the previous stage. This means that, although it is a confused and angry time, the child is still able to bring loving feelings to bear. The child may destructively hold on to faecal matter, or aggressively push it out, but he may also hold on to it with care and evacuate it with love and pride. The parent's ability to be consistently fair is essential if the child is to overcome these conflicting desires without being left with an abiding sense of shame and doubt in his own goodness, or in the validity of his feelings, thoughts, ideas or wishes. The parents, and by extension older members of the family, teach discrimination in choice and action through their interventions and by their example. If this is poorly done and there are meaningless experiences of shame, there may well be a consequent lack of trust, leaving the child obsessively, stubbornly and minutely controlling of his environment.

Gradually the battles diminish in intensity as the child accepts the attitudes of his parents and the outside world. They become part of his internal world and, as he strives for cleanliness, unwelcome wishes are defended against. He becomes more cooperative and has less need to insist on his rights. No longer is there such intense ambivalence that he answers 'Yo!' or 'Nes!' to requests or offers of treats and excursions, as one child I knew did at this age. She would also, in response to the question 'Would you like to come for a walk?' firmly answer 'No!' whilst pulling on her coat and walking out of the door. From the self-control which the child learns at this stage comes a sense of self-respect and personal worth. This permits a good will, a rightness of purpose towards others, to emerge.

We can see from the stages already discussed that each is linked to the next. It is evident that the achievements of one stage are necessary to the child's ability to continue to grow and develop in the next. Each stage follows upon its predecessor like building blocks (see figure 1.1). Whilst this is self-evidently true it will also have become apparent that each stage overlaps with the next. There are several strands which may run throughout them all. Erik Erikson (1965) illustrated this point and drew attention to it when he produced his 'Epigenetic Chart', and Anna Freud (1966) refers to it in her 'Concept of Developmental Lines'.

THE AGE OF RIVALRY AND OF EAGER COOPERATION

The child becomes very active at this age and seems to possess an over-abundance of energy. He uses this to explore the world, which he does with vigour and excitement. Because of this surfeit disappointments, though keenly felt, do not overwhelm him. Accidents may happen, he often tumbles still, but his profound inquisitiveness, together with the powerful drive to learn, and his continuing demand that mother should keep him safe, soon have him up and running again, or climbing, jumping, rolling or hopping, and so on.

At this stage we see how children fall for the parent of the opposite sex. This is the age when the daughter says to her father: 'I'm going to marry you when I grow up.' Sons say the same thing to their mothers. There is a wish to own the parent of the opposite sex completely. In order to manage this, the parent of the same sex is cast out. One little girl I knew used to climb into her parents' bed each Sunday

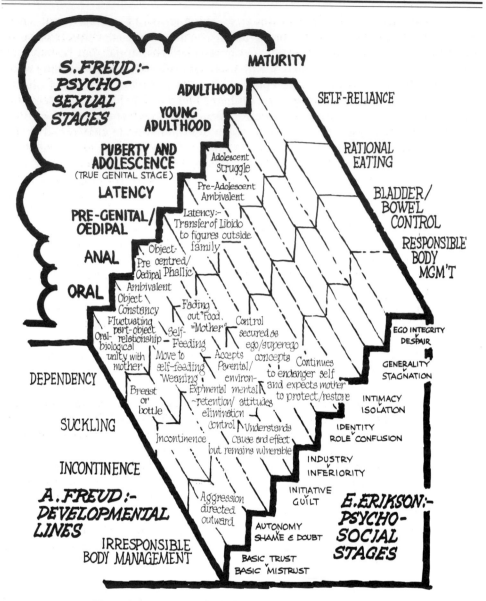

Fig. 1.1 An interrelating view of developmental theories

morning for a cuddle. Invariably she would wriggle into the space between them. Her parents had recognised her growing attachment to her father for some time and had wondered when, or if, they would see any sign of her attempting to oust her mother. Their little girl did not fail them. One morning, after throwing her arms lovingly around her father, she looked over her shoulder at her mother and in a firm, clear voice said: 'It's all right, you can go and make the tea now!'

We do not always see or hear evidence of this attachment. This may be because we are too close to see the wood for the trees, or because, for a variety of reasons, much of what happens is hidden from view within the child's inner world. These 'oedipal' preoccupations bring with them the incest taboo which is internalised by the child as a powerful injunction which may only be broken with dire results. This must cause the child considerable anxiety which he deals with by withdrawing into a clearer identification with the parent of the same sex. The boy-child will do things that his father does; the girl-child emulates her mother. These days the distinctions are not as clear-cut as once they were. Thankfully, it is increasingly the norm that men and women share tasks, professions, skills and responsibilities, so the boy-child may identify with his father by cleaning his room and the girl may involve herself more in her mother's world by pretending to repair a mechanical device.

During this time the superego (which if translated from the original German becomes the 'over-I' – that which watches over me) continues to develop. Klein (1927) suggests that superego development begins during the first months of life, and is related to the child's bad feelings that he has hurt his mother by imaginatively evacuating his bad feelings, thoughts and impulses into her. The child is sorry for this, wishes to make reparation, and strives not to repeat this damaging process. This implies the formation of an internal 'watcher' who intervenes to prevent aggressive impulses being allowed expression.

This notion provides the basis to an understanding of the major psychoses. The statements which many schizophrenic patients make illustrate the lack, or confusion, of boundaries between inside and outside, self and other, which is characteristic of the first stage of emotional development. For example, 'I made the lights come on with my eyes' or 'It's my fault that the Jonestown people died; I failed to veil my power'. These statements show a confused notion of what is real and unreal, what can be done and not, what is fact and what is fantasy. They also show that, for these patients, there exists a notion that something inside can be pushed out – in the latter case, the power to kill, or violent destructive feelings.

It is important that we begin to form a picture of how this happens, for splitting and projection are important processes that we need to be aware of in any group, and they are the processes which precede the formation of the conscience, or superego. But leaving aside splitting and projection for the moment, we can recognise the role of the conscience in the following example. It is taken from a mother and baby observation when the child was a little over 12 months old. She was walking by this time, but still crawled occasionally. She had begun to talk and had a small vocabulary of words.

●   . . . Heather's Mum had left us in the livingroom whilst she went to the kitchen. Heather spent some time smiling at me and pulling faces, then she walked until she stumbled upon a building block, whereupon she crawled. The TV set was plugged in but not switched on and Heather crawled towards it rapidly at first, slowing down more the nearer she got. As she approached within arm's length she reached out her right hand to the plug but I heard her say 'No!' to herself and again 'No!' over and over, louder each time. She pulled away from the plug and sat up, crying in distress before repeating her actions.

The observer had made no comment (although he would have intervened to protect the child). Consequently, we can see that it was an inner voice – a conscience – which was at war with Heather's impulsive inquisitiveness. We can see that she had 'internalised' her mother, so that the Mummy outside, who would say 'No' to her about certain things, was represented in Heather's inner world. This inner representation was quite solid; it did not need the immediate external presence of her mother to confirm it.

The formation of the superego continues throughout this stage and on into subsequent stages until it reaches a peak in this stage of rivalry and cooperation; the oedipal stage of psychosexual development, or the stage of Initiative versus Guilt (Erikson, 1965) in psychosocial terms.

During this time the child becomes increasingly keen on cooperating and working with other children to make or do things. There is an increasing willingness to share and to be equal which is related to the child's relinquishing his demands to have his mother all to himself or to win the parent of the opposite sex.

SUMMARY

Work, which was begun in the first weeks and months of life and was continued into the anal phase (the stage of ambivalence and wilful self-determination), achieves a resolution in this oedipal stage. During the first (oral) stage the baby is increasingly able to see his mother as separate and is able to release her from his demand that she be ever-present. This is achieved gradually as the baby becomes more aware of his mother as a continuing presence in his inner world. Later, during the anal phase, the toddler battles within himself and with others to resolve the conflict between retaining and eliminating feelings, bodily products and people. The outcome of this phase is an increasing acceptance of his mother as independent of his wishes, and the establishment of a sense of self-respect.

We can see that not only does one stage build upon and merge with the next, but also, issues from the earliest stages of life continue to change, to be modified and to develop throughout later stages. The particular issue chosen here is the process of individuation as the child becomes increasingly independent and needs his mother less. Each stage brings with it new challenges and adventures and new hope as the child is given another and yet another chance to work over aspects of the same issue time after time.

This hope is something which is carried into adulthood as we continue to be given opportunities to rework incomplete or unsatisfactory experiences. Our children offer us this chance as their experiences resonate with those from our own childhood. Individually we grow through further developmental stages which allow us opportunities to reconcile our continuing conflicts and unresolved experiences. This augurs well for the prospect of successful treatment as it means the therapist's work will be aided by natural processes.

References

Bion W R (1962) *Learning from Experience*. London: Heinemann.
Erikson E H (1965) *Childhood and Society*. Harmondsworth: Penguin Books.
Freud A (1966) *Normality and Pathology in Childhood*. London: The Hogarth Press and the Institute of Psycho-Analysis.

Klein M (1927) Paper for Symposium on Child Analysis. In: *Love, Guilt and Reparation and other Works*. London: The Hogarth Press and the Institute of Psycho-Analysis.
Klein M (1946) Notes on some schizoid mechanisms. In: *Envy and Gratitude*. London: The Hogarth Press and the Institute of Psycho-Analysis.
Klein M (1952) On observing the behaviour of young infants. In: *Envy and Gratitude*. London: The Hogarth Press and the Institute of Psycho-Analysis.

Further Reading

Saltzberger-Wittenburg I (1970) *Psychoanalytic Insight and Relationships*. London: Routledge and Kegan Paul.
Winnicott D W (1964) *The Child, The Family and the Outside World*. Harmondsworth: Penguin Books.
Winnicott D W (1974) *Playing and Reality*. Harmondsworth: Penguin Books.

2

Individual and

Family Development

Families grow through a series of developmental stages in much the same way as individuals do. These stages bring with them a series of crises, the intensity of which will be directly related to how effectively each preceding stage has been managed.

The parents will find that resonances are established between their own childhood experiences and the current experiences of their children. In consequence they will find themselves re-experiencing emotions that belong to an earlier time in their lives. In addition, each parent brings similarities and differences of experience and character which may produce conflict and tension between them that is felt throughout the family and influences their whole existence.

The family is the first social group to which we belong. Our experience of this group will influence our behaviour in all other groups which we join throughout our lives. Each of us, as members of a profession, belong to a group which is composed of members of that profession. Every time we sit with friends over a drink we have formed a group. A choir is a group, so is a football team. Any gathering of more than three people is a group.

As all groups are governed by the same processes, we can identify these in every group – in a therapy group, in a group of friends around a table in the pub, and so on.

Unless otherwise stated, where groups are referred to in the text, it is intended that the reader should think of groups in the wider sense, as defined above. The pattern of relationships begun in the family continues into all the other groups to which we subsequently belong. The individual brings with him experiences, prohibitions, permissions and approval for certain ways of relating which were learned in his family of origin. This 'learned' behaviour will be recreated in all groups, even when it is inappropriate, unless it is successfully challenged and the individual is helped to develop other more appropriate ways of relating.

If the individual has enjoyed satisfactory experiences throughout childhood there will be sufficient flexibility to accommodate others without feeling anxious or overwhelmed. But if early experiences have been unsatisfactory then problems occur as the individual unconsciously recreates his family of origin with members of the group.

This process of relating unconsciously to another 'as if' he or she were a significant person in one's past is known as 'transference'. It was Ferenczi (1916), a psychoanalyst and admirer of Freud's work, who expanded the idea of transference to include phenomena which were apparent outside of the analytic situation. In other words, people in everyday life are constantly transferring their own unconscious feelings towards important people from their past onto other people in the present.

We are all familiar with the way we sometimes take an instant like or dislike to another, or how we can say, 'I don't like that name'. If we think about it, it is often because we have known someone in the past who looked like, sounded like or walked like our new acquaintance. The favour or distaste with which we view new people is based upon our like or dislike of past associates. What we have done is to project the image we have of our past associate onto the new acquaintance and then we have responded as if the projection were a fact.

These processes of transference and projection are important to the foundation of all relationships, including marriage.

In chapter 1 we followed the development of the child up to the oedipal stage, or just before he first went to school. Later in this chapter we shall return to look at the impact that starting school has on him and on his family. We shall also look at adolescence, again from the family's viewpoint. Before we do, we take a step into the past to look at some of the processes which influence the choice of marriage partner and examine some of the family's developmental stages.

COURTSHIP AND MARRIAGE

When a man and a woman meet and find a mutual attraction they each bring to the budding relationship a set of values, attitudes, opinions and beliefs which were learned in their families of origin. They, or others, will have challenged many of these attitudes and views, particularly during adolescence. They also bring their current experiences of life – their experiences of increasing individuation and of separation from their families of birth.

Gradually and increasingly, as they talk, they each become more open with, and consequently more vulnerable to, the other. Each will measure the other against values which, especially during adolescence, are passionately held. Out of the common ground that is found a bridge is built linking them. Each will see in the other admired characteristics which he wishes to share or emulate, or which he respects yet feels to be beyond his aspirations. The similarities that are found may encourage each of them to deny, in themselves and in each other, feelings and wishes which make them feel uncomfortable. Some couples hide these feelings from themselves and from each other, forcing them out of conscious thought and into remote areas of the mind. Sometimes unwelcome thoughts and impulses are excluded before they become consciously available. They are sifted out by something which Freud (1917) called 'The Watcher at the Threshold'. He was writing of the faculty we all have to withhold from our sentient selves thoughts, feelings or impulses which would cause us distress if they become available to our conscious minds.

Robin Skynner (1983), amongst others, writes about a screen behind which we conceal aspects of ourselves that we have learned during childhood are unacceptable to our parents and other important people. In this sense the 'watcher' is an internalised parent.

Occasionally, we find that the sense of self-criticism is overdeveloped in some people. This may be because they had overcritical parents or, if this is not the case, it is due to constitutional factors. In other words, some people are born feeling more persecuted than others. A 'good enough mother' (Winnicott, 1965) will successfully influence such a child so that his sense of persecution diminishes. But where circumstance, or the mother, is inadequate, then the sense of persecution may grow until the persecuted child becomes a guilt-ridden, self-critical adult.

Once the unwanted or unacceptable aspects of the self are removed to a place of concealment the individual is left with only those characteristics which were considered admirable by his family. In this way the wife who found in childhood that she received more love and attention when she behaved in a demure and feminine way will invest the forceful part of herself in her husband, who, having learned that 'big boys don't cry' or display any 'sensitive' feeling, will invest these parts of himself in his wife. This process is known as projective identification (Klein 1946), and is a process to which we have recourse throughout our lives.

Ogden (1979) describes projective identification as having three phases. The first is a fantasy stage during which the baby imagines that he can split off an unwanted or endangered part of himself and push it outward into another. The second is an induction stage when the baby behaves in such a way that the intended recipient is made to experience the same feelings which the baby wishes to rid himself of. The third is a metabolisation stage when the recipient inwardly processes the projection and returns it in modified form to the baby.

To illustrate this let us consider what happens when the baby (or the adult, since the use of projective identification is not confined to infancy) experiences considerable discomfort from an impulse, thought or feeling which so alarms him that he wants to rid himself of it. Unconsciously he imagines that he can evacuate it and deposit it with his mother. He cries or struggles, whines or whimpers in such a way that he evokes within his mother a feeling akin to the one he wants to be rid of.

The mother returns the unwanted feeling in modified form, that is in a form which the baby can manage. She does this in thousands of different ways. She might cuddle her baby and gently laugh at his temper. She might be a little bit impatient with her baby when he is older and he can deal with it. She might speak to her baby in a voice that is both gentle and firm. She might hold him and comfort him for as long as he needs. She might remove the breast that he bites and only return it when he stops.

We have all said at some time 'He made me angry', or we have felt sad while watching a moving play or a film. We know that others can make us feel in a particular way. The baby uses the same sort of skill as the actor to elicit the desired response.

Dupont (1984) suggested that one of the primary functions of projective identification, in addition to allowing the baby to rid himself of unwanted feelings, is to serve as a primitive, pre-verbal form of communication. The mother then brings her intuitive ability to bear (Wright, 1987) to understand the communication. She thinks about what her baby is feeling, feels some of it herself and remembers consciously and unconsciously her own experiences of infancy as they are stimulated within her by her empathy with her child.

The following example shows how projection works in a very ordinary way, in most marriages.

A couple I knew well got married some time ago. Before their wedding they both had their own accommodation, both worked, had bills to pay and rooms to decorate, and both did well at it. When they married the husband took on the management of the family finances because he and his wife agreed that she was 'hopeless' with money. The wife took on responsibility for designing, colour schemes and so on as they decided that his taste was 'awful'. In truth he was a little more organised with money than his wife, but she was quite able; and his choice of colours was always pleasing, though not as splendid as hers. They both recognised a greater ability in the other for the skills identified. Then they invested their own ability in that area in their partner. Consequently the partner's skill seemed enhanced and their own skill in that area seemed diminished. In fact his colour schemes did get wilder and her budgeting did become very sloppy. Thus they were convinced of the accuracy of their perceptions of each other.

When the projection is not returned, as happened in this marriage, there is an inevitable depletion of resources. If he holds her aggressive qualities, for example, while she has his tender abilities, neither has the opportunity to work on any of these areas of difficulty, since they are invested in the partner. Consequently, the relationship, and the individuals within it, stagnate unless and until a crisis occurs which is beyond the scope of the couple to deal with, and one or both break down emotionally or psychologically.

When two peole who have the same hidden characteristics meet, they may find in each other only those attributes they have been taught to admire and to emulate. They become two as if they were halves of the same soul. When opposites attract it is because one has hidden those characteristics that the other displays and reveals those traits that the other conceals. They are reciprocal opposites. At the beginning of any relationship this is to be expected, but when it continues into a boundary-less future we begin to see problems. Couples who are unable to move from the original position of unconditional mutual regard may often be viewed by others, and see themselves, as an ideal couple. They may never row or argue. But it is simply impossible never to have a conflict of views or difference of opinion with a lifetime partner. What happens in these cases is that conflict is denied and avoided. This is possible because of the acceptance of the roles which they occupied when they first met. In other words, those attracted by similarities may unite to exclude aspects of themselves and of each other which, in childhood, they were taught were unacceptable. Those attracted by differences will be able to invest in each other the personal characteristics which they learned were unacceptable in themselves and were to be admired in others.

The same applies with those couples whose relationship is based upon shared similarities. They may stagnate because they encourage each other to deny feelings or aspects of themselves which cause discomfort or emotional pain.

With couples who base their relationship on such flimsy foundations deeper feelings remain concealed and are withheld. They touch each other only superficially, and similarly their involvement with the world at large is tangential and inert.

To be able to become truly close to others we must first become intimate with ourselves. This stage of development enables this fundamental issue to be reworked. It is an ability or inability which began in infancy when the baby had to learn to trust his mother enough to hold him safely in her arms and in her mind so that he could enjoy her comforting presence.

We have looked at the couple who conceal unwanted aspects of themselves and at the couple who invest unwanted characteristics in each other. It is probable that the majority of couples have relationships that lie somewhere between these two extremes.

At the same time as the couple are getting to know each other and moving along the road to a more complete integration of the self, each partner is separating from home and family. Inevitably this will stir feelings and memories, though not always consciously available, of other and earlier separations.

Where these have been satisfactory and there has been no undue distress through loss or abandonment, then the couple will be able to help each other to negotiate this step with care and consideration. Even if there was a distressing loss in childhood, if the partner has been helped by a constant caring other (perhaps a father, older brother or sister, an aunt or family friend) then this step can be managed without undue difficulty. If, however, separations have been fraught, or feelings to do with loss were disallowed or not recognised, then separation becomes a problem. Separation anxieties may manifest themselves in many ways. There are no rules which confine the responses of the individual. For example:

● One young man, who had experienced several separations during his childhood used to make many physically intimate and romantic but emotionally distant relationships as he could not allow himself to feel close. The feeling of emotional closeness brought with it the anxiety that he faced an impending loss.

And again:

● A young woman who had spent her entire childhood moving between hospital and a children's home, with brief interludes at home with her parents, could not allow herself any gentle feelings. She was gruff and apparently hostile for much of the time during the first year of therapy. For her to allow herself to be gentle meant that she opened the door to other feelings which left her vulnerable.

Some couples may flee the emotional pain which accompanies the separation from their respective families of origin, by immersing themselves defensively in the safety of their loving partnership, so that they feel none of the sadness of loss. In consequence the bonds of love are forged by denial and avoidance as the couple are joined by a chain whose links are of repression and unacknowledged anxiety.

One girl, a member of an outpatient group for teenagers, spoke very eloquently of the difficulties of this time. She said that even when she was fifteen she had felt a lot safer than she did now. Then she had still been at school – legally she had to be there. If things went wrong at home then the state was obliged to provide her with a place of safety. Now that she was older she had to be responsible for herself. There were choices that she had to make. She was at college and was finding the work hard although she was academically able. She could leave college and get a job, but she had no way of knowing whether or not she could manage to hold a job down. The possibilities and opportunities both excited and alarmed her.

We are always given more chances to grow and develop, to come to terms with internal conflicts and past experiences. There is always another opportunity to improve upon the achievements of the previous stage. The attractions which initially bring a couple together continue into marriage, as do the negotiations begun in courtship. These negotiations concern what each finds acceptable or otherwise in the character or the behaviour of the other, and the rights and responsibilities of each.

Adjustments have to be made. How much of the housework is to be shared; who cooks and plans which meals; which friends are welcome or not; do they continue to have separate nights out with their friends; and so on?

The couple's ability to achieve a comfortable and appropriate compromise is influenced by their earlier experiences and is mediated by the differences in those experiences which each of them bring to the relationship.

Perhaps the wife's fierce independence and determination not to be ruled by another were established early in childhood as a response to overcritical, demanding and controlling parents. Her husband's experience of a more fair and thoughtful style of parenting may help him to respond firmly, fairly and considerately so that, over time, she is able to relinquish her insistent demand for her absolute independence thus enabling them both to move into a more emotionally intimate and complete relationship.

Perhaps his continuing need of her constant presence is rooted in a failure of attachment to his mother. Her experience of a good mother who was emotionally and physically available may help her to tolerate such smothering contact without her needing to withdraw her emotional presence. Again, over time, he will be helped to feel sure of her continuing love, even in her absence.

In both cases work begun in childhood continues into adulthood and enriches their experiences both individually and as a couple.

PARENTHOOD

As the day of birth approaches the mother and father to be rehearse their roles for the future. They buy babyclothes, a cot, a pram; a new room is prepared for the baby and names are chosen. When the baby arrives it is a time of intense pride and pleasure for the parents and a time of celebration for all. Everyone congratulates the couple on their new arrival. It is a happy time, but it is also the beginning of a momentous change in their lives.

Many people are not prepared for the changes that parenthood brings. Even when couples have sensibly and carefully thought through what they expect it will mean, they can never be wholly prepared. Parenthood is wonderful but it is not a bed of roses.

The new and beloved baby disrupts their lives twenty-four hours a day, every day. The baby's needs are paramount and must be met. Yet even as they recognise, acknowledge and accept this they may sometimes feel dissatisfaction with and resentment towards each other and their baby. Both may well dislike themselves for having such negative feelings at what should be a happy and contented time, yet be unable to conceal or contain them wholly. It will become increasingly difficult for each of them to maintain an equilibrium, particularly as they succumb to the increasing burden of tiredness which is added to by each successive night of disturbed sleep.

The couple is now a threesome. Emotional space has to be found for the baby in a way which does not leave either parent feeling excluded. Three is always a difficult number to manage as it is so easy for it to become a pair and one left over. This is particularly noticeable in children's games. Inevitably one will always be left out, or will be picked on by the other two, or will be given the parts in the game that nobody else wants.

There will be faint but influential echoes from the parents' own infancy that will be felt as vibrations which shake the concealing dust of the years from incompletely resolved feelings and issues. Old rivalries will be rekindled and sleeping jealousies awoken. They will be experienced as feelings rather than remembered as memories. They colour the way that the parents feel about, react to and behave towards each other. Rivalries from babyhood with brothers and sisters will be played out in the present as if one's partner was really the envied brother or sister. These feelings are difficult to manage, partly because the parents don't recognise their roots in past relationships, but also because society conspires to pretend that caring for babies is as soft and warmly fluffy as the advertisements suggest.

The feelings themselves are often unpleasant, having to do with rage, anger, impatience, frustration and blame. As well as being the rekindled embers of the fires of jealous competition, they are a return to the feelings of infancy when storms of anxious emotion raged unharnessed by modifying experience.

Most parents know what it feels like to despair of ever being able to help their distressed infant to settle, and what it is like to feel almost overwhelmed themselves with a distress that is similar to their baby's. This is the result of the process of projective identification which was described earlier. The distress that the baby wants to be rid of has been evoked in the parents so that they now feel what their baby is feeling. This evoked feeling awakens other similar feelings that the parent has experienced in the past, so that the projected feeling is enhanced by the corresponding feeling from the parent's own childhood. In this way the parent is helped to understand more fully what the baby needs help with.

Unfortunately, where the parent has had insufficient help in coping with overwhelming feelings during his own childhood, this process can leave him feeling just as helpless, frightened, overwhelmed and angry as he was in infancy. In consequence his ability to help his child will be as impaired as his ability to manage his own feelings. This is the sort of circumstance which leads to baby battering.

Every parent is touched by feelings of jealousy for the relationship that the child has with his or her partner, and by anxieties of being swamped by the more primitive feelings discussed above. Most parents manage to deal with these emotions sensitively, effectively and appropriately. But even when there is difficulty it is possible for the parents to get help in dealing with unresolved areas. The case example which follows illustrates how this might happen.

The Watson Family

Mr and Mrs Watson were a young couple who had been married for several years before deciding that they wanted a child. They had thought about it carefully. They both came from large families and were used to having younger children around so they knew what to expect. They had no illusions that it was going to be easy, but felt that they might find it easier than most because of their experience as older children in looking after their younger brothers and sisters. They were consequently both very upset when Mrs Watson began to have problems in looking after their baby daughter. She became extremely agitated and anxious when her daughter cried for more than a few minutes.

They explained to their therapist that she had become frightened that she would do something to harm her baby, particularly when she was on her own, and would shut her away in an upstairs room when she cried. She did this to keep the baby safe and to distance herself from the distress that her baby caused in her.

Over a fairly brief time the therapist was able to help them to understand why she was so distressed and why she could not cope.

Her own mother used to leave her babies to cry, not because she was unduly distressed herself, but because she thought it was good for them to exercise their lungs. She believed that her babies would be spoiled if she picked them up when they cried. Mrs Watson knew that this had happened as she was an older child and had witnessed her mother's behaviour with her younger brothers and sisters.

When Mrs Watson's baby cried a feeling of distress was provoked in her that was the baby's distress and an echo of the pain that Mrs Watson had felt when she was a baby herself. She felt an added panic as she used to worry for her younger brothers and sisters when they cried inconsolably and were ignored by her mother. She wanted to help them but couldn't as she had been too small and now she felt unable to help her own child. The child in her had been awoken so that she felt the same impotence with her baby as she had felt with her brothers and sisters.

Once the initial adjustments are made and the new family is able to feel that they are a unit, the stresses diminish tremendously. Yet throughout their baby's childhood the parents will continue to be reminded of feelings that they first experienced as children themselves. As well as enabling the parents to understand their children better, these echoes stimulate their potential for continuing growth.

They have the opportunity to rework incomplete experiences within the marital rather than the maternal relationship.

GOING TO SCHOOL

We usually find that families present with problems at times which coincide with a new developmental stage. The presenting problems are often symbols of underlying circumstances, from a parallel time in the parent's past, which remain unresolved. During this stage in the family's development the issues are mainly to do with separation and the management of feelings of loss. Every developmental stage includes elements of this central concern.

Through weaning the baby loses the breast and the intense closeness to its mother. During toilet training the toddler relinquishes some part of his consistent demand for his mother. In the oedipal stage the child eventually forgoes the demand to exclusive rights over his mother. When the child goes to school he will feel the sadness of loss keenly. He also feels the excitement of a new challenge and the pleasure associated with growing up.

These feelings are in conflict with each other to some extent and the child has to resolve this conflict whilst also coming to terms with having to do without his mother for long periods of time and sharing his teacher with many other children. He also has to make relationships with a number of strangers and this may cause anxiety too.

Most people experience a small touch of concern whenever meeting a new group of people, it is the same for children.

The parents experience reciprocal feelings of loss and concern. When their child starts school they are reminded that childhood is short and he is already on the road to independence. Their concern is for their child's feelings, for his ability to make friends and to tolerate being apart from his parents for such a long time each day. They are also concerned because their child represents them amongst people who may not know them and will judge them according to how their child behaves.

Through their child the parents become involved in a wider society of other children, their parents and their teachers. The child and, through him his parents, are exposed to a number of new influences. Their way of parenting is set against the parenting styles of others. Differences emerge and have to be dealt with. Children and parents learn from each other what is fair and what is not, what is acceptable and what is not. Through their child's involvement in the outside world the parents modify their views and their behaviour so that they are in step with the rest of society. All groups have this normative function.

If a child is to be able to move out of the home into the outside world successfully he must first have had the satisfactory experiences of intimate attachment upon which trust is built. This is initially established within the maternal relationship, is extended into the relationship with his father and thence to the rest of the family.

Where there has been a failure of attachment it becomes difficult for the child to leave home and form new relationships. Because there is not a sufficiently strong bond the child will cling to his mother and continue to need her physical presence. Such children may fail to make relationships with others, or only be able to engage in superficial and peripheral involvement in which busy activity substitutes for close contact.

PUBERTY, ADOLESCENCE AND MIDDLE AGE

The move to senior school coincides with the onset of puberty for most children. It is a stormy time during which much happens.

Moving to senior school is a major milestone and signals tremendous changes in the life of the child and his family. Often he has to travel miles to a distant school where he is faced with new pupils, new teachers, new friends and new enemies. Expectations change, there is a greater emphasis on work, with most children being expected to take work home with them. Home life may need to be reorganised to accommodate the demands of the school timetable and the need for study space. Once again, the family faces a new society of parents and teachers.

This move marks the beginning of the last phase of the child's school career and the final years of childhood. Physical changes begin: body hair appears; boys find their voices breaking and deepening; girls have their first period.

This time is the bridge between childhood and adulthood. It is a time when children search for a personal identity through exploring new ideas and challenging their parents' value-system.

As part of the impetus to discover themselves young people identify with musicians or footballers, older cousins or friends, and try to emulate them. They become critical of and dissatisfied with their parents. They distance themselves from their parents and their parents' generation. At times this can become quite extreme, yet it is a necessary precursor to the establishment of a personal sense of identity and it is preparation for the final separation from home. Old ties must be tried and tested, or cut, before the adolescent can begin to feel that he owns himself.

It is necessary for the teenager to put some distance between himself and the parent of the opposite sex. Until now the boy's mother or the girl's father has been the most important person in his or her life. Now that they are sexually mature the incest taboo is felt more keenly so that temptation must be removed even if it means denigrating the loved parent. These forces and their controls operate at an unconscious level so that the family may be aware only of the rows, the silences and the time spent in separate rooms throughout the house. It is a tumultuous time for the parents when they find their values and even the fact of their love for their children challenged.

The parents will be reviewing their own situation too, for they are approaching middle age. Their role as parents is nearly over, their children will not need them in a few more years. What then, does the future hold?

Many women face a sense of self-doubt, a lack of self-esteem, a feeling that the best years have gone and with them a sense of purpose. The mother may doubt that she will ever find work or feel useful again. She may feel unattractive, and compare herself unfavourably with her youthful, vigorous and sexually mature daughter. There may be a sense of having attained nothing, of having achieved none of the goals set in her own youth.

Men see their sons overtake them in strength and prowess and find themselves failing. There may be an awareness of not having gone as far or as high at work as they planned in the zest of youth. Younger men get the coveted promotion, the challenging project. Both parents need to recognise that they will soon be a couple again. They have to relinquish their responsibility for their children and allow them increasing independence. They must do so knowing that they are losing them in the process. If they try to cling then they might force their children to abandon them altogether.

FULL CIRCLE

The latter part of this stage is also the beginning of the courtship stage when the foundations of a new family are laid down. The parents must face the loss of their children and the end of their youth. As this separation reverberates with the memories and feelings of earlier separations, the facility with which the parents can help their children to separate depends upon the quality of the early relationship and how it was managed.

In the next chapter we shall look more closely at the family as a mutually responsive unit and, borrowing from structural and systemic theories of the composition of the family, we shall describe the relationships that are amongst the first we ever form.

References

Dupont M A (1984) On primary communication. *International Review of PsychoAnalysis*, **11**: 303–310.

Ferenczi S (1916) *Contributions to Psycho-Analysis*. Boston: Richard Badger.

Freud S (1917) Resistance and repression. In: *Introductory Lectures on Psycho-Analysis*, vol. 1, Harmondsworth: Penguin Books.

Klein M (1946) Notes on some schizoid mechanisms. In: *Envy and Gratitude*. London: Hogarth Press and The Institute of Psycho-Analysis.

Ogden T H (1979) On projective identification. *International Journal of Psycho-Analysis*, **60**: 357–373.

Skynner R and Cleese J (1983) *Families and How to Survive Them*. London: Methuen.

Winnicott D W (1965) *The Family and Individual Development*. London: Tavistock.

3

The Family as a Group

In chapters 1 and 2 we looked at individual and family development and at the close relationship which exists between them. Individual development influences family development and, in turn, the development of the individual is affected by family influences. We have begun to build up an idea of how the family operates as a unit whose rules are formed and reformed in response to the influence each member has upon it at various stages in its lifecycle. In this chapter we look more closely at the structure of the family, its communication systems, and the ways in which roles are allocated or adopted. We shall think also about the underlying factors which govern the family.

FAMILY STRUCTURES

If we examine any family we can see a clear and readily identifiable hierarchy, with the parents positioned at the pinnacle and the children occupying positions lower down. The places which the children occupy in this hierarchy are governed by a number of factors – age, emotional maturity, common sense, intelligence, and so on. Teenage children occupy a higher level in the family hierarchy than pre-pubertal children. These older children can be expected to be more sensible and to behave more responsibly than their younger brothers and sisters. Consequently they will be given more freedom, more independence than the others. At the same time, they will be expected to take on more responsibility for themselves, their schoolwork, the tidiness of their rooms, their younger siblings, and so forth.

So we can see that the hierarchical structure of the family is not based upon power but upon what is sensible and appropriate. One's place in that structure is related to age, level of maturity, being sensible, the social system of which the family forms a part, and to the belief system of that particular family.

This 'belief system' can be described as those attitudes, ideas, opinions and judgements which the parents hold to be true and which govern the behaviour of family members towards each other and the quality of the family's relationship with society at large. Many of the attitudes which make up the belief system will have been formed in the parents' own childhood and so are inherited from their families of origin and are modified in their family of procreation. Each parent, in bringing his or her family's views into the marriage, brings influence to bear on the views or beliefs of his (or her) partner. Thus, in a healthy family we have a mutuality of influence which enables or stimulates change and inhibits stagnation.

Figure 3.1 shows a simple family hierarchy. The teenage and younger children, whose rights and responsibilities may be very different, have equal access to their parents.

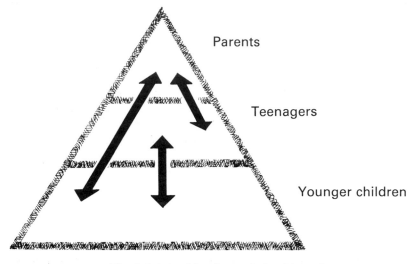

Fig. 3.1 A healthy, interrelating hierarchy

If figure 3.1 represents the norm then we can illustrate more rigid structures by steepening the triangle as in figure 3.2.

Fig. 3.2 A steepened, unresponsive and remote hierarchy

We can see that each level rests on the one below with the parents paramount and the teenagers blocking the younger children's access to them. In this way the parents are distanced from the younger children and there is an implied primacy of the teenagers over the younger members.

In such steeply organised structures we often find that the parents are rigid and unyielding. This means that the family is bound by rules which preclude a closer, warmer, more human contact.

If we remember the flatter triangle we can see that the parents are in closer, less impeded contact with their children; in fact, they seem almost equally close to all their children, with any differences minimal. Herein lies a clue to what happens if we flatten the triangle still further as in figure 3.3.

Fig. 3.3 A flattened, chaotic hierarchy

In figure 3.3 the distinctions between levels in the hierarchy have become almost nonexistent. In such a family we would see that the rights and responsibilities of the parents would be little different from those of the children, who would be allowed to make decisions beyond their years.

If we review the different types of structure we can see that extremes of each kind bring their own problems. The steepened hierarchy creates distance and emotional deprivation, whilst the extremely flattened hierarchy produces chaos and uncertainty. Both extremes can lead to emotional or mental disturbance in family members.

A family which has a hierarchy which is flattened sufficiently to allow emotional warmth and ease of access to the parents must also retain enough depth to protect the integrity of each of its members.

These descriptions are merely a simplified introduction to the complexities of family structures, which may be construed in a number of ways. For example, another useful approach to the family is to consider it as a group which is further divided into sub-groups. The parents form one sub-group, the teenagers another, and the younger children a third.

We can help ourselves to think of the family as a distinct unit which is capable of interacting with other families if we picture the family surrounded by an invisible barrier that allows inward and outward communication whilst preventing unwelcome intrusion. By extending this imagery to the sub-groups within the family we can picture how it is possible for each of them to relate comfortably, openly and safely with the others. Figure 3.4 illustrates this.

Fig. 3.4 Clear boundaries

Figure 3.4 shows a family with permeable or 'clear' boundaries between each of its sub-groups, and between the total unit and the outside world. The boundaries overlap slightly and there is sufficient space for communications to pass.

Families differ, as we have seen, so we need to find a way of representing these differences graphically. This can be done by drawing in the various types of boundary structure.

Rigid families, with steepened hierarchies, would be drawn with unbroken lines surrounding them (figure 3.5). Each sub-system is remote from its neighbour and ordinary communication has an intrusive quality when moving from a higher to a lower sub-system, whilst it fails when moving upward.

Overinvolved families with extremely flattened hierarchies and diffuse or wide open boundaries would be depicted as in figure 3.6. The boundaries overlap greatly and communication has no clear direction.

Of course, no one family will fall so neatly into a stereotype that it fits any of these figures perfectly. If we think of the types of boundary as points on a line or continuum we can see more readily how a family will fit somewhere along it, tending towards one extreme or the other at various times in its life, whilst occupying a more or less central position for most of the time.

The continuum is depicted in figure 3.7.

In chapter 2 we saw how families grow through a series of developmental stages which correspond to many of the milestones in the life of the individual. Each family responds in its own way to these crises. Some may become more open, others more closed as each family struggles with the changes that disturb its balance. These attempts to regain equilibrium by opening or closing boundaries move the family's footing to one side or another of the central, healthiest point of the continuum, between rigidity and overinvolvement.

Fig. 3.5 Rigid boundaries

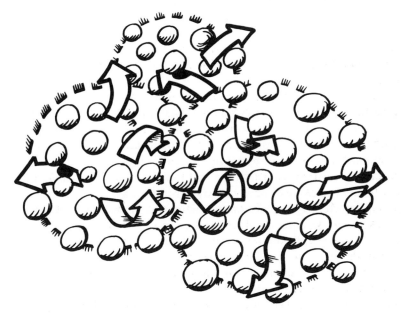

Fig. 3.6 Diffuse boundaries

This is well illustrated by two families who were referred to a family therapy clinic. Both families were seeking help with their teenage daughters who were having problems. But, as we shall see, the circumstances and the structure of the boundaries defining the family systems were very different.

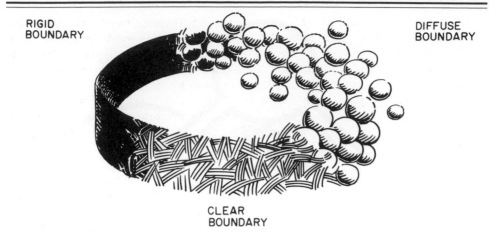

RIGID
BOUNDARY

DIFFUSE
BOUNDARY

CLEAR
BOUNDARY

Fig. 3.7 Diagram to show the boundary types merging and blending

The Maples

Mr and Mrs Maple had both been married before. Mr Maple had children from his first marrige who lived with his ex-wife and visited him for holidays and at weekends. Mrs Maple had a daughter, Sally, who lived with her and Mr Maple, only visiting her natural father infrequently. Her mother and stepfather had been married for a long time and Sally thought of him as her real father. At 14 years Sally was a small, slightly built, timorous and shy girl. Her parents were worried because she had difficulty getting to school. When she did get there she was often frightened and would phone her parents and beg them to collect her and bring her home.

When they attended their first appointment their therapist had no more information than this. His first task was to help the family to feel reasonably at ease and to get as much additional information as he could. He began by asking the family what the problem was and how each of them saw it. It is useful to know what points the family agree and disagree upon.

Mr Maple began by saying that they had talked about the problem until 2 a.m. the previous night and now knew what the trouble was.

The therapist asked again what the problem was. He needed to know whether or not the family were in agreement before hearing their views on its cause.

Their initial comments supported the information the therapist had received from the Educational Psychologist: Sally had problems getting to school.

One important point emerges from this – the family saw Sally as the identified or 'index' patient. If we consider the family to be an interacting structure then we can view any family member with problems to be representing the problems of the family on its behalf. This person is the identified patient, i.e. the person identified by the family as the sick member or the one with the problems. The problem which manifests itself will often be symbolic of, or give clues to, the nature of the difficulties that the family is struggling with. In this case it seemed clear that as Sally was having difficulty in being away from her family, the difficulties were to do with being close or with being distant.

The therapist encouraged the Maples to give him their views on what lay behind Sally's 'school phobia'. Mr Maple did most of the talking whilst Mrs Maple sat close to Sally who sat between her mother and father with her finger on her lips. Frequently throughout this time, and during the remainder of the first part of the session, Mrs Maple pulled Sally's hand away from her face.

This was another piece of information which tended to support the therapist's speculations about the nature of the problem. Sally sat closer to her mother than to her father. Mrs Maple nervously clutched at her daughter's hand and pulled her finger from her lips unnecessarily. In this way Mrs Maple invaded her daughter's personal space. Such closeness between a mother and her child is entirely appropriate when the child is very young, but most children will begin to protest against too intense an involvement much earlier, during the latency years and even earlier – during the anal stage – so there was plainly something unusual in this behaviour. Even if we accept that the therapy situation was stressful for Sally and that her mother was trying to be supportive, the matter of the interference in her personal space remains.

The therapist considered that perhaps Sally and her mother were overinvolved. It also seemed possible that Sally occupied a space between her parents in their emotional life as well as on the settee. The therapist contemplated these matters whilst listening to Mr Maple's account of the prevous night's discussion.

He learned that the family had moved to the area to run a small catering business together. The family included Mrs Maple's parents – she was their only child and they were very close. Mr and Mrs Maple, Sally and her maternal grandparents had always lived together. They had shared a large house in north London, all of the adults had good jobs and between them they brought a great deal of money into the house.

Upon closer questioning it became apparent that, although it was true that they had shared a house, the grandparents in effect had a self-contained apartment whilst Mr and Mrs Maple lived with Sally in their own flat.

It was significant that Mr Maple spoke of the income brought in by the four adults as if it was shared between them (in the same way that a married couple shares an income) and that he said that they lived together when in fact they had flats in the same house.

Mrs Maple was an only child and so was her daughter. Perhaps the similarities between the generations went even further? On the basis of the history that Mr Maple had given so far, it seemed that Mrs Maple and her parents had not managed to separate effectively and that there was too close a relationship between them.

Mr Maple continued with his story. They had gathered from Sally that she found it hard and felt very lonely to think of the four of them at home together whilst she was on her own in a strange school with strange people many miles away, and with no way of returning home except by school bus at the end of the day. There was no public transport; they now lived in a rural area which was radically different from what they were used to. When they had lived in London, Sally had not minded being at school. Things had been very different then; all of the adults had been out at work in different parts of the metropolis, so she had not felt left out. There was a good public transport system and she could return home without relying upon school transport.

The therapist was interested to hear this; it substantiated many of his speculations. The problem was focused upon being distant and being close in emotional terms. The distance between home and school served to highlight an area of conflict which hitherto had been disguised by the living arrangements of the family in their London house and by the proximity of home to school. The problem was symbolic of an unacknowledged and partly unconscious anxiety about separation.

Where the contact between a mother and her child has been close enough to help the child to feel safely held, and intuitive enough to allow sufficient distance for him to deal with just enough distress and discomfort on his own, then the child is able to tolerate separation from his mother for increasingly long periods of time. The inadequately attached individual's inability to separate is often confused with devotion. Those who have had the closest and most satisfying of loving relationships with their parents will find it easier to separate. The pain of parting may be acute but parting is more possible. In this family it seemed very clear that the problem was continued from one generation to the next. It was evident that Mrs Maple loved her daughter – this was not in doubt, love is not the same thing as attachment. Attachment has to do with the instillation in the baby of an inner sense of security. This is based on many things, including the certainty that the mother will always return and will always be able to do something which is 'good enough' (Winnicott, 1965) to help the baby feel safe and well.

Compare this with the examples from chapter 1 of the different results produced by the care given to Kay and to Carol by their mothers. Carol's mother was always close beside her but Carol was eventually to suffer from such undifferentiated closeness. The 'good enough mother', like Kay's, will do some things which may leave her baby feeling distressed and alone for a time but not for too long or too short a time. Leaving her baby for too long would make him feel overwhelmed by the distress which pervades his whole being. Leaving him for not long enough would be to risk producing a frightened child who is not able to manage without his mother's constant support. A 'good enough mother' will get things wrong from time to time but she will get other things right and so compensate for any mistakes over time.

Before continuing with Mr Maple's account of the late-night discussion, it will be useful to focus on one or two points which emerge from this case study.

We have described the resonance which is established between the feelings of the child and those of his parents at successive developmental stages and it has been suggested that the process of development takes place over a lifetime.

The first point is readily established. Mrs Maple and Sally were both anxious and they gave every indication of living inside each other's skin, of being undifferentiated. Mrs Maple was so intimately in touch with her daughter's distress that she did not have to imagine what it was like to be so upset; she experienced that distress herself.

Sally was approaching adolescence whilst her parents were entering middle age and her grandparents had reached retirement. They each had developmental obstacles to negotiate. As Sally began a stage in her life which would normally lead her towards increasing independence, her parents were embarking upon a career which would lead them to become a couple again rather than a family, and her grandparents were dealing with the loss of relationships at work, facing old age and, eventually, death.

Each of these stages brings with it the need to separate and to negotiate new relationships. Sally eventually will go out with boys, and her parents will have to relinquish their parental role to become a couple once more. Her grandparents face the loss of a life-long partner. All of these changes bring with them anxieties to do with loss and separation; Sally's parents and her grandparents were colluding to resist this alarming process. They made conscious decisions which were to do with the family finances, the deteriorating quality of life in a London borough, and so on. These conscious decisions were irresistably influenced by unconscious imperatives to avoid the pain of loss that growing up a little more would incur for all of them.

In order to avoid this loss, the family moved closer together than it had ever been in terms of its boundary structures. The family had always been one which leaned towards the diffuse end of the continuum and now it went even further towards this extreme to stave off the approach of loss. The very open boundary between the Maples and the maternal grandparents ceased to exist at all. They began to have all their meals together, they lived in the same house, shared a living room, bathroom and kitchen. They even shared the income that the catering business brought. The only space that they did not share was their bedrooms.

All of this activity, which was unconsciously intended to hold the inevitable at bay, failed. It failed because it was an attempt to deal at the surface with events which were occurring at a deep level in the inner world of each of them individually. It also failed because Sally had to go to school many miles away. She consequently felt as if she had been cast out by the new unit of parents and grandparents.

The Maples' intention had been to resist the inevitable by bringing the three generations of their family into closer proximity. To achieve this they had moved to their new rural location. But the result was to move Sally to an uncomfortable distance away from the home so that the original intent was frustrated.

Sally's (and consequently the family's) presenting symptom was school phobia, the product of which was intended to be the unification of the family by bringing them together under one roof for twenty-four hours a day if Sally stayed home from school. The effect, as the therapist heard from the parents, was to create disunity amongst them as it became increasingly difficult to deny the differences which had always existed.

If we return to the session we find that Mr Maple spoke of the family's decision to sell up the business because they believed Sally's problem was caused by the distance between home and school. This seems to show that another of the boundaries which map the family structure had been breached.

Sally had effectively usurped, or had been given, a responsibility and authority which was rightly the province of the parents. There was an apparent repetition of this in the relationship between the parents and the grandparents; they had left any decision about where they should move to Sally's parents. Their authority was invested in the parents, whose authority, in turn, was invested in Sally.

When the therapist asked how Sally had got on at her previous school he had been told she was fine but that she had been anxious about attending her primary school. The therapist asked about other out-of-home activities such as youth club or the Guides, and was told that Sally had attended a variety of these extracurricular activities but her interest in each lasted for only a short time before she wanted to stop. During this time the parents frequently contradicted each other so that the therapist was able to focus upon their disagreement and begin to bring it out into the open.

There was a pretense that everyone was in agreement with everything in order that differences might be concealed and separateness avoided. Furthermore, these differences highlighted an internal conflict that the therapist voiced for Sally. This was that part of her wanted very much to grow up and become independent of her parents and to enjoy the company of others of her own age, whilst another part of her became anxious at the thought that she was leaving her mother behind.

We shall leave the Maples here with their blurred boundaries, unresolved conflicts and flattened hierarchy and move on to look at the Birch family.

The Birch Family

When the Birches first came to the clinic only the mother and fifteen-year-old daughter Mandy attended. This was the mother's second marriage; her relationship with Mandy's father had deteriorated over some time and to such an extent that, for the children's sake, they had separated and divorced three years earlier. Their therapist asked them to explain, in their own words, what the problem was as they saw it.

He noted that Mrs Birch sat upon the settee and Mandy sat at quite a distance from her in an armchair.

Mrs Birch began talking in a firm, clear voice and, in a professional manner, described the difficulties she and her friend had been having with Mandy. The therapist clarified that this friend was her new partner and that they lived together. This caused Mrs Birch some discomfort but it was essential that the therapist establish the principle of frank, honest and open communication.

Already the therapist had begun to form a hazy picture of the family's boundary structure. The way that Mandy and her mother sat apart from each other; the way that Mrs Birch's explanations and descriptions of their troubles sounded like a report given by one professional to another rather than the concerns of a worried mother; the way in which Mrs Birch talked about her partner – all pointed towards closed boundaries. The therapist kept this in the back of his mind as the session proceeded.

Mrs Birch talked of the breakdown of her marriage and of how Mandy had failed to cope adequately with this. She had been and still was close to her father but unlike her sisters had not been able to give expression to her feelings of loss, when he left. Mandy was the eldest of three girls and had never mixed well with them, nor had she been close to her mother.

The therapist asked how Mandy saw things and she could only answer very briefly, almost monosyllabicly, that she liked her father.

Mrs Birch told the therapist that Mandy had been stealing things from them. She said Mandy told her that she had never taken anything from her purse and was indignant and horrified that they thought she could have done such a thing. She

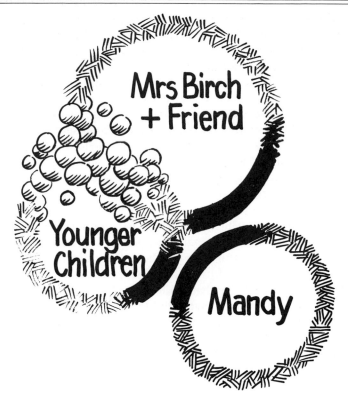

Fig. 3.8 The Birch family

eventually admitted to having stolen from bottles and other savings boxes. Money was tight and Mandy had taken quite a lot.

The therapist asked Mandy what she had done with the money. She said that she had spent it on 'things'. After further questioning (Mandy was very reticent about giving much away) it turned out that she had spent the money on nice things – clothes for herself and so on.

Mrs Birch explained that when her husband had left she had done all that she could to keep the house on. For the children's sake she tried to keep things together. She worked part-time and sewed all the children's clothes herself. The other girls accepted how difficult things were and managed to reconcile themselves to their straitened circumstances. They did not complain as Mandy did. However, the younger girls were still in junior school whilst Mandy was a teenager.

Mrs Birch told the therapist that her new partner and she shared the view that children needed discipline and they had agreed together that Mandy should be grounded until she had earned their trust once more. However, they had allowed Mandy to go out with her father over the holiday break, so she did not feel that they were being inordinately severe. Mrs Birch said that sometimes she wanted to cuddle Mandy but Mandy resisted this. Mrs Birch thought Mandy might feel she was too big now. Mandy admitted to wanting a cuddle sometimes but she felt stupid so couldn't ask for one.

Mrs Birch wondered if some of this was her fault. When her marriage had ended she had insisted that, if her ex-husband wanted to see the children, he had to see them all together. She had done this because she wanted to be fair, to make sure that the girls each had the same amount of time with their father. Now she realised that Mandy must have felt as if she were being penalised. She was much older than her sisters and in many respects it was easier for her father to look after her or to take her with him when he want on a business journey.

Whilst Mrs Birch was talking the therapist recognised that this had been impossible for Mrs Birch to see at the time when her world was falling apart and she was struggling as hard as she knew how to keep it all together. She had always been a person for whom rules and discipline were important so it is predictable that she would veer towards the rigid end of the continuum in an attempt to hold things together.

The seating arrangements which Mandy and her mother adopted illustrated the boundary arrangements and said something about the nature of the problem. Mandy sat completely apart from her mother. They did not touch and seldom looked at each other – they had little contact with each other at all. It was almost possible to see the walls that they had built around themselves and between each other. The therapist could also see that both Mandy and her mother were distressed by their circumstances. Mrs Birch was often close to tears despite her attempt to adopt a professional tone and manner. Mandy seemed worried and scared, she had the look of a creature which, sidling up for comfort and affection, is nervous because it expects a scolding.

Once again the problem was to do with closeness and distance, as it had been with the Maples. But where the Maples had organised their boundary structures in a diffuse way because of their anxieties about being apart, the Birches constructed firm boundaries because of fears to do with closeness. There was both a wish for and a fear of closeness.

Sometimes we fail as professionals because of an inability to recognise that two things which are contradictory can both be true at the same time. Most of our lives are spent dealing with or working through conflicts of one kind or another or in resolving the conflicts which are inherent in each of our developmental stages. In this instance Mandy and her mother wanted, but felt extremely anxious about, closeness with each other.

Figure 3.8 shows that it is possible to have a variety of boundary structures within the same family. The boundary between Mandy and her mother and 'stepfather' is rigid. Communication between them is practically impossible, but the boundary between the 'parents' and the younger children is much more open, even though it still tends toward the rigid. The younger children had not yet reached adolescence, the age when all children are impelled toward greater independence, whilst Mandy had. They did not challenge the authority of their parents in the same way that Mandy did. Consequently, it was possible for the parents to feel safely in control of the younger ones and so remain open to them, whilst Mandy posed a threat to their fragile authority.

Boundaries may be used as defences which protect the individual, or the sub-system, from vulnerability. Those who rigidify their boundaries signal, from behind an apparently impregnable bastion (which gives the semblance of strength), that there is considerable anxiety about being too open to others.

The therapist acknowledged that he was aware of some of the distress that lay behind the distance that this mother and daughter created between themselves. He talked about how difficult it sometimes is to give or ask for care or even to recognise it when the need is too great.

Mrs Birch was able to respond to this by saying that she had some idea of how her daughter might feel and that she only wanted the best for her. She went on to inform the therapist that her own childhood had been a difficult one during which she had experienced considerable distress.

Mrs Birch had begun to acknowledge that some of her daughter's problems were related to her own childhood difficulties. We can suppose that the problems the mother experienced in her own childhood predisposed her to manage her life in a controlled and rigid way in order to dispel the possibility of similar difficulties in the present. Something extremely distressing had happened to her which left her feeling vulnerable, badly hurt, exposed, and needing to wrap herself in a defensive shield so that she would not be hurt again.

Mandy's stealing was a response to a feeling of being shut out by her mother. The money she took and spent on 'nice things' symbolised the nice things she felt she didn't get from her mother and substituted for the love she needed. It was an intrusion by stealth into her mother's space from which she was otherwise forcibly excluded by her mother's rules, regulations and rigid boundaries.

The therapist tried to help Mandy and her mother to understand some of this by talking with them about the money standing in the place of love and by saying that sometimes it could seem that there was not enough to go round and had to be guarded. Mrs Birch told him that she often felt as if she didn't have enough inside to be able to give sufficient to her children, so she had to be firm about sharing everything equally.

Several things were happening here. Mrs Birch was influenced by her own experiences of childhood to withhold the love that she felt was in such short supply. She placed it within the vault made of her rules and protected it with stalwart outer defensive boundaries. These boundary walls also made it impossible for her to give affection to or receive it from Mandy at those times when either wanted to express their love. The mother felt so depleted that her daughter's desperate attempts to steal the love she needed was felt as an assault upon extremely limited resources. The consequence of this was that the mother redoubled her vigilance, re-formed her boundaries and retrenched her position as if she were besieged. The therapist had to be careful to do nothing that would make either feel too vulnerable while helping them face their needs and the anxieties these stimulated in both of them.

Each attempt by Mandy to get close to her mother had evoked the pain that lay hidden behind the barriers and had increased the distance between them that had caused Mandy to steal. If they were left to their own devices the situation could only worsen and leave a lasting rift between them. Amongst other things this would mean that Mandy would be left to negotiate her transition into young womanhood without the guiding hand of her mother. It would also mean that Mandy would be left needing to come to terms with unresolved issues at some later stage, and that her mother would have missed this opportunity to work out some of the pain which remained from her own childhood.

In the case of both of the families we have discussed it would have been possible to predict the kind of boundaries they would form under stress. There were already clues in the family background, in the history and in the way they presented themselves to the therapist which suggested the preferred form of defence.

Before we conclude this chapter it would be as well to remember that all families construct boundaries of one sort or another between themselves and the outside world and that this is appropriate and healthy. Not all boundaries are dysfunctional barriers between the generations, one family and another, or one group within the family and another.

We have seen how two mothers carried experiences from their own family of origin into their families of procreation. This was, perhaps, most clearly seen in the relationship between Mrs Maple, her parents and her daughter. We all carry influences from our family or origin into our marriages or partnerships and into each and every group to which we belong. This can be helpful as we each then influence one another through the different ways we have of thinking, feeling and dealing with problems that we learned in our original families. It is part of the impetus towards growth and maturity which continues throughout life.

In the next chapter we shall look at the ways in which families influence and in turn are influenced by the world outside, and begin to look at the normative function of groups which was briefly hinted at in the preceding paragraph.

Reference

Winnicott D W (1965) *The Family and Individual Development*. London: Tavistock.

4

The Family Within

and the

World Outside

In the first chapters we have looked at the relationship of the developmental stages to family members; here we examine how the family accompanies the individual in each group in which he participates. We shall, of course, be looking at the *unconscious* representative of the family which peoples the inner world and influences all of our contacts with others.

In chapter 1 we saw how the infant internalises an image of his mother. He is enabled to do so by her constancy and predictable presence. His external view of his mother becomes an inward representation as his mental image of her is strengthened by each shared moment. This process of introjection – the taking inside of oneself of aspects of another – continues throughout the whole of one's life. Subsequently, important others, such as the child's father, or his brothers and sisters, find their way into his inner world in the same way. These representatives bring into the unconscious aspects which they possess in reality. Thus if a father is cheerful and confident of his child's ability then his internalised representative will be felt as supportive. If, however, the father is disapproving and forbidding then his internalised presence will be critical and is felt as persecuting.

The same rule applies to all members of the child's family, and is influenced by the innate characteristics with which we are all born: Melanie Klein (1946) referred to them as 'constitutional factors'. This means that each child is born with differing capacities for dealing with distress. In other words, some babies are born happy and contented from the start, whilst others are easily upset and hard to console. The child who is born with a sound sense of inner strength and goodness will be less adversely affected by a critical father than the child who is born with a reduced capacity for contentment. Such a child is likely to be strongly influenced by a critical father whose disapproval will tend to confirm the child's sense of dis-ease.

The discontented child is favourably influenced by parents, and other relatives, who are able to offer a reassuring presence. In this way his sense of innate distress is modified, diminishes and becomes less influential. In this case the internalised family is beneficial to the individual.

When the child becomes an adult and moves out into the world, he assesses each new person against the backcloth of his internal family. This largely unconscious process subtly influences his receptivity to each new person and affects his responses. We have already seen how these projective processes work between individuals through projective identification and transference (i.e. relating to a third person as if he or she were an important figure from one's inner world), now we shall see how this occurs in group situations.

We have to remember that we are considering more than two people at the same time. As one person responds to covert influences from his own past, another will be similarly affected by his individual past, and so on. As this is the same for everyone it is evident that there is a tremendous variety of influences which touch every group. As a result there has to be a great deal of negotiation when any group of individuals meets before anything constructive can be done. This is one reason why councils, committees and parliaments have well-established procedures. Instead of having to decide who should lead each meeting (which will vary every time depending on who is present) rules are agreed which determine this without the need for discussion. For instance, the Speaker or his Deputy presides over the House of Commons; he decides who will speak and so on, and even this decision is governed by well-recognised conventions.

Whilst there are undoubted difficulties surrounding the formation of any group (rivalries, potential for hostility, jealousies and competitiveness, etc.), there are powerful gains to be made and wholesome rewards. Many of the benefits derive from the same variety of influences that have potential for chaos and confusion.

For example, although John may treat Ann as if she were his selfish and unconcerned mother, Ann may respond in her own way – with care and warmth. If she is able to do this consistently, without succumbing to John's unconscious attempts (through projective identification) to manipulate her into responding to him selfishly, then he will gradually be able to respond warmly himself. He will have internalised a warm and caring figure who helps to thaw the icy image of a cold and selfish mother.

Ann will find it easier to maintain her personal qualities in the face of John's attacks in a group rather than in a one-to-one relationship with him. The group will have a variety of views of her each different from each other, as well as from John's view; this will enable her to keep a balanced image of herself. However, if Ann responds selfishly then the situation will deteriorate, with John becoming convinced of the correctness of his original view, and both responding defensively, aggressively and with each occupying artificial and entrenched positions in relation to the other.

Let us look at some accounts from treatment so that we can see how the individual brings the family into the group.

In the first example a young woman brought her family into the group in the form of a pattern of behaviour which she repeated in all group situations.

The group of six adolescents had been meeting for only a short time and had not yet become established as a cohesive unit. There were four young women, and two men. Kathy was talking to Mary, who sat beside her. She was perched on the edge of her chair with her body turned towards Mary, to whom she spoke in a mumbled whisper. The conversation seemed to be very secretive, but in a way that demanded the attention of the others, so that the secrecy became a taunting exclusion or an invitation to take notice.

As the group had only been running for a matter of a few weeks one of the two therapists decided to take the lead and intervene. He hoped to set the tone of the meeting by teaching the members good group practice through his example. He intended to confront Kathy's behaviour. Having challenged the way she was excluding the rest of the group he wanted to help her and the others to feel a little more comfortable.

The therapist had several ideas about what was happening at that moment. First, there was the matter of Kathy's behaviour and what that might mean individually. He had noticed in earlier sessions that she tended to isolate one person at a time and speak exclusively with him (or her), holding him with a fixed gaze that seemed to make the recipient feel pleased and embarrassed all at once. It also seemed that it was exceptionally difficult to break eye contact with her without great effort and apparent rudeness. This behaviour recurred each week and so had some significance; it was not merely a response to a single event in the life of the group, it was part of Kathy's personal repertoire and it was dysfunctional as it made others feel uncomfortable. It might be intended to create a special bond between Kathy and the recipient, but as it excluded the others and made the recipient so uncomfortable that she would avoid Kathy if at all possible, the therapist assumed with a reasonable degree of certainty, that he was witnessing something that was part of Kathy's problem with relationships. Her desire to be close was so intense, demanding and excluding that she drove people away.

Secondly, there was the group's response to her behaviour. The others all remained silent and stared at the floor, avoiding any contact at all. It seemed to the therapist that this was not just a common awkwardness but also had to do with a wish to escape being captured by Kathy's gaze. Consequently it was reasonably certain that as the group wished to avoid dealing with this problem, it would shirk other difficult issues too. The group members seemed happy to leave the focus of the discomfort with Mary and uneasy about abandoning her to deal with Kathy on her own. None of them wished to intervene lest it draw attention to themselves. In the present circumstances the attention that they would have received could only have provoked anxiety.

The therapist considered that the group was directly avoiding Kathy and that it was also avoiding the more common discomfort faced at the beginning of all groups. This has to do with issues of trust and mistrust. (Cf. the development of the individual in chapter 1, with particular reference to Erikson's chart of Psycho-Social Development, summarised in figure 4.1.) Early in the life of the group the members have not yet discovered enough about each other and the potential of the therapist to feel sufficiently comfortable to be open with each other. The group also needs time to learn what its purpose is.

This was the third idea that the therapist had in mind. The group was at the very beginning of its life so he would have expected to see evidence of this 'newness' in the way they communicated. He would have expected too to see the kind of one-to-one conversation in which Kathy had engaged Mary as a sort of regression which occurs at the beginning of all groups.

The notion of regression is a familiar one. By it, we understand that the individual is returning to an earlier developmental stage when faced with an unmanageable degree of stress. The behaviour which this group exhibited can be understood as a regression to an earlier stage of development when, as infants,

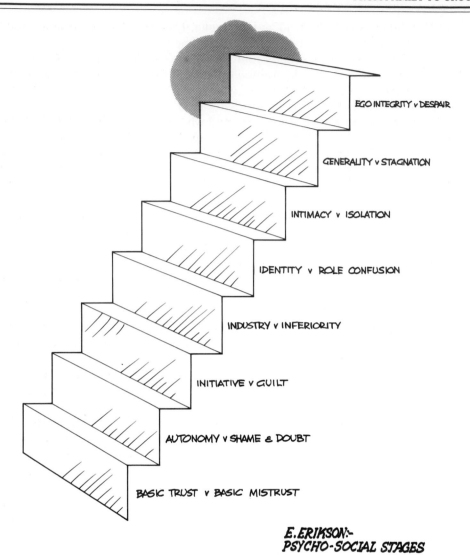

EGO INTEGRITY v DESPAIR

GENERALITY v STAGNATION

INTIMACY v ISOLATION

IDENTITY v ROLE CONFUSION

INDUSTRY v INFERIORITY

INITIATIVE v GUILT

AUTONOMY v SHAME & DOUBT

BASIC TRUST v BASIC MISTRUST

E.ERIKSON:-
PSYCHO-SOCIAL STAGES

Fig. 4.1

each of the members related almost exclusively with only one other – mother. Seen in this light, it is a return to an aspect of the maternal relationship.

We can view it in another way too – as each member of the group using earlier experiences as a template which guides their responses in each new situation. In this sense the various stages of the group's development mirror aspects of the development of the individual within his family. This is another way in which the family is brought into the group.

Let us return now to the group of adolescents.

The therapist asked Kathy what she was talking about, adding that it was very difficult to hear her. Kathy's response was to turn her back on him more firmly and otherwise to ignore his question. She continued talking to Mary in a quiet voice.

The second therapist, a woman, made a similar intervention and this time Kathy replied.

This pattern of ignoring the male therapist and responding to the female therapist had occurred in earlier sessions and could thus be regarded as significant. Not only was Kathy segregating one member of the group from the rest, she was also splitting the two therapists.

The therapists knew that Kathy's behaviour had caused her difficulty at school and had led her to become isolated. They also knew that her parents were divided in their response to her. They were isolated from Kathy's mother's family too. Again, there was evidence of a split, with the mother's family generally being regarded as good and the father's family being seen as uninvolved, unhelpful, thoughtless and uncaring.

Kathy was recreating in the group forms of relating which were learned within the family. Thus, as was stated at the beginning of this case, she brought her family into the group as a pattern that influenced her relationships with the group. The therapists were able to resist these primitive splitting manoeuvres and eventually managed to bring Kathy into the group in a more healthy way as the group became more trusting.

The following extracts show some clear examples of transference, that is one member of the group treating the group therapist or another group member as if he were a significant figure from the past. We shall also find examples of projection; i.e. an unwanted personal characteristic is seen as belonging to another.

This was an adult group with nine members – six women and three men, with a male therapist. The ages of the group members ranged from the early twenties to the late forties.

This particular session was well advanced when the therapist remarked that the group had ignored the absence of one of its members and remarked that this might have influenced the topics of conversation that day. They had been talking about death, accidents, car breakdowns and mourning but had not referred directly to the empty chair or the person who should have occupied it. Mike, a middle-aged man, had exploded verbally at this and had said that the therapist was grossly unfair, he was always picking on them, never had a kind word to say to or about them, always thought he knew best and would never admit that he was wrong.

Mike himself was always scrupulous about saying that he could be wrong whenever he gave an opinion or voiced an idea. Yet, whenever he said 'mind you, I could be wrong', he always conveyed the feeling that this was highly unlikely. His assertion of the possibility of his being wrong served as a warning not to challenge him but, having said it, he could rest assured of his own fairness.

Mike had identified one of his own shortcomings – his difficulty in admitting that he could be wrong – as belonging to the therapist. He had projected his unwanted controlling self onto the therapist. The group was able to bring this home to him by pointing out that the therapist had merely voiced the fact that they had not talked about the absent member directly. Many of them were able to make the connection between the verbal material of the session and their own feelings of concern for the absent member. They pointed out to Mike that the therapist had tacitly acknowledged his fallibility by saying that the absence 'might' have affected their choice of material that day; he had not been categorically certain that he was correct. Mike knew that when *he* said 'might' he meant 'do not challenge me' and so he attributed this sort of prohibitive control to the therapist too.

The group also voiced their feelings about the therapist. They saw him as able to accept his mistakes and own up to them, and as being thoughtful and careful of their feelings. They saw him as being a caring and helpful person but also as one who could be very confronting at times. This corresponded very little – if it corresponded at all – with Mike's view and, consequently, because he was so at odds with the majority, he had to revise his opinion. This meant that he increasingly saw the therapist as he really was, and became less influenced by the hostile and critical internalised father with whom he had confused the person of the therapist.

Over the following weeks Mike was able to note for himself when his perception of the therapist was influenced by his internalised father, to recognise the distortion that these transferred feelings caused, and to correct their influence on him.

During another of this group's sessions Patty, one of the younger women, spoke directly to Madge, one of the older women. She said that she did not really know whether or not her feelings had become apparent to the rest of the group, but she had been feeling hostile towards her. Having got to know her better within and through the group she now realised that her hostility had been misdirected. Madge was not a justifiable focus for her anger. The events of the previous weeks, when the group had been talking about distortions and transferred feelings, had had a powerful effect on her. The issues with which the group had struggled had touched her deeply as she began to realise that she saw Madge reflected in the darkly distorting mirrors of her own mind. She realised that not only had she seen Madge through the image of her mother which she interposed between herself and Madge, but also that the image she fostered of her mother was incomplete, and disregarded the care that her mother had given her as a child and continued to give her still. Consequently she was helped to see that the feelings which influenced her behaviour towards her mother, Madge and others were themselves distorted by a self-protective skin which had reduced her ability to be in touch with others and to tolerate any criticism. Anyone who had tried to help by offering criticism, even when it was constructive, had been seen as interfering and hostile to her. This protective skin was also intended to obviate the need for self-criticism. She had invested in the person of Madge (through the process of projection) her hostility, her anger and a persecutory form of guilt-invoking self-criticism. She now realised that this is exactly what she had done and continued to do with her mother. That is, she had turned her mother into a nasty, persecuting harridan in her own mind.

There are two points worthy of note here. First, although Patty had not directly participated in the events that had taken place within the group, she had been intensely and intimately involved in them.

Just as each of us might gain something from a particular instance and generalise from it into many other situations, thereby increasing the benefit we receive from one piece of learning, so might we 'particularise' from general circumstances.

Patty had been able to take relevant aspects of the group's experience, and of Mike's experience, and apply them to her particular circumstances and learn from them. She was helped in this through the group's functioning as a forum for self-examination and honest appraisal. It also helped that the group failed to conform to her expectations that it would respond to her as her family had. The group itself was aided in this valuable function by virtue of the fact that it was composed of a group of strangers who had been selected for the group by the therapist. In this respect it differed from most other groups to which we belong.

When we choose friends we make choices which, like our choice of partner, are influenced by past experiences. Consequently, even though it is our friends who might wish to help us most, they are often the people who can help us least as they conform to the influences which defined their selection as friends in the first place. Just as couples support each other by enhancing valued personal attributes and aiding the concealment of unacceptable aspects, so friends support each other in the same way. Such support, whilst helpful in the short term, becomes a hindrance to the resolution of real problems in the long term.

The therapeutic group, being composed of strangers, suffers less from these constraints. Patty had not been able to 'recreate' her family in the group although, as we have seen, she tried. As it was different from her family, the group enabled her to become aware of a dysfunctional form of relating which had hindered her relations with everybody else until this time. Because the group was conducted in a thoughtful, firmly confronting and tolerant style, Patty was able to face these issues within herself and to work with them towards a successful outcome in which she was more tolerant, less hostile and felt the need to disown her unwanted aspects much less than before.

Secondly, Patty began to realise that she used to invest her mother with negative and hostile qualities. Here she differs from Mike. Mike's father was critical and persecuting, while Patty's mother was not – at least not to the extent described by Patty initially. So, whilst we can see that both Patty and Mike transferred feelings which belonged to a parent onto the person of another, in Patty's case her view of her mother was coloured by the influence of her own negative constituent feelings. These made Patty think of her mother as 'bad'. She then responded to her mother as if she really were 'bad'.

Parents are often anxious that they have somehow failed their children. Sadly, this is frequently true, but it is important that we recognise that it is not always the case, and even where it is true, it is not necessarily the whole truth. Patty's case illustrates this very well. Her mother had not failed her; Patty was born a distressed child. However, Patty's mother did not have the personal resources necessary to mediate, or to mitigate wholly, the disabling influence of Patty's constituent elements. The bad feelings she was born with and which she feared would overwhelm her remained with her into adulthood and were dealt with projectively by her. As her mother had been turned into a bad, critical and persecuting presence in her mind, when she transferred aspects of her relations with her mother onto another then that person was seen as bad, critical and persecuting too.

Through these two examples we have seen how we each bring our family of origin and other formative influences into each and every group to which subsequently we belong. It is essential to any understanding we gain about the workings of groups that we recognise the simple truth that group processes occur in all group situations. These processes are not the sole prerogative of treatment groups and they do not require that a group be comprised of patients before they occur.

In her classic paper 'The Functioning of Social Systems as a Defence against Anxiety' (1976), Isabel Menzies reviewed her research into the organisation of an orthopaedic hospital. Much of the paper is concerned with the effect of the social system upon the children who were patients in one of the wards, but she also examined the influence of this system on the staff, particularly the nurses. She showed, through a painstaking analysis of the material she observed, staff interactions, the rate of attrition amongst student nurses, the way in which patient-related and other ward tasks were organised, that the staff were influenced by their own unconscious processes. Much of the effort which was consciously intended to improve staff efficiency in the execution of their duties was unconsciously designed to avoid the anxiety that the intimate contact with patients evoked in the nurses. For example, all nurses are familiar, although they might dislike it and try to behave differently, with such phrases as: 'Go and take a bed pan to the fractured femur in bed 3.' Or 'Keep a close eye on the CCF in bed 2.' Such terminology reduces the individual to the component part which brings him into hospital for the care he needs. It leaves the nurse with the simplified task of dealing with only a part of the person and spares her any need to make contact with the emotional life of the patient. As a consequence the nurse is not faced quite so directly with her own feelings about the patient or with her feelings about what she is doing to him, which might be painful or embarrassing. Unfortunately, it also leaves the patient feeling frightened and unhelped. Perhaps the honorific 'Angels' is more accurate than at first it seems. It conveys a generous commitment to others and a remote and non-human distance!

The primary unconscious mechanism which is used in this situation is that of 'splitting'. This is a very primitive mechanism which is first employed in infancy and is a part of the process of projective identification, as we have seen. The infant is threatened by a disturbing or anxiety-provoking feeling and wishes to be rid of it. In order to achieve this he fantasises or imagines that it is possible to 'split off' a part of himself and push it outwards.

When the nurse talks about the 'femur' or the 'CCF', she is employing the same mechanism. Unconsciously she is splitting off the major part of her patient so that he becomes less than he is – a heart or a leg, a 'non-person'.

We can see then that even professional groups, who consider carefully the way in which they organise their functions, are prey to the same processes that influence therapeutic groups. Even groups whose members are all trained and experienced group analysts exhibit the same processes as groups formed of people in emotional difficulty.

It is clear then that all groups in any society are governed by the same principles. As all societies are made up of a number of ever-extending and overlapping groups we can adduce that the whole of society is influenced by the phenomena we have described. It would be foolhardy to suggest that whole societies behave in the same way that a family of four or a group of eight does. This would not be possible, there are too many different factors. The members of small groups and families know each other quite intimately; they see each other most days for much of the day. This obviously is not the case for the whole of a society. However, one group may touch another through a shared interest, shared space or by having a member in common. Here there are similarities with the small group; contact is regular, individuals are known, and so on. In this way the whole of a society is influenced through overlapping membership, shared interest, shared space, and so on.

If we think of society as a lake whose still and flat surface is disturbed by two separate individuals each of whom throws a pebble into its depths from opposite banks, then we begin to form an idea of how it is that groups many miles apart can influence each other. The ripples from each of the stones spread in ever-widening circles until they touch and overlap, eventually spreading into each other.

The same splitting mechanisms that Menzies described may also operate at a national level. If we take the miners' strike of 1983–84 as an example we see that the country was divided into two camps: those who saw the miners as troublemakers and enemies of law and order, and those who saw the government as the enemy of the working man which would deprive him of his right to work. The police were seen as either hardpressed and valiant upholders of the law or as agents of a harsh and unsympathetic government which was determined to suppress all opposition.

If we examine newspaper reports of the speeches made by members of the opposing factions, we can find considerable evidence to support these observations. Each side saw the other as the repository of the source of all things bad, and itself as the true champion of a beleaguered people; the fountainhead from whence flowed all things good. Any group or individual who attempted to put a more balanced view was either ignored or ridiculed for owning ill-formed and poorly considered opinions, or for lacking the moral fibre to have courage in any conviction. Whilst this is obviously a simplified account of the dynamics of those months, it is clear that the mechanisms we have defined did operate as part of the forces impelling the country at that time.

Splitting occurs through the vehicle of interconnectedness as described above, but it is aided dramatically by the national press. The influence which the press exerts is great, but it is tempered by the fact that people choose to read the paper that most closely corresponds to their own values, prejudices and opinions.

This chapter began with an illustration of how the family enters the group through transference, projective identification and repetition compulsion (the compulsion to repeat in the present aspects of an earlier relationship). We have ended it by showing how the group then enters into society through overlapping membership of other groups and via communication up and down hierarchies. We have seen how the more primitive mental mechanisms can operate equally in a group or on an individual basis. Furthermore, we have found that these same mental mechanisms may be used by whole nations, particularly at times of acute crisis (e.g. the Third Reich and the rise of Fascism).

This latter observation is offered for the sake of interest and completeness; it is of very little use to most of us to think in terms of the place of the group within the nation and how it might influence its life. However, we do need to consider the impact of the immediate society upon the group. By this I mean we need to be aware of the influence that the day hospital, inpatient unit, hostel, outpatient department, social service department and so on, has on the group and its conductor. Consequently, we would be wise to bear in mind the routes by which the group can be affected and the unconscious determinants of the need of the immediate society to influence and effect the group (Menzies, 1976).

Before we move on to look at the life of the group in more detail, we shall examine the relationship between psychopathology and ordinary human emotional development and consider why psychotherapy can be helpful in treating distressed or disturbed patients.

References

Klein M (1946) Notes on some schizoid mechanisms. In: *Envy and Gratitude*. London: Hogarth Press and The Institute of Psycho-Analysis.

Menzies I E P (1976) *The Functioning of Social Systems as a Defence against Anxiety*. London: Tavistock.

Psychopathology

and

Psychotherapy

In the preceding chapters we followed the individual through the nurturing relationship with his mother into wider relationships, first with his family and then with an ever-expanding society outside the home.

In this chapter we shall look at the individual to identify the impact that experience has upon him and how it influences his psychological make-up. In addition, we shall establish an understanding of the impact of psychotherapy upon the psychopathology of the individual.

If we return to the psychosexual stages of development outlined by Freud we can use them to identify certain areas in which the individual may become stuck.

We are all familiar with the descriptive diagnoses which are given to individuals, often rather loosely and pejoratively, in everyday life: 'He's an oral personality,' may be said of the individual who is perceived as greedily taking all that comes his way, or who is seen to be anxiously watching whilst others help themselves to the dishes of food before they reach him.

There are others that are often used with more distaste, more venom: 'She's anally fixated, the mean so and so.' This description is often used to insult and also to define the person who is reluctant to part with anything that she possesses. It is meant to bring to mind the infant who refuses to relinquish bodily products during potty training and to imply something sordid and unhealthy about the person.

There are, of course, many similar offensive phrases in common usage, so that we can see how the notion of psychological types has become widely accepted. Unfortunately, they are more often used to insult and to pigeon-hole someone than to understand or acknowledge a personal difficulty.

We need to be able to think in terms of developmental stages and to use our knowledge of these stages to understand 'fixated' behaviour without using our understanding in an offensive or an insulting way. It is useful to remember that such abuse often indicates a defensive posture; in other words, the dismissive or critical remark may conceal an unwillingness to face up to a similar aspect in oneself.

We also need to bear in mind the positions described by Klein (1946) (see chapter 1) and the way in which the individual may move into and out of them at various times in his life. These movements are influenced by the state of the inner world, and this in turn is affected by events in the external world. The impact which any of these circumstances may have is governed by the interplay between them, by the extent to which constituent elements have been modified through the early maternal relationship, and by the relative strength of opposing constituent elements in the first place. To this we must add the experience of the individual at each successive stage of development as these experiences may predispose him to respond in a particular and characteristic way.

We know that many real-life events produce degrees of stress which affect the individual's security and comfort. T H Holmes and R H Rahe published a social readjustment scale in 1967 (*Journal of Psychosomatic Research*, vol. 11, Pergamon Press) which rates the level of stress induced by a number of life-situations (figure 5.1). The stressor which carries the highest factor of stress is the loss of a spouse (stress value 100). The scale identifies other factors such as:

- *Marriage* Stress value 50
- *Retirement* Stress value 45
- *Change of job* Stress value 36
- *Moving home* Stress value 20

Fig. 5.1 Stress factors

The impact that these stress factors have upon the individual depends upon many things – his relationships with others, particularly his life partner; upon the number of stressors which coincide; and upon the level of his emotional stability and maturity.

We can see then that psychopathology is not a constant, it is fluid and responsive to both internal and external changes, and it is because it is so that it is possible to help people to change through the medium of psychotherapy.

We can, of course, detect instances of sticking points in others and in ourselves which may take the form of a character trait (e.g. obsessionality, carelessness or greed) or a behaviour which is repeated over and over (e.g. the person who falls in and out of love regularly, but who fails in any long-term relationships), but these may be influenced by experience.

Before we can use this knowledge successfully, we need to have a clearer idea of the personality types which relate to the various developmental stages and of the behaviour associated with them. Also we need to bear in mind Klein's theories of the paranoid schizoid and depressive positions. We shall begin by investigating three differing personality types.

PERSONALITY TYPES

The Depressive Personality

We are all familiar with the person who sees the world as through a glass darkly, whose vision is occluded by grey mists, and for whom anything which gleams does so merely to conceal the cloud which lurks behind it. We are used to dividing the world into pessimists and optimists, the former finding the glass half empty the latter finding it half full. This commonplace definition of the difference between the two types also serves to illustrate the fact that circumstances may be interpreted in either a hopeful or a despairing way, and that the view one takes can have very little to do with objective fact and much more to do with the state of mind of the observer. The person who takes the negative view may be said to be a depressive personality.

It will be evident that there is an element of the depressive personality in all of us, and that there is a range of types from the extreme to the relatively minor which coexist within this descriptive banding. This is because each of us has come to terms, to a greater or a lesser degree, with the realisation in infancy that the mother, whom we invested with our own bad feelings, is the same mother who provides us with all of our good and satisfactory experiences. This dawning awareness is believed to invoke a feeling of remorse for having attacked the mother in imagination, or in reality through biting or greedily depleting the breast of milk. The feeling of remorse carries with it depressive feelings of sadness and guilt.

Guilt is one of the features of depressive illness, and is often associated with extremely minor incidents from the past. For example, one patient who was profoundly depressed repeatedly confessed to having stolen five pence from her mother's purse as a child. The misdemeanour was small but was associated with other feelings of having robbed her mother in some basic way of good things which she could not replace. Most of us are able to resolve these feelings through the process of reparation which is characterised by an idealisation of the mother by the baby. The baby tries to repair the damage he feels he has caused by expressing his newfound view of his mother as a Madonna who can do no wrong, and by returning to her some of the good feelings he feels he has stolen.

One baby who was observed from three days old was uncomfortable and demanding of his mother. He expressed his displeasure with her through his angry crying and through his apparently insatiable demand for her breast. Even when he was not feeding he crossly sought the nipple, searching with his mouth whilst making increasingly angry and impatient cries until his mother put him to her breast. This behaviour continued until he was three months old, when a small change became evident. He no longer needed such constant contact with his mother's breast and was willing to try to deal with his need for the reassuring presence of the nipple in his mouth by seeking and using his thumb and fingers as a substitute.

Later, at around four months, there was another change in his behaviour. He began to notice his mother in a different way, as a separate person with whom he could have a social contact that was not entirely based upon the feeding relationship. This became apparent through his adoration of her; through his filling his time with her with generous smiles and looks, by cooing and gurgling at her in a loving way, by treating her breasts with gentleness and respect, and by holding her eyes with his own worshipful gaze as he fed from her.

This new behaviour was reparative and expressed his remorse for having been so hostile and demanding in the first months. The mother's willingness to accept this contrition and to respond to the change in the baby's behaviour with smiles, warm looks and soft words of her own did much to release the baby from the overwhelming sense of having damaged her and his relationship with her. This in turn instilled a sense of hopefulness in the child that damage can be repaired and that the future does not have to be as bleak and full of despair as he may once have feared. Older children continue to make these penitential gestures through doing the housework, helping with the washing up, and so on.

It would seem that the patient who continued to feel overwhelming guilt about her theft of the coin had not, for whatever reason, had the chance to make amends to her mother, or her attempts at reparation had been spurned, leaving her full of guilt and with the feeling that it was never possible to have hope in the future.

Indeed, another patient, a middle-aged woman, described her attempts as a child to make her mother notice her with affection. She would spend all of her holidays cleaning their large house in the hope that her mother would notice and praise her for her helpfulness. She failed. Instead of praise she received criticism for having dusted carelessly or for having missed some dirt on the windows, and so forth. This same patient also spoke of her current difficulties; her days were spent looking forward to mealtimes, yet when they came she was filled with anxiety lest she eat too much. She was persecuted by a sense that she was too greedy and that she never did manage to put things right with her mother. Although she had never made any self-destructive attacks upon herself she doubted whether she would ever be able to enjoy life and she contemplated suicide.

Both of these women were depressive personalities, each suffered from various symptoms of depressive illness, although the latter had never been hospitalised while the former had, on several occasions.

In our work with people in psychotherapy groups we shall come across many who experience a similarly grave degree of difficulty, but not all people who may be said to have 'depressive personalities' will be as deeply troubled as these two women, though they may still suffer a large measure of distress. Those who work in psychiatric hospitals and especially in acute admission units will work with many people who, like the first woman, are suffering from what the psychiatrists term endogenous depression. This is regarded as a psychotic illness. Such patients may find it difficult to participate in groups because the extreme nature of their depression leaves them mute and lacking in curiosity or any interest in the world at large. They might also feel unworthy (as did both women described above) and believe that no one could find them interesting or attractive. This absence of self-esteem is a key characteristic of the depressive personality (Storr 1979) and is not necessarily linked to current, external reality, although its extreme quality is often stimulated by the sort of external event listed earlier.

Even though such people find it difficult to participate in groups, this should not mean that they are excluded from them. In particular this applies to ward or unit 'community meetings'. These meetings are of great value to the therapeutic and anti-institutionalising aspect of the ward, unit or community hostel. Through them the patients have a voice by which they may find some self-reliance and through this self-reliance they may achieve greater autonomy and a feeling of personal strength, ability and individuality.

Such meetings are intended to deal with 'housekeeping' matters. They are the venue in which the members of the community can talk of important interpersonal issues – who is it who has taken more than a fair share of the tea, coffee, bread and other domestic supplies? Or how can we best deal with Miriam's disruptive and demanding behaviour or Harold's frightening aggression? They are safe places to which can be brought any issue that impinges on the life of the community. Their therapeutic value lies in the opportunity that they offer to their members to think about themselves and the effect they have upon others, and the chance they give to confront interpersonal matters in such a way that changes can begin in the behaviour of the individual.

To disallow membership to those who are profoundly depressed would be to deprive them of these opportunities. Other members of the community would be denied the help they need to think about depressed people and to continue to relate to them despite any lack of response from them. Also it would create the circumstances which would confirm unworthiness in the depressed person through the fact of his exclusion.

The Somatising Personality

Much of the early work of psychoanalysis was undertaken with 'hysterical' patients who displayed a wide variety of fascinating and hitherto inexplicable symptoms. The term has fallen into disrepute, quite understandably, although when used correctly it has diagnostic value and is not derisory or denigrating. Nowadays the sort of profound symptoms that were seen in those early days are rare; at one time it seemed that patients with hysterical paralysis, with blindness or amnesia, or with gross disturbances of behaviour, abounded. However, we do see many patients whose primary symptoms are mainly physical, even when there is no identifiable physical cause. These patients may be *somatising* emotional issues, i.e. experiencing emotional disturbances as physical debility, or dis-ease.

Many feminists have suggested that such gross symptoms were related to the inferior status of women in those times (from which it was difficult to escape) particularly in the rigidly ordered middle or professional classes, and it was mostly women who suffered in this way, except in times of war. At these times, particularly during the First World War, there was a tremendous increase in the number of men who exhibited hysterical symptoms. They were described as being 'shell-shocked' in the First War and 'battle-fatigued' in the Second World War.

It is interesting to note that men who showed symptoms of paralysis without physical cause should be termed 'shell-shocked' whilst women with similar symptoms were called 'histrionic' or 'hysterical', both of which are pejorative terms in common usage. Indeed, work was done during and after the First World War on the nervous systems of deceased 'shell-shocked' men to try to establish where the physical damage was done.

The author's experience would seem to bear out the views of the feminists. He has only ever seen two young women with so-called 'hysterical' paralysis and they both belonged to rigidly formal families who proscribed the behaviour of their female members, offering them no outlet outside the home. Both of these families belonged to a very unbending social structure which guarded their women and forbade them personal liberty and other freedoms.

Today the diagnosis of 'hysteria' or 'hysterical personality' is seldom used, although there are people still who suffer from a symptom or an ailment of some sort which serves a useful purpose and who may be understood to 'somatise', or to render as physical, emotional difficulties.

The value of the symptom is often related to avoidance of conflict and consequently is useful only in those terms. It is not useful to the health, emotional stability or growth of the person. Very often there is a gain to the sufferer, however shortlived and ultimately destructive it may be. The headaches, bad back or gastric discomfort initially produce sympathy in those close to the sufferer. If they continue, as mostly they do, then very often those who are close will begin to identify patterns in the symptoms. They will see that the symptoms appear to be designed to elicit sympathy at times when the sufferer might be expected to face a situation which he would find difficult. Very often such people will profess great disappointment that they are once again rendered incapable of joining in or doing something.

One of the most salient and most often disregarded features of this personality type is that the sufferer is not consciously aware of the gains his symptoms produce. He is also unaware that his symptoms are of psychosomatic origin. He cannot see what others can see all too easily after a time – there is a discrepancy between what he says he wants or wishes to do and what his behaviour shows he really wants. For example, the man who says he desperately loves his wife, but who is always impotent with her, or the women who becomes ill each time she succeeds in getting the job she says she wants so much.

The description of the somatising personality given above is similar in many respects to the description of the consequences of the poorly resolved oedipal stage given by Erikson (1965). Erikson suggests that the symptom allows the individual, who has defensively denied his guilt-evoking, thwarted impulses by promoting a false and inflated self, to retire with some sense of his ability intact. He can believe that, but for his symptoms, he would have done this or that, or been a tremendous success in this area or that field.

For example, one man of middle years would boast of how he would have been a valued member of the Officers' Mess if only he had taken up advice to enlist in the

Regular Army. He would also talk of his potential as an academic as if he had selflessly renounced his rightful place in the Halls of Academe. He would blame his circumstances on his new wife, managing to convey the impression that but for her and his continuing devotion to her despite her unacceptable behaviour, he would be a notable success. The truth of the matter was that he had been married once before, that marriage had failed, as had his business, and he had failed to get the qualifications he needed for university. His own inadequacy was consequently invested in his second wife. She was the centre of all that was wrong with his world. She was like a paralysed limb for him; if only he had not been disabled by this useless appendage he would have shown the world his mettle.

This was a particularly interesting complication in a man with a somatising personality; he was able to consider himself entirely whole and competent by investing his sickness in his wife.

Some people who may be considered as being character types that fit in with this group are much more seriously disabled. In extreme cases the conflict between aggressive impulses and the guilt they invoke produces a response that is more disabling than denial and the overcompensatory showing-off which the frightened, somatising person indulges in instead of fleeing as he wishes to.

The Borderline Personality

Some people produce fantasies which have a delusional and quite psychotic quality whilst retaining a grasp on reality. True psychotic delusions are said not to be amenable to rational argument or to the immediate changing influence of interpretation, as the fantasies of those with a 'borderline personality' may be. The term is descriptive of those who do not suffer from a clearly definable psychotic illness, but who nevertheless portray some of the symptoms of psychosis from time to time. Or as in Steiner's (1979) description: 'One might say that these are patients who are not frankly psychotic but who use psychotic mechanisms . . .'

It seems as if some internal structures, some boundaries that are intended to keep one aspect of the mind separate from another, have become hazy or permeable, allowing an intermingling of influences. The ability of such people to respond to interpretation causes them similar difficulties of tolerance from others as those who manifest their difficulties with physical symptoms. It can seem to their physicians, nurses and others that they are 'putting it on' or 'play-acting'. Somehow the fantasy, delusion or behaviour does not seem real. There is not the same quality of conviction that is seen in true psychotic illness. Even so, their problems are real, and they do need help.

One young woman presented with exceptionally aggressive behaviour, particularly verbally. During the first months of therapy she would try to take control of the session from her therapist. She talked of being a member of the security forces, having been recruited as a child. She also believed that she had been 'turned' by the KGB. Her fantasies continued, deepening in their resonance with her unconscious as she spoke.

She said she was the Bride of Christ, that she had done something awful and was now the Whore of Babylon. She was, she said, now an evil witch who had turned from her true nature and from her responsibilities and had failed in her mission to save the world. From being the Chosen of God she had become the Handmaiden of the Devil. Christ had come to her when she was a child, he had taught her to talk before she was one year old. One day he came to her to tell her that he was going to take back her little sister, who at that time was a tiny baby only a few weeks old. At the same time he said he had been preparing to split her mother and father, for her father was an evil man belonging to an anti-Christian sect. He would arrange for her to go with her mother to her mother's family elsewhere in the country.

When she first spoke of these matters she was firm and certain, sure that she was giving a lucid account of events which had actually happened. She resisted any interpretations insisting that her therapist listen to her without interruption. She seemed to believe these fantasies, yet when her therapist made interpretations, and insisted upon doing so, she would listen and make sense of what he said. She was able to experience relief that her therapist was able to understand from her fantasy that she was horrified by the murderous feelings she had harboured against her baby sister and her father when she was little more than an infant herself.

Her fantasies of purity and of her mission to save the world from evil (characterised in her story by witches and by Russia) indicated a wish to resolve her own 'bad' self. But there was a failure in her ability to do so. Even Christ became contaminated by her destructive impulses when she displaced her murderous wishes onto him; she 'saved' her sister by intervening with Him. We can see that there was a tremendous impulse towards stopping or rectifying the destructive effects of the 'bad' part of herself. Yet somehow there was a failure to manage this adequately. Her reparative drive was deflected so that her good intentions became polluted by destructive impulses. Consequently she had never been able to feel that she had truly made amends for her infantile destructive behaviour towards her mother. She was forever living on the boundary between the paranoid schizoid and the depressive positions. As soon as she began to feel guilt and grief for her actions she moved back from this step towards mourning and depression and into the more primitive position of blaming others for her problems. She would, for example, blame her therapist for interrupting her with interpretations and say that therapy and the therapist were useless.

This behaviour could have been either a transference of feelings that she had towards her mother who may have been unable to hold her aggressive feelings, or a projection of her own failure to face or take back into herself destructive feelings which were perceived as a threat to her existence. If it were the former then it may be that her mother was inadequate in some way, could not tolerate her own bad feelings, and thus defensively left these feelings for her daughter to deal with by herself. If it were the latter then it would be likely that she was born with a strongly persecutory inner-world which her mother, even though she tried, could not mitigate wholly.

In fact it was probably a mixture of both. Her mother was not able to manage her, and although she made extravagant statements of what she would do to help, she did less than one would expect of a concerned parent. But she was not a bad or neglectful mother in many other ways, so perhaps there was a strength to the constitutional, persecutory elements with which her daughter was born that foiled her best efforts to help.

There were times when even her therapist became unsure about this patient.

Somehow, despite her protestations that she believed what she was reporting had happened, it seemed that it was unreal to her too, as if she were acting a part. It became hard to believe in her distress so that her family, their GP and many friends became first distressed on her behalf and later unconvinced of her distress and critical of her inability to cope. Such is the quality of confusion which these people bring into their lives. But it would be wrong to assume a conscious and deliberate manipulation of circumstances to suit the individual's needs.

One of the things that this patient dreaded most was 'being stuck' with her 'overbearing mother' for the rest of her life. This was the last thing that she wanted. Yet she behaved in a way which ensured that she would ever be dependent upon her mother.

There is a similarity here with the somatising personality who protests his love of his wife and can never express it physically because of his impotence. Both are unable to do the thing they most want to do, which must lead us to question which contains the truth; their words or their actions?

It would probably be true to say that both their words and their actions contain aspects of the truth. We all know what it's like to try to make a choice between two alternatives. Because we choose one it does not mean that we did not want the other.

It would seem that this young woman was unable to break free of her family, particularly her mother, as she had not yet been able to feel either that she had achieved that degree of closeness that we all need, or that she had resolved her infantile guilt. She continued to beat herself against her unyielding parents like a moth against a lamp. As Anthony Storr writes in *The Art of Psychotherapy*:

● It has often seemed to me that, if human beings have not been given what they need at the appropriate stage in their development, they are left with a compulsive hunger which drives them to try and obtain what has been missing. (1979, pp.91–2)

Many psychotherapists would agree with this statement. The role of the psychotherapist is not to fulfil the need of the individual for a more satisfying experience of childhood; this is not possible once childhood is over. But it is possible to help the patient or client to come to terms with early, unsatisfactory experiences, and it is possible to provide an experience which is rich in many of the qualities denied to the patient in his childhood.

The first of these qualities – constancy and continuing commitment – enables a developing sense of trust to become established in the mind of the patient. He is able, gradually, to begin to believe that his therapist is not going to let him down or become overwhelmed by his more negative feelings, and neither is he likely to be driven away by his threatening, hostile or otherwise unacceptable behaviour.

During a period of therapy there are many other qualities that become apparent and which further the work of therapist and patient together. The attention that the therapist pays to boundaries such as the beginning and ending of sessions at the agreed times, and the interest that he will pay to fluctuations in the patient's behaviour at these times, all help to create an environment of trust and a feeling of security in the patient. This feeling of trust and security, which is initially established in external reality, eventually is experienced as an inner certainty. After a time the concern and interest that the therapist has in his patient enable a sense of personal worth, a feeling of being valued and of having been cared for to establish a powerful and positive presence in the inner world of the patient.

How does this actually happen? We can do no more than take a brief glimpse at one part of the therapy of one patient. But it will, I hope, be enough to illustrate how the therapist can help the patient to face herself and her problems, whilst directly influencing her inner world.

Let us look again at the young woman who was tortured by religious fantasies. Each session she would verbally abuse her therapist and insist that he should make no interpretations of her material. She would tell him that if he listened to her then he would learn a lot more about psychotherapy than he had ever learned from his training. Her therapist gently but firmly stayed within his role and carried on interpreting the material of the session. This went on for some time with the patient becoming belligerent and bullying and quite abusive to her therapist. One day she threatened to walk out if the therapist did not do as she told him. Her therapist quite rightly continued to do his job of informing her of what he understood of the unconscious processes that lay behind what she was telling him. At this she jumped to her feet and, slamming the door behind her, ran downstairs and stood crying loudly in the hallway of the clinic.

Her therapist debated with himself about what he should do, but gave his patient time in which to return if she meant to, or to leave if that was what she had intended. It became clear that what she intended was to stay where she was, crying as loudly as she could. The therapist decided that perhaps his patient needed a way of returning to him; it did not seem likely that she would do so on her own. He went downstairs and told her that he would wait in his room for her return. He was still willing to work with her if that was her wish, if she felt that she could not return to the session that day, then he would be available for her the next week, but he would not discuss anything further with her outside of his room. He said that these matters were confidential and private and should be protected.

The young woman tried to engage him in a discussion at the foot of the stairs, but the therapist reminded her that he would only talk with her in his room and went back upstairs. She followed muttering that she supposed he thought he had won some kind of victory, but he had another think coming. When they were back in the room the therapist interpreted her anxiety that somehow he would engulf or ensnare her if she did things his way.

The next week this young woman was able to be in touch with her sadness and her remorse for having attacked him so savagely. She was able, for many sessions thereafter, to make use of her therapy in a more fulfilling way.

There were many different varieties of the sort of behaviour described above throughout this patient's treatment. A problem or anxiety has to be reworked time after time before the lesson is finally learned. It is the same for all of us, but each time we gain a little more.

What had happened in this session that was of such value to the patient? The therapist had paid attention to a number of issues. He was aware of the challenge to his value as a therapist and the way that patient denigrated him and attempted to prevent him from doing his job. He was concerned to know what lay behind that and it seemed to him that there was an anxiety on the part of the patient that he would try to take her over just as she was trying to with him. It seemed to him that if he were to challenge or interpret this demanding behaviour directly it would only get them into a quarrel about who was doing what to whom and who started it anyway. So he decided to continue to interpret the verbal material in the session, only interpreting when he was reasonably certain he had something of value to offer. In doing this as gently as possible, he could maintain his therapeutic effectiveness and preserve the boundaries of the session. This meant that his patient could push harder and harder to try to make him relinquish his ground. This was a form of testing-out behaviour in which the patient was unconsciously driven to challenge whether her therapist could really manage her aggressive, impulsive and demanding feelings without giving up, or being overwhelmed by her. She found that he could. All her attacks had left her knowing that he could safely manage her negative impulses. Also she discovered that she could begin to feel safe with him; the need to feel wholly accepted, the good with the bad, was also being met. Consequently, her inner world, which was peopled with evil and malicious figures who persecuted her and meant her harm became a changed reality. For now, she had in her mind a picture of someone who could help her with her alarming inner world and begin to make it safe for her. He had not been overwhelmed by her bad feelings so she could begin to believe that they were not as powerful as she had feared, and in this way they became more manageable for her too.

As has already been said, this is but a very small fragment of the psychotherapy of one person. But it is possible to generalise from it and to see how psychotherapy provides the circumstances in which change can occur.

In the next part we shall be discussing, amongst other things, those factors which, as part of the group experience, enable the individuals who comprise the group to change.

References

Klein M (1946) Notes on some schizoid mechanisms. In: *Envy and Gratitude*. London: The Hogarth Press and The Institute of Psycho-Analysis.

Erikson E H (1965) *Childhood and Society*. Harmondsworth: Penguin Books.

Holmes T H and Rahe R H (1967) The Social Readjustment Rating Scale. *Journal of Psychosomatic Research*, **11**: 213–218.

Steiner J (1979) The border between the paranoid-schizoid and the depressive positions in the borderline patient. *British Journal of Medical Psychology*, **52**: 385–391.

Storr A (1979) *The Art of Psychotherapy*. London: Secker and Warburg with Heinemann.

PART II
The Life of the Group

6

Stages in the Life of a Group

In part I we looked at the life of the individual as he gradually made contact with others beyond the maternal relationship, first with other members of his own family and then with individuals and groups outside the family. In this part we shall discuss the life of the group proper, with particular reference to therapy groups, bearing in mind that all sorts of groups, both formal and informal, replicate the patterns that we shall discover in the following chapters. In this chapter we examine the developing life of the group more directly.

We shall see that the group grows in much the same way as the individual does, experiencing an infantile stage of acute dependence, a stage of adolescent rebellion and a more mature adult stage. In some degree it also resembles the development of the family (Foulkes and Anthony, 1957), growing through a series of crises which affect the lives of all of the members of the group. It would be odd if this were not so. After all, the group is composed of people each of whom brings individual and family experiences, and it is a human trait to use past experience as a template for each new circumstance.

When any new group forms there is an initial return to the sort of dependency which was experienced in the maternal relationship. There is a period in which the therapist is deferred to by all the members of the group.

As has already been stated, this process, and all the processes discussed in this chapter, occur in all groups whether they are therapy groups, groups of students in a classroom, or the committees of multinational companies. They happen in the wards of all our hospitals whether they are general or psychiatric hospitals, and they happen in all residential settings, in all homes and hostels. These processes occur in playgroups, mother and toddler groups, in anxiety management, social skills and other problem-centred groups; in fact, they occur in each and every gathering of people everywhere.

The conductor or facilitator may be a teacher, the chair of a committee, or the nurse in charge of a ward. It will usually be someone who is regarded as having more knowledge, responsibility and information and who is seen as having more authority than the others present. These supposed (or real) qualities enable others to place themselves in the care of the conductor, that is, in a dependency relationship. There are many reasons why this might happen and it is important to note that, whilst it is undoubtedly an attempt to avoid the anxiety we all face in new and untested circumstances, the dependency relationship, initially at least, is not based on a feeling of trust that the conductor can deal with the anxiety; rather, it is based on the panicky feeling the individual has that he can't cope and the hope that the conductor can. Trust takes time to establish within any relationship and there are many levels and qualities of trust.

This early group experience is very similar to Erikson's (1965) description of the First Age of Man (infancy) which is characterised by the conflict between Basic Trust and Basic Mistrust. One of the themes of Erikson's work is that we are allowed many chances to rework issues which remain unresolved. Each time we join a new group of any sort we are faced again with the opportunity to come to terms with this and other issues as the group grows.

This theme of recurring opportunity is one which characterises the life of the group. Time after time the group is offered the chance to work over important formative issues.

There is a number of different views of group development and it is interesting and heartening to note that, whilst they may focus on different aspects of group life and use a different vocabulary to describe their observations, there are many points of agreement between them. Many of the different structures that are described are attempts to form an inclusive theory which identifies the behaviour that will be seen at each stage, as well as providing a description of group development.

MODELS OF GROUP DEVELOPMENT

We shall start with Bion's (1961) view of group life as it establishes clearly the notion of cycles of experience within a developing organism. These cyclical experiences exist within and alongside the linear progression of the group, so that it becomes possible to have a view of groups which describes how a group can return to earlier or more primitive forms of relating without losing its developmental gains.

Bion describes each group as having two aspects; the work group and the basic assumptions group.

1. The *work group* is the more sophisticated of the two and quite simply is the aspect of the group which is prepared to work by confronting painful or difficult issues.

2. The *basic assumptions group* is that aspect of the group which is anxious and which uses a variety of unconscious devices to avoid working on conflict and other painful experiences.

There are three types of Basic Assumption described by Bion: dependency, pairing and fight/flight. We can simplify Bion's description in the following way:

The *dependency group* looks to the conductor for all things, and consequently denies much knowledge or skill and avoids the work task. In a sense the group is saying, 'Look after us' and 'You do all the work for us, we can't do it, we're too little.'

The *pairing group* encourages two of the members of the group to communicate or make some form of contact on behalf of the whole group, with the other members staying out of it. The purpose once again is to enable the group to avoid the task of the group, which in the early days is getting to know each other so that an initial trust may be established.

The *fight/flight group* tends to avoid the work task by fleeing from it, perhaps by using strategies which are intended to focus attention elsewhere, or by creating a fight between one member and another or between the conductor and one group member. The skilful conductor refuses either to flee or fight, but chooses to examine the process. These Basic Assumptions recur throughout the life of the group, facing it with the same issues again and again, with the consequence that the group has many opportunities to work through problem areas in ever greater depth.

Others have identified three basic stages of group life. Schutz (1958) described cycles of group phenomena which were centred on issues to do with *inclusion* and *exclusion*, *control* and *affection*. Gradually, the group moves towards dealing with issues related to affection or intimacy, having already worked through issues to do with the inclusion and exclusion of others, and issues of control. The attention of the group will be centred on one or another of these issues throughout its life and the level at which the group will work on them will deepen as the group matures. Any termination, such as the departure of a group member, the ending of the group, a holiday or other absence, provokes a reversal, and intimacy gives way to issues of control which, in turn, give way to the group's focusing on issues of inclusion and exclusion once more, though in increasing depth each time.

Whittaker and Leiberman (1965) pointed to a resurgence of basic themes under an expanding social scene within the group, so that issues are seen with greater clarity and in greater depth as the group develops. They also acknowledge a *formative* and an *established* phase of group development.

Yalom (1970) illustrates three stages of *orientation*, *conflict* and *cohesiveness*.

The orientation stage is marked by the search for meaning in the group – it has to discover its own purpose and undertake the task of each member getting to know the others. These two early concerns are of paramount importance and, inevitably, they are inextricably linked. Before the group can discover its purpose it must find out about its members' wishes in this respect and this means that the group must begin to find out about each other.

The conflict stage is characterised by a power-play being worked out in the group. The group moves on from a concern with finding meaning and purpose to a preoccupation with position, rights and power, and gradually establishes a hierarchical structure. The conductor should concern himself with helping the group to recognise these processes and to discover their meaning. An overwhelming concern with one's position in the group and a consuming determination to be the one with the power, may signify an underlying fear of trusting any relationship. On the other hand, an eager or passive willingness to submit to the will of others may indicate a paralysing inability to accept one's own aggressive, assertive or competitive qualities. In either case the individual is incomplete and unhappy.

In the final stage of group cohesiveness the group concerns itself with issues of intimacy. Individuals become committed to the group and it carries a high value. In some ways it can become idealised and the group strives to maintain cohesiveness, sometimes at the expense of dealing with the genuine conflicts that arise. This idealisation bears a resemblance to the depressive position described by Klein (1946; see also p.7 above). If the conductor can recognise rather than share in the idealisation of the group, he will be able to help it to discover and deal with the feelings of guilt, blame and sorrow that remain from this time.

Tuckman (1965) reviewed fifty articles dealing with the formation and development of groups and concluded by suggesting that there are four stages which fit the literature on the subject. Many people will be familiar with them even if they are not familiar with Tuckman's paper.

1. *Forming*   The group is characterised by its concern with issues related to a need for orientation and dependence, and a wish to test the group, its boundaries, and the ability of the conductor to contain the group.

2. *Storming*   The group is concerned with conflicts and with polarisation around interpersonal issues.

3. *Norming*   Group cohesion is established and the group feels able to express intimate and personal opinions.

4. *Performing*   The group is able to focus upon the task, roles are functional and flexible, the group structure is resolved and is supportive of the task.

Most researchers identify stages of intimacy, power, performance and separation, as we have seen through our brief look at the findings of Yalom and Tuckman. We now need to put some meat on the bare bones of the stages as described above, and to do this we shall use Levine's (1979) description of phases in the life of the group. Levine suggests that the life of the group can be divided into four phases and three crises as follows:

Phases

1.   In the *parallel phase* the direction of communication is towards the therapist. Consequently, behaviour which is apparently intended for another group member is meant for the therapist.

During this phase the group has not yet established a structure or an identity and the main tasks are those of establishing mutual contact (forming) and the working through of anxieties to do with trust. It is evident that unless the group can learn to trust each other and the therapist, then any sense of cohesiveness is impossible to achieve.

This phase also has clear elements of dependency upon the therapist which can be compared with the dependency of the child upon his mother. In this sense it can be regarded as regressive, yet it is also normal (cf. Anna Freud 1966). It is related to how each of us first began to make sense of the world; we proceeded from a relationship with one other, our mother or some other primary caregiver, towards a widening system of relationships (as shown in chapters 1–4). As discussed earlier, the early patterns established in the development of the individual provide a template for the development of all future relationships.

The parallel phase corresponds to the Basic Assumption group *dependency*, described by Bion. It also bears a similarity to Erikson's stage of psychosocial development, *Basic Trust* v. *Basic Mistrust*.

2. In the *inclusion phase* communications directly to the therapist decrease and there is a corresponding increase in communications between group members, coupled with the formation of relationships between individuals in the group. It proceeds from pairing and sub-groupings and ends with most members having a relationship with each other. During this phase there are many struggles for power and control (storming) which underlie the main task.

Once again we can see the operation of the 'developmental template'. There is an obvious similarity between this phase and the individual child who moves out of the almost exclusive relationship with his mother into the wider circle of relationships within the family. It corresponds with Erikson's psychosocial stage of *Autonomy* v. *Shame and Doubt*, the stage of *Ambivalence and Wilful Self-determination* discussed in chapter 1, and has similarities with Bion's Basic Assumption Group *pairing*.

3. The *mutality phase* brings a capacity for intimate relationships (norming). It is the operating phase (performing) of the group and most of the group's time will be spent in this phase. All of the members are included in the group and empathy deepens. It corresponds to Bion's description of the Work Group, to Yalom's *cohesiveness*, to the extended *established* phase identified by Whitaker and Lieberman, and to Schutz's advanced cycle when issues of *affection* predominate.

4. The *termination phase* is arrived at by the group coming to an end, a member leaving, a series of absences, holidays or other similar events. It is a phase which can occur during any of the other phases, and it involves a regression to the inclusion phase. Where the precipitating factors are sufficiently profound and disturb the equilibrium of the group dramatically, then the group may be propelled into a return to the parallel phase. Unless events have denuded the group of most of its established members, the regression to an earlier phase will be brief and the work done in this earlier phase will be of a more intimate nature than was possible when the group first passed through it.

This phase is similar to Bion's Basic Assumption group with aspects of *fight/flight*, *pairing*, and, potentially, a return to *dependency*.

If we pause for reflection for a moment we can see that this view of group development substantiates that of Whitaker and Lierberman that the group is 'characterised by the recurrence of basic themes under progressively expanding cultural conditions' (Proposition 18, 1965; see also figure 6.1). It also has similarities with Anna Freud's (1966) concept of developmental lines in that it recognises that developmental issues are seldom entirely worked through within the developmental stage most closely identified with them. They continue to be worked on in subsequent stages which bring their own emphasis and flavour to bear upon the focus of attention. In this way one developmental issue will be worked over from several different angles. Again, there is a similarity between this concept and Erikson's 'Epigenetic Chart' in which he suggests that each stage depends upon the successful negotiation of preceding stages, and also enables incompleted work to be reviewed.

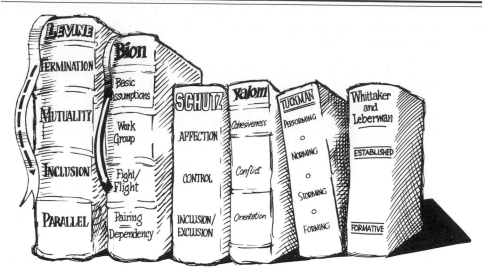

Fig. 6.1 Interrelating stages in group development, by author

We may deduce from all this that the ordinary experiences of life offer opportunities to continue our development, both as individuals and as members of any number of groups which occur naturally throughout our lives. We can add that the therapy group provides an experience which is intensified, with the consequence that each member is confronted with unresolved issues and the opportunity to deal with them within a compressed time span. The group is rather like a greenhouse in which the gardener, or therapist, provides conditions which are as near ideal as possible for the plants to grow. It is not to be compared with the commercial grower who forces plants to early maturity under hothouse conditions.

The Three Crises

1. The first is the *authority crisis* in which the power and authority of the therapist is challenged.

The resolution of this crisis marks the end of the parallel phase and the beginning of the inclusion phase.

If the therapist does not relinquish power appropriately, or if the group fails to accept power unto itself, the crisis remains unresolved.

The group may move to the inclusion phase without having resolved the authority crisis, but, if this happens, the quality of communications and of relationships will be shallower.

If power is wrested from the therapist without his consent the group does not experience its own authority as real.

If the therapist relinquishes his authority before the group is ready, then the group will return it to him.

This is reminiscent of the anal stage of individual development with its struggles and ambivalence. The small child needs increased independence from his parents at the same time as needing their continuing safe and appropriate care to ensure that he is not overwhelmed by his imperative wishes. Once again there are similarities with Basic Assumption *fight/flight*.

2. The authority crisis is followed by an *intimacy crisis* which begins at the end of the inclusion phase and draws to a conclusion at the beginning of the mutuality phase. It is a process which may recur and is influenced in this by events which stimulate the termination phase – absences, holidays and other separations. Here we are reminded of Basic Assumption *pairing* and of Schutz's description of the group's concern with issues to do with *inclusion* and *exclusion*.

3. The *separation crisis* may occur at any time in the life of the group and is provoked by the absences or breaks which tilt the group into the termination phase. It has a cumulative effect, and levels of response to it are deepened each time a separation crisis occurs. The separation crisis resonates with other separations experienced by group members, again in increasing depth.

Levine also identifies the following as being basic to the development of all groups.

Principles of Group Development

1. In any process of group formation there is an initial binding together of the members.

2. The transfer of sufficient power from the therapist to the members is fundamental to the success of the process of binding together.

3. Struggles for control require a shift of power from the therapist to the members and are a consequence of this shift.

4. The establishment of group cohesiveness is the direct result of the resolution of the struggle for control.

5. Power ceases to be a major issue once group cohesiveness has been achieved.

6. The direction of communication, interaction and relationships move from the therapist to the members and thence from member to member.

Now that we have introduced the theory of group development it would be helpful to see what happens in practice. Each group has its own particular identity which is given to it by its members. Consequently it would be impossible to point to one piece of behaviour and say that this is what will be seen in all groups. Each group is distinctive, and whilst governed by universal processes, will portray them in its own way. What we can do here is to present a number of events from a variety of groups which illuminate some of the processes described.

THE EARLY SESSIONS

This group, a training group, had not met before and after a while began by asking the therapist what they should do – should they ask each others' names? Would it be helpful to introduce themselves and identify their professional roles? This uncertainty continued for some time, with the therapist merely saying that it was up to them; his task was simply to help them understand what they did as a group and perhaps help them to discover why.

After a time the group fell silent, but this was shortlived as it was interrupted by Jill, one of the group members, asking what hobbies others had. This time there were no takers, the group talked instead of how difficult it was to talk.

Again there was a silence. It was broken by Bill, who wanted to know why there was a table in the centre of the room. Again this remark was addressed to the therapist who invited the group to respond to the question themselves, and wondered why the question was being asked.

Bill said that he found that the table got in the way of their discussion – it inhibited them and blocked communication. Jill asked if she should remove it. The question was put to the group, and as none of the members gave a distinct or audible reply Jill prepared to remove the table from the centre of the room.

The therapist intervened directly to say that the group had not discovered why it was so concerned with the table and that it should stay.

We can see many of the early group processes in this brief example.

First, the direction of communication was towards the therapist; all of the questions were put to him, at least initially. Even when the questions were apparently asked of other group members it was plain that there was a great deal of interest in what the therapist might think. This was made evident by the tone of voice of the questioner, the direction of attention of the other group members and the kind of question that was asked or comment made. This corresponds to Levine's *parallel phase*.

Secondly, there was a number of attempts at reducing the anxiety that each felt about not knowing the others by asking for fairly shallow information to do with names, roles, and so on. This was related to anxieties to do with issues of trust. It was an attempt to deny uncertainty by treating the group as a purely social situation in which the members could enjoy a conversation, and by pretending that everyone would be easier if each could be identified by name and role. This surface information was meant to stand for the deeper knowledge and understanding that could only come with experience of each other over time. Had the therapist allowed the group to continue with this self-deception then the group may not have managed to confront other, deeper issues later in its life.

Thirdly, there were elements of an early striving for power and control. The group knew that the therapist had placed the table there for a reason, and had asked what this might be. The therapist was not being mean or churlish by not giving the information required; he genuinely wanted to know what lay behind the interest. If he had responded to the surface question he would not have discovered the underlying anxiety. It was also difficult for the group to focus on why they were interested and so the members preferred to remove the apparent cause of their concern to working on the underlying conflicts. If we remember Bill's remarks we can see that the table became imbued with the group's difficulties in talking. Obviously it was not the table which created this problem, but the newness of the circumstances and other concerns of which the group members were not conscious. The group allowed Jill to assume that they agreed that the table should be removed; the group was asked, not the therapist (although it was plain that the group was greatly interested in what the therapist might do). We can see that the group was attempting to take some power from the therapist by removing the table. Once again, the group knew that the therapist had placed it there and had assumed he had a reason, so removing it was a direct challenge to his authority.

Fourthly, there are several examples of Basic Assumption *flight*. Attempting to remove the table without confronting what lay behind the wish to do so, talking about hobbies and roles, and breaking the silences with chit-chat are three examples of this.

Fifthly (and this is related to the first point), it is clear that the group is also operating within Basic Assumption *dependency*. The group is overwhelmingly interested in what the therapist might say or think and repeatedly looks to him for information about how they should proceed. It is interesting to note that many members of this group had been facilitating other groups themselves for some years, so they were not unaware of group processes or of how groups work, yet still they relied upon the therapist for a lead.

THE LATER SESSIONS

This group had been together for a little longer, but had not yet achieved the prolonged established phase described by Whitaker and Lieberman.

One of the members, Tom, was absent. During the previous meeting he had angered some of the other members by refusing to comply with a group attitude. In other words he held a view about several matters which ran counter to the view accepted by the majority in the group.

Mary spoke to Jane with whom she had a rapport which was based upon some perceived similarities of personality and belief. She said that she had been really angry with Tom, that she was glad that he was not there because that meant that the group could now get down to work.

The conversation passed between the two of them for quite some time, until the therapist pointed out that none of the other members had joined in. Two other members of the group spoke up in much the same vein as Mary and Jane and a conversation between them followed, again for quite a long time. There were two other members present who had not yet said anything. The therapist intervened again, this time to wonder if the group was blaming the absent member for the difficulty they were having themselves in being able to work. He pointed out that they had been talking for half the session about the work they could do without Tom, yet they had not done any work.

Again we can see some of the processes which we described in the first part of this chapter.

1. The initial direction of communication was between two of the members for some time, only later widening to include two more members. Even then two further members had not participated. This is characteristic of the *inclusion phase* of development.

2. With the point 1 in mind, we can see that initially there is a pairing with only two of the members talking. This is very like the Basic Assumption *pairing* which is intended as a defence on the part of the group against the anxiety of dealing with the real task.

3. We can see that this was relatively early in the life of the group and that the session belonged to the *inclusion phase* because the rapport that Mary and Jane assumed was based upon perceived similarities; they had not yet got to know each other well and had 'paired' defensively. The purpose of this defensive pairing was to protect each from the uncertain qualities of the group and to hold in abeyance any need to examine areas of conflict that might exist between them. In fact in later sessions they were to discover important areas of hostility which they were able to understand and resolve. Had the therapist gone along with their assumption of being 'like minds' they would never have been able to do that work.

This same group, in later sessions, was to work well together. Tom did in fact prove to be an inhibiting factor in the development of the group, but even his reluctance to participate did not destroy the confidence and trust that the group was able to establish. Because of his apparent off-handedness there was a risk that he would continue to be excluded as he excluded himself. However he was included, the group continued to be prepared to listen to what he said and to share with him their feelings, thoughts, fears and ideas. By this time the group was characterised by an openness of communication – no one was excluded from the discussion, and most often the group would struggle with difficult experiences. This is characteristic of the *mutuality phase* of the group's development and it is what Bion meant when he wrote of the Work Group, the group behaves in an adult and workmanlike fashion and faces areas of conflict and difficulty.

Finally, let us look at one group which was well established and had achieved the mutuality phase some time previously.

This session was immediately prior to a planned holiday, which the group had been aware of for some months. Not all the members arrived on time, but as they came they brought with them stories of car crashes in which they presumed people to have died, funerals that they had glimpsed on their journeys in to the group, tales of friends or relatives who were leaving their home town or village and who were not expected to return, and so on. Gradually, the flurry of early comments slowed and eventually only three of the group were left talking about the mother of one of them who was ill and causing some worry. The rest of the group remained silent.

Once again we can see several processes in this slice from the life of a group.

First, the issue of separation was plainly of great concern to the group as was illustrated actively by several members arriving late. In other words, there was an unconscious expression of some of the anxiety which was felt about the ensuing holiday break.

Secondly, some flavour of the depth of the anxiety is shown in the topics chosen, again in an unconscious, unpremeditated way. Each member of the group had a story to tell of profound and sometimes tragic or violent loss. One or two members had spoken in other sessions of funerals, or of car accidents, or of friends moving away, but this had not provoked such a welter of similar or related stories from the other members of the group before. It is reasonable to assume that these stories were stimulated by the holiday – an important event in the life of the group, which apparently resonated with other, earlier, or more important separations.

Thirdly, after a short time only three members of the group were left talking. This represented a return to the *inclusion phase* of the group as a response to anxieties to do with loss and ending; if the group is to take a break then is it safe to let yourself talk about or reveal, even to yourself, feelings which might cause distress? This is characteristic of the *termination phase* of the group's development.

Fourthly, this was not the first break the group had experienced. The depth at which the group was able to work was increased by the work done around the earlier breaks. The member who spoke of her sick mother was able to reveal some of the ambivalent feelings she had – her mother had been intrusive and burdensome to her for most of her life, sometimes she hoped that she would die. This enabled another member to share some of the grief and guilt she bore over the tragic loss of her young husband.

In this particular session the therapist was able to interpret sufficient of the group's anxiety for them to be able to manage to knuckle down to facing some of the more painful issues it had been avoiding. The session ended with the group returning to its Work Group aspect, as shown by the widening response from other members and the willingness to share experiences of painful separation with each other.

In chapter 7 we shall look at some of the phenomena that occur in groups and examine their purpose, function or meaning.

References

Bion W R (1961) *Experiences in Groups*. London: Tavistock.

Erikson E H (1965) *Childhood and Society*. Harmondsworth: Penguin Books.

Foulkes S H and Anthony E J (1957) *Group Psychotherapy. The Psycho-Analytic Approach*. London: Maresfield Reprints.

Freud A (1966) *Normality and Pathology in Childhood*. London: The Hogarth Press and The Institute of Psycho-Analysis.

Klein M (1946) Notes on some schizoid mechanisms. In: *Envy and Gratitude*. London: The Hogarth Press and The Institute of Psycho-Analysis.

Levine B (1979) *Group Psychotherapy, Practice and Development*. New York: Prentice-Hall.

Schutz W C (1958) *FIRO: A Three Dimensional Theory of Interpersonal Behaviour*. New York: Holt, Rinehart and Winston.

Tuckman B W (1965) Developmental sequence in small groups. *Psychological Bulletin*, **63**: 384–399.

Whitaker D S and Lieberman M A (1965) *Psychotherapy through the Group Process*. London: Tavistock.

Yalom I D (1970) *The Theory and Practice of Group Psychotherapy*. New York: Basic Books.

7

What Happens in Groups?

The processes discussed in chapter 6 describe how the group develops. Within this progression towards maturity there exist other phenomena which also contribute to the life of the group. In one sense it is difficult to separate them from the maturational processes as they are interdependent; they exist as recurring events that have an influence on and are in turn influenced by the stage or phase which the group has achieved. In another sense, because of the distinctive features that they possess, it becomes possible to describe them and to place their value to the group.

In any group we see examples of these phenomena, but unless we have foreknowledge of them they can be difficult to perceive and it can be hard to understand their significance. In this chapter we shall examine some of the most important, and discuss their relevance to group development. They are also related to the curative factors which are discussed in chapter 8.

Many of the phenomena discussed were first described by S H Foulkes and E J Anthony (1957) and S H Foulkes (1975). Foulkes' contribution to our understanding of groups is tremendous. He was one of the early pioneers who applied his understanding of psychoanalysis to his work with groups. Together with other interested colleagues he established the Group Analytic Society (London) and later, the Institute of Group Analysis to provide a training for the increasing number of people from a variety of professions who were interested in increasing their knowledge of group work. In a tribute, written after Foulkes' death in 1976, Martin Grotjahn, an American colleague, acknowledged Foulkes' central role in the development of group analytic therapy: '. . . Michael Foulkes' great gifts and devotion were shown as an original thinker, teacher, therapist and group leader' (Grotjahn, 1978, p. 6).

We could do much worse, then, than to use his work to help us in our own understanding of groups. Before we begin our survey of group phenomenology it is as well to remind ourselves once again that: 'It should be emphasised that the spontaneous dynamisms observed in the treatment situation exist in all other life groups' (Foulkes and Anthony, 1957, p. 147).

MIRRORING

Just like the infant who first sees himself reflected in his mother's eyes, so the individual in a group sees himself reflected in the views and attitudes which others in the group hold towards him. This phenomenon deals, in essence, with the residual infantile narcissism, or self-love, of the individual by making available to him views other than his own. He is increasingly able to see himself as others do and, by taking within himself (*introjecting*) the vision others have of him, or by externalising his own inner vision, is able to reduce the self-centred focus which hitherto was an integral and limiting part of his personality (figure 7.1).

Fig. 7.1 The group as mirror

CONDENSER PHENOMENA

When there is a series of associative links, provided by the group in an unpremeditated and unconscious way, there is often a sudden discharge of primitive material. By primitive material we mean impulses, fantasies, fears or feelings of a deeply unconscious or infantile nature.

In the last chapter we observed the experience of a group facing a holiday break. The group members had arrived in fits and starts and most had stories to tell of accidents, funerals, illnesses, leavings and other losses. These were the unconscious associative links which led to the discharge of primitive material which followed, and which is described here.

One of the members, Mary, had spoken about her mother's illness and had been met with some sympathy which acknowledged her worry and concern for her mother. When Jane spoke up empathetically to acknowledge her feelings about the death of her young husband, and her worry that she could have done more, Mary burst into tears and confessed to the group that sometimes she wished that her mother was dead. Jane became pale at this point and cried quietly, but was visibly shaking with her sobbing. The mood in the group became very quiet and several members seemed moved to the point of tears. Michael spoke with great difficulty about a brother he had lost as a child. His brother had been younger than himself and he had felt that he had been displaced from his central position in the family by him. His brother had died when only three years old in a traffic accident when they had been playing in the street outside the family home. Michael had always thought it was his fault because he had often wished his brother dead, and, even though he had only been five years old himself, he felt he should have taken better care of his brother. It was as if he believed that his wishing his brother dead had caused the car to run him down.

This feeling of responsibility for the death or injury caused to others was shared largely throughout the group.

This was a 'condenser phenomenon'; the stage achieved by the group, the influence of feelings associated with the break in group treatment, the association of links together with the very immediate feelings of one of the group in regard of her sick mother, all combined to produce a discharge of powerful primitive material. In one sense, although it was powerful material which could be worked on within the group, it was also a flight from owning up to the angry and destructive feelings which were felt towards the group therapist for his taking a break.

CHAIN PHENOMENA

This is a process which is very similar to free association in individual psychoanalytic treatment. It consists of a series of stories which are capped by another member. Where they have to do with fears and worries, and when the group has achieved the established or mutuality phase, then it is a helpful phenomenon. But when the group is young and there is still considerable competition for attention, then it can become quite negative. In the former instance the level at which the group is communicating may be deepened and this, in turn, can lead to a development in the maturity of the group. The therapist would do well to allow the group to complete their own associations lest he inhibit or halt the chain. In the latter case, where the associations are made competitively ('My problem is worse than yours') then it becomes divisive and potentially destructive of the group (figure 7.2). The therapist would help the group by interpreting in this situation.

We are familiar with this phenomenon in everyday life, it is what children are doing when they say 'My house is better than yours' or 'I got a better present than you for my birthday'. This a boastfulness which measures and takes pride in possessions and in feelings and in people ('my Daddy is better than yours'), but it can become quite pathological when there is a boastful comparison made about deprivations, because it relates to the views individuals have about the composition of their inner worlds.

Fig. 7.2 'No, mine was worse . . .'

RESONANCE

When Foulkes and Anthony (1957) wrote about this they referred specifically to the likelihood that the individual member would respond to any group event by unconsciously associating it with the stage of psychosexual development at which he is 'fixated'.

By 'fixated' we mean that the individual has not wholly worked through a developmental stage and will respond to life or group situations in a way that is associated with that stage. For example, the individual who has not worked through the anal stage successfully may respond to a group event, such as a holiday, by attempting to control the therapist or the group by his behaviour, or the pre-genitally fixated individual might respond to the same event by attempting to split the therapist 'father' from the group 'mother'.

This term may also be used to describe other forms of experience which reverberate with the individual and the group. For example, experiences in the group may resonate with experiences outside the group, the present may resonate with the past in other ways than those already described. In addition, the individual in the group may respond to group events in the same way that he relates to events in his family of origin, or the group may be influenced in its behaviour and preoccupations by local or national events. In many cases there may be a confluence of factors with which the group resonates.

One example which illustrates this occurred during a period when there was a great deal of national interest in the pay award which was to be granted to the nursing profession. The group became preoccupied with the feeling that they were not 'getting enough', that they worked hard and that the rewards of the group experience were not commensurate with the effort and commitment they gave it. In one sense this is a resonance with the anxiety of the infant that his efforts are not being met with sufficient food to sustain him; in another sense it can be seen as a resonance with the national concern with the nurses' pay award; they should be rewarded for their dedication and hard work, but the belief was that they might not be.

THE STRANGER EFFECT

This relates to what happens when a newcomer is introduced to an existing group. What happens will depend on a number of factors, including: the kind of person the newcomer is – shy or aggressive; the state or stage of the group – whether it has achieved a state of basic cohesiveness or not; the kind of people who populate the group as established members, and whether they are welcoming or not. These factors, and many others, will determine the sort of reception that the newcomer receives initially. If he is aggressive, or the group is feeling exposed and vulnerable, then he may be met with battles and hostility; if he is quiet then he may be met with a wary tolerance; if the group is well integrated then he may be met with considerable understanding and a welcoming attitude. But however he is met, he, and the group, will feel his strangeness until he becomes fully assimilated.

This 'strangeness' will probably manifest itself as an uncertainty on his part about how he should conduct himself; he will wish to discover the unwritten rules of the group. The therapy group should have none, other than one basic rule which is that members should be prepared to face the various issues which come to light in the course of the group and acknowledge their own feelings. Of course, there is one basic rule which applies to the whole of human life – feelings should not be expressed through violence.

On their part the group may include the newcomer, but on a sort of probation, until they are ready to include him wholly.

This phenomenon has to do with a return to the earlier stages of the group when concerns to do with the conflict between *Basic Trust* v. *Basic Mistrust* were paramount. For the existing group members it allows another chance to rework some of these issues whilst discovering if the newcomer can be trusted with confidential and intimate matters. It is a defence against the persecutory anxieties of the infant, whilst also being a way of containing those anxieties until the newcomer has been able to imbibe sufficient of the group ethos to be influenced by it.

SUB-GROUPING

The sub-group or pair is formed by the group splitting into smaller factions in response to some group event and is often based upon a shared affinity or perceived similarity (presenting symptoms, a shared profession or job, sharing transport to the group, and so on). This has similarities with Levine's (1979) description of the processes which occur within the *inclusion* phase of group development, with its characteristics of pairings and small groupings when communications take place. We are also reminded of the *termination* phase in which an event, usually to do with some form of separation, will precipitate the group back into the *inclusion* phase for a time.

This phenomenon may form the basis for an unhealthy, fixed allocation of roles within the group, at least for a time. It can relate to the notion of the 'in-group' and the 'out-group'; 'We are the in-group because we are hardworking and conscientious. They are the out-group because they don't do as we do.' It is related to the processes of splitting, projective identification and mutual projection, upon which the allocation of roles within the group is based.

SPLITTING

This is a term which is in common usage and is often understood to mean the manipulative process of turning one against another, for example, when a child says to his father, 'Mummy said that I can stay up to watch the film if it's all right with you', and then says to his mother, 'Daddy says I can watch the film', when what his mother really said was, 'Well, I don't really think so, but we'll see what daddy thinks.' It is a process enshrined in the doctrine 'divide and rule'.

The basis to this process lies within the early infantile experience. It is founded upon the baby's need to protect himself against the frightening destructive impulses and feelings which cause him great distress and persecutory anxiety (see chapter 1). It is a primitive mental defence mechanism which lies behind the more complex mental defence mechanisms of later years. The baby, feeling his fragile sense of possessing something good and comforting at his core, fantasises that it is possible to split one part of himself away from the rest in order to separate and thereby keep safe the valued, but threatened 'good' parts.

In the group situation we may notice it in individuals who are only thoughtful and never angry, or who always help others to deal with difficulties but never acknowledge their own. In the first case the persons concerned have split off their own angry parts to protect the caring side of themselves, and in the second these people have split off their own needy aspects and have dealt with them as if they really did belong to another.

Splitting may also become apparent as a division in the group between those who work and those who don't, those who understand and those who don't, those who attend and those who take unplanned absences. It can also become manifest as a division between the group and the therapist. The variations are many, but the roots reside in the infantile experience.

PROJECTIVE IDENTIFICATION

This is possibly the most important of any of the group phenomena. Along with splitting it forms the heart of many of the other processes that occur in groups. Again it is a process which is founded in the infantile experience.

It was first described by Klein (1946) as a method used by the infant to deal with persecutory anxieties about bad parts of the self. It is related to splitting in this way; the fantasy that it is possible to split off one part of the self from the rest is a necessary precursor to the notion that it is possible to push out a part of oneself into the mother. (See p.17 for a more detailed account of this process.)

In chapter 1 we discussed this process in relation to human emotional development in its aspect as a defensive measure. This is not the sole purpose of projective identification. Klein (1946) tells us that the baby also expels good parts of the self into the mother. This may be to protect the good parts of the self from the rage of the bad feelings which are felt to remain in the baby, but it might also be related at times to the baby's wish to give the mother something good. At these times the projected good feelings have the significance of gifts. If the infant does this too much, he may begin to feel that he has lost valuable parts of himself and feel consequently weakened and disabled. If this occurs he identifies his mother with the ideal qualities which he associated with the good feelings he has projected; this can be the basis to an over-dependent relationship with the mother. As we have seen in earlier chapters, the quality of his relationship with his mother may be, and often is, repeated in later relationships. In the group this may mean that such an individual would imaginatively endow a recipient (initially this is likely to be the therapist but it may be any group member) with the ideal qualities and repeat the negatively dependent relationship he had with his mother within the group.

This process is not confined to the sort of needy individual described above, we all use it in small ways in our everyday lives. In the group it may occur in a variety of ways. Recall the first session of the group described in chapter 6 when one of the group commented that the table was preventing the group from communicating and we can detect the presence of projective processes. It is obvious that, unless the table were really a vast structure which obscured the group's view, or possessed some sound-absorbing qualities, it could not have interfered with the group's ability to communicate. Consequently we can conclude that the table had become imbued with qualities given to it by the group member in question. In other words, he had split off a part of himself which caused him difficulty in talking, pushed it out, in fantasy, into the table, and then responded to the table as if it were responsible for his problems with communicating. Further, the other group members responded as if it were really true that the table had stopped them from talking, by offering to remove it in order to facilitate a flow of conversation. This has something of the dimensions of a group folly – even the therapist had to think hard to be able to retain a clear perception of what was really happening.

We can see that there was an initial process of projective identification undertaken by Bill that was later taken up by the group which colluded with his fantasy and added another – that it was Bill's problem which prevented the group from working. We begin to be able to see how roles are allocated in groups; if the therapist had not been careful, Bill might have been blamed or *scapegoated* by the group for their inability to work.

MUTUAL PROJECTION

This phenomenon is based upon projective identification and is a development of it. As the members become more familiar with each other we see that the group begin to allocate roles.

In one such group, a so-called 'leader-less' group, the allocation of roles became quite extreme and was certainly anti-therapeutic, if not actively harmful to the well-being of its members. A small group of adults had been meeting once a week for over a year. Over a period of time the members had become almost caricatures of themselves. One member, who was of an anxious disposition, became identified as the 'sick' member. The rest of the group treated him carefully and gently in a way that prevented him from being anything other than 'sick'. Another, who was assertive, became identified as the 'angry' member, so any comment she made was regarded as an angry response, even if it were thoughtful, or caring, or sad, and so on. Yet another was seen as 'helpful and caring' and anything he said was regarded in this light, even if he was expressing angry feelings. The identification of individuals with roles, which then confined them, continued throughout the whole of this group.

If we think about this we can see that, whilst it might be nice to be thought of as caring, after a while it can become a diminishing experience. John may be of an anxious disposition yet still be able to respond to life with a full range of feelings. However, if the group identifies his anxiety as his single most important quality and responds to him in ways that avoid making him anxious, they disallow normal social intercourse between him and the rest of the group. He becomes incomplete, an empty shell of a person who becomes more and more anxious as he is maintained in this position by the projections of the rest of the group.

Mary might be an angry person and still be able to feel sad, or generous, or thoughtful, but if the group prevents her from expressing warm and gentle feelings, or refuses to hear them, then she is likely to become more and more angry over time. She becomes diminished, there is a whole world of feeling which is forbidden a response, her emotional horizons are effectively foreshortened and this outward difficulty becomes represented in her inner world. She will feel depleted of good and warm feelings and will begin to feel angry for the slightest reason. She will feel an increasing anxiety about this 'bad' side of herself and there will be a concomitant feeling of persecution.

Similarly, if Tom is angry and expresses this anger, yet is only ever responded to as if he had made a caring remark, he must begin to feel disregarded, unrecognised and easily dismissed.

The difference between projective identification and mutual projection is that the latter, as the name implies, is reciprocal (Main 1966). The process by which the projection is achieved is the same, but in mutual projection there is an element of trading. For example, in the illustrations given above, John was anxious, Mary was angry and Tom was caring. Each had invested in the others a part of themselves which the recipient owned to a greater degree. In other words, John and Tom invested some of their angry feelings in Mary as she was obviously more able to manage angry feelings than they were. Mary invested some of her gentler feelings in Tom to protect them from her anger and because he was more comfortable with gentle feelings. Tom invested his anxious feelings in John and was therefore more able to be caring, and so on.

There is nothing magical about this, it happens in quite a straightforward way. The individual in the group is used to dealing with some of his unwanted aspects by imaginatively pushing them outward (projection). He evokes the projected feeling, or its representative, in the recipient in much the same way as the baby does – through non-verbal communication, the tone of voice, the juxtaposition of words. Children often do this sort of thing to each other. The little boy who teasingly mimics his sister beyond the point of fun and makes her angry can only be responding to the 'bad' or cruel part of himself. There is something destructive or angry in this sort of teasing, if we think about it. Consequently, when his sister has become angry, we often see that the little boy becomes more relaxed, more comfortable with himself, because he has evoked in his sister the feeling that made him uncomfortable. Since he can see that his sister is angry, he can believe that he has rid himself of his angry feeling by pushing it into her.

In the group this happens between all of the members. Processes of mutual projection occur in all groups, and although the example given here is of an extreme type, it is necessary that the therapist be aware of it. When it does happen the projection will usually only hold when it matches a significant aspect in the recipient. If the recipient cannot manage his own angry feelings then the anger of others will not be successfully projected. In other words, for the projection to stick there must be a 'hook' in the recipient to hang it on. It occurs in families and in couples and when it is repeated in the group it may be seen as an attempt to recreate, in the group, a situation that first existed within the family of origin. It is a defensive phenomenon and it inhibits growth.

SCAPEGOATING

This is a process which is related to mutual projection and is enabled by projective identification.

The biblical scapegoat was used by the Tribes of Israel as a repository for all of their sins. As the members of the tribe touched the goat they placed their wrongs on the back of the animal. Having done this they then cast the creature out into the desert. (It is to be assumed that the goat would eventually find its way back into the herd once the fuss had died down.)

The scapegoat of the group serves a similar function. Just as the biblical goat symbolically absorbed the wrongs of the tribe, so the scapegoat serves the group. The role of the scapegoat is to act as a recipient for all of the hostile and guilty feelings the group have. He may be chosen because of some particular attribute he has, or because he is somehow different from the rest because of age, size, colour, creed, nationality or some other such difference. He is chosen because the group is afraid to attack the true focus of their feelings, very often the therapist, who is himself the target of transferred feelings to do with an important authority figure, such as a parent. The group will attack and ultimately cast out the scapegoat, unless the therapist is able to help the group to recognise the unconscious part of their behaviour.

It is often quite easy to see when the group is involved in scapegoating, for all of the criticisms, hostility and invective (or most of them) will be directed towards one member. It is not always as easy to identify the concealed attack upon the authority figure.

In one group this became quite apparent. The therapist was a clergyman and one of the group members was also a clergyman who attended one day in his clerical garb of black and white collar. This was, perhaps, the basic difference upon which he was selected; none of the others in the group were members of the clergy. The group criticised him, the work of the priesthood, his distance from the 'real' world, his lack of understanding, and so on. It was not until the therapist pointed out the unwarranted quality of the hostility and the unprovoked nature of the attack that the group were able to step back and examine what they had been doing. The therapist was able to show that the group knew that he was a clergyman too, and to interpret that the group might be feeling that he failed to understand them and was out of touch. He also wondered whether they were familiar with that feeling in other areas of their lives. This was, of course, a reference to the transference of feelings of being uncared for by an important figure, such as a parent, onto the person of the therapist. The therapist did not interpret this directly, but enabled the group to make the discovery themselves by providing them with the necessary information.

In the last few examples we have described phenomena which illustrate how the group can affect its members negatively. Whilst these phenomena do have a negative quality, a knowledge of them enables the therapist to help the group to deal with them. The process of working with them is of therapeutic benefit to the group. Perhaps, for the sake of balance, it would be useful now to examine one or two processes which have a positive effect.

TRIANGULATION

This term has been used in two different ways. In one usage it identifies the process by which the individual member of the group draws upon the many and varied views which others within the group have of him, in order to establish a clearer or more accurate view of himself in his own mind. This is a lengthy business that happens throughout the life of the group. It employs processes of *introjection* and *identification*, whereby the individual copies admired aspects, usually of a favoured other (but in this situation it is his own, previously unrecognised, admirable qualities that he emulates) in order to feel that he is like the object of his admiration.

It has also been used to describe the process in which a conflict that exists between two parties is diverted into a third party, who then enacts the conflict in some way (figure 7.3). It has most often been used by family therapists to acknowledge the parental conflict that may lie behind a child's problem. In this sense it is the outcome of projective processes, and has similarities with the phenomenon of scapegoating.

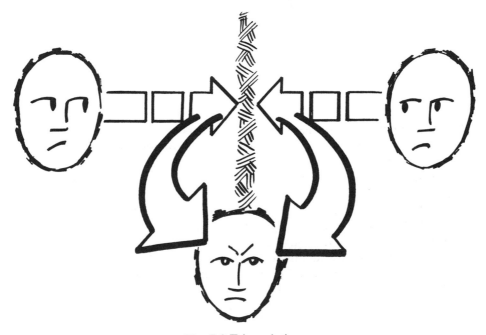

Fig. 7.3 Triangulation

SEE-SAW

This refreshingly unscientific term has been borrowed from a valued colleague, and it effectively describes the to-ing and fro-ing of opinion that takes place in the group. For example, one member might express a fairly extreme view that the group (or any focus for the group's attention) is useless. Another will reply that, on the contrary, the group is of inestimable value, whereupon a third might respond that, it was sometimes, if rarely, helpful; and a fourth may say that he found it helpful quite often. Eventually the members would agree that the group was sometimes quite helpful and at other times not and that this would depend upon many things, including one's own state of mind. We can see how the spread of opinion in the group swings wildly from one extreme of opinion to another, until gradually more reasonable opinions are expressed, the swing becomes shorter and the see-saw comes to rest in a balanced position.

This phenomenon helps the group to deal with the primitive process of *splitting*. Through the group's ability to contain within it a number of differing views, and because of the spirit of freedom of expression and of enquiry that the therapist fosters, the individual in the group is enabled to relinquish his extreme position. He is helped to take back on board a part of himself with which he was previously uncomfortable.

If we look at the simple example above, the first complainant was helped to own the feeling of being useless, which he had identified as the group's uselessness. The group had fulfilled the same function for him as the mother does for the baby when she *metabolises* the baby's projection (Ogden, 1979; see also p. 17 above). They had effectively reduced the quality of anxiety inherent in the feeling of uselessness and returned the projection to the complainant, through not agreeing with his jaundiced perception.

There are other identifiable phenomena that occur in groups, but we have described the most important and related them to the life of the group and to the family, as appropriate. In the next chapter we shall look at the factors in groups that help people change. In order to do so, we shall need to draw on both our understanding of group development and of group phenomena.

References

Foulkes S H (1975) *Group-Analytic Psychotherapy, Method and Principles.* London: Gordon and Breach.

Foulkes S H and Anthony E J (1957) *Group Psychotherapy, The Psycho-Analytic Approach.* London: Maresfield Reprints.

Grotjahn M (1978) A walk with Michael Foulkes. In: *Group Therapy 1978; An Overview.* New York: Stratton Intercontinental Medical Book Corporation.

Klein M (1946) Notes on some schizoid mechanisms. In: *Envy and Gratitude.* London: The Hogarth Press and The Institute of Psycho-Analysis.

Levine B (1979) *Group Psychotherapy, Practice and Development.* New York: Prentice Hall.

Main T F (1966) Mutual projection in a marriage. *Comprehensive Psychiatry*, **7** (5): 432–449.

Ogden T H (1979) On projective identification. *International Journal of Psycho-Analysis*, **60**: 357–373.

8

Therapeutic Properties
of Groups

A number of researchers have studied the therapeutic properties of groups and have identified many of them. It is important to acknowledge at the outset that these 'therapeutic properties', which may be named and described individually, are really parts of a larger process. They are related to the development of the group from dependence towards maturity and to the group phenomena described in chapter 7. They are interdependent, interactive and mutually influential.

For example, Yalom (1970) lists what he describes as eleven primary therapeutic factors. If we take one of these, 'the corrective recapitulation of the primary family group', and study it, we can see that Yalom means us to understand that the experiences which we had in our family of origin may be re-enacted in the family which we create in the group. The family we create in the group, at least in our own minds, has many, if not all the characteristics of our original family. The group allows us the chance to experience again many of the influences that formed our lives. Over and above this it offers the opportunity to explore, to understand and to come to terms with, the feelings and responses which formed part of each experience.

What must happen within the group for this to occur?

Feelings which are related to a member of one's own family must be *transferred* to a member of the group, or to the group at large. Then there must be a *projection* of the characteristics of the family member onto the person of the group member. So we can see, even at this simplified level, that this one factor is dependent upon at least two of the group phenomena described in chapter 7.

A number of therapeutic properties must be linked. Before the individual can safely react openly and with feeling it has to be plain that the group can be trusted, there needs to be a feeling that 'we are all in this together', and a realisation that 'I'm not the only one', along with a belief that it is possible for things to change. These qualities relate to Yalom's primary therapeutic factors of *'instillation of hope'* (change is possible), *'universality'* (I am not alone) and *'group cohesiveness'* (we are working together, or we trust in the unity of the group's purpose).

Before any of these can develop the group has to be brought together by the therapist. We shall be examining the role of the therapist from a different perspective in chapter 9, but it is essential to note his contribution to the therapeutic process here.

THE ROLE OF THE THERAPIST

It is the therapist's responsibility to select a group of people who will be able to understand each other and work together. He enables them to become psychologically-minded through the stance that he takes, and the attitude of non-critical inquiry that he fosters, whilst establishing honesty as the basis for all communication within the group. At the same time he ensures the group and its members freedom and individuality.

He establishes the early norms of freedom of communication, the open communication of feelings, and a style of listening which is attentive and non-critical. Other researchers (Truax and Carkhuff, 1967) have identified the need for appropriate empathy and non-possessive warmth. He must translate non-verbal communication into verbal language. Because he works honestly and openly to deal with the problems and anxieties which are feared, the group feels safe with him. The trust that is thus established by the therapist enables the group to develop as a cohesive, therapeutic entity. Consequently, the way he acts is often more important than what he says; the effective therapist looks for ways to help the group to discover knowledge for themselves and avoids making profound interpretations (Foulkes and Anthony, 1957; Yalom, 1970). This suggests the next of the therapeutic properties.

Interpretation

Interpretation is one of the basic tools of the psychodynamic psychotherapist. It is the means by which he helps to bring to consciousness material which was previously unconscious or unavailable to the conscious influence of the individual. This same material, though unavailable to the conscious influences the individual might like to bring to bear, itself strongly influences the responses of the individual in every sphere of his life. This includes impulses, feelings and past experiences which reside in the unconscious mind. Each of these shapes how we think or feel in the present and affects our relationships with others and the outside world. Consequently, we need to make this material available to the conscious mind of our patients in order that it might be faced and its effects understood. Making this material available does not effect a cure. It is not sufficient to present something to the conscious mind once. We need to find the same truth time and time again before we can deal with it effectively.

A colleague tells the story of a friend who had been in analysis for some years. One day, after a series of interpretations, the friend experienced the ringing bells and flashing lights of understanding.

'But why didn't you tell me this before?' he asked in frustration.

His analyst replied: 'What do you think I've been telling you for the past three years?'

Obviously there was a great deal of work which had needed to be done before the patient had been able to assimilate the lessons he learned in his analysis, and this is true of all of us. Another colleague would point out that it took a while for a lesson to be learned, but when it was it would stay with us until eventually we would realise that we had forgotten it, whereupon we would have to learn it all over again.

In the group situation the depth at which interpretations operate increases with the deepening commitment of the group. As the group becomes a more cohesive unit (see Group Cohesiveness, p. 67) it takes on some of the conductor's interpreting role. Foulkes and Anthony (1957) acknowledge that interpretations from group members can be useful, or they can be merely an attempt to copy the therapist. At other times they can be a hindrance to the work of the group and constitute a defence against other painful issues by drawing the attention of the group and the therapist to other matters. Foulkes (1975) recognises that interpretation does not depend on conscious, verbal communication. He suggests that interpretations take place all the time in a group, consciously or unconsciously, through the stance one takes or the attitude one adopts, through actions or in words, deliberately or accidentally, and that all the members of the group participate in interpreting in this way.

The therapist will pay particular attention to the group process, by which we mean the quality or kind, or the nature of the interactions and relationships that develop in the group. He may draw attention to this process by interpreting the behaviour of the group, for example;

● It seems to me that the air of casualness is a little unreal, I think there may be something happening; John has not stopped looking out of the window, three of you are looking anywhere but at each other and no one wants to interrupt Mary's story about her shopping trip. The story sounds amusing but no one is laughing.

The therapist's purpose is to enable the group to become aware that something is happening and to leave the group the task of discovering what it might be. People learn better if they are enabled to make their own discoveries. The therapist's job is to provide the conditions necessary to fulfil this task. This brings us to consider the next of the therapeutic properties of groups, which is an amalgam of several other therapeutic factors which, when brought together, enable the group to feel contained.

Containment

This relates to the quality of care that the 'good enough mother' (Winnicott, 1974) gives to her child. Winnicott called this process 'holding', which effectively conjures a picture of the mother holding her child with affection, with sympathy, with thoughtfulness and with feeling. Containment (Bion, 1970) suggests the requirement of 'keeping something within' a little more strongly. The ability of the therapist to 'keep within' himself his own anxieties and to hold on to the group's anxieties enables the group to survive the first stressful weeks of meetings. Where the therapist is not able to contain sufficient of the group's anxiety then there is a risk that the members, or some of them, may deal with it by resorting to primitive defences such as *flight*.

The use of the word 'containment' should not suggest that the therapist tries to take away all of the anxiety for the group. He deals with the group's anxiety by allowing them to experience anxiety, by tolerating it in himself, by indicating that he is not overwhelmed by it, and by being able to continue to work despite it. He does not rush to reassure the group, nor does he wish to take all the anxiety away. If we remember the description of the way Baby Kay was mothered (pp. 5–6) we can see a good model for handling anxiety in the group. Baby Kay was allowed to cry a little, but was also given the degree of support she needed to deal with too much anxiety. Her mother was there with her, but did not take over the management of her anxiety for her. This enabled Kay to learn that anxiety and other bad feelings would not necessarily overwhelm her, even if it seemed that they might, and that she could deal with her anxiety herself.

By contrast, because Carol's mother (pp. 6–7) was unable to allow her to experience the distress of any bad feeling, Carol could not manage any of the anxiety she faced in the world at large when she grew up. Because her mother had protected her from painful feelings and uncomfortable circumstances, she had not learned that she could cope with them. Consequently, this meant that everything she faced caused her unbearable distress.

The group therapist who responds to the group's anxiety by effectively taking it away will (as Carol's mother) make the group feel better for a time. There will, at least initially, be a sense of relief expressed within the group. However, the group will eventually come to feel so increasingly anxious that its members may fail to attend, or will leave for one reason or another (*flight*), before any real work has taken place. This increase in anxiety would be related to a growing, unconscious awareness that the therapist is not managing and cannot manage the group's anxiety. He would have shown them so time and again by avoiding it himself and encouraging the group to avoid it with him. Instead of providing a relationship which reassures through constantly facing up to anxiety, the relationship becomes one which ultimately alarms; it is as if the therapist were saying: 'This really is unmanageable, this is really frightening.'

Alternatively, he might be left with a group which thinks him wonderful, because he makes the members feel a little better for the time that the group meets, but he would find that none of his patients really improves. Carol loved her mother and felt better with her, but she could not live an ordinary life, she could only feel safe when close to her mother and so was devastated when her mother died.

Containment is therapeutic in its own right. As we have seen, the individual is helped to manage his difficult feelings through this process, he is able to feel safely held. This is an experience which may begin to rectify an unsatisfactory experience within the maternal relationship during the early months of life and later.

The therapist who contains the group's bad feelings enables it to develop the trust that is needed before it is possible to deal with personal problems. Indeed, a lack of basic trust is itself a causative factor in the problems of many.

Initially, the therapist is responsible for this process of containment, but as it matures, this is another function which the group adopts. Once the foundations have been laid then trust deepens throughout the life of the group, enabling the members to explore and experience personal and relationship issues of an increasingly profound nature.

This brings us to the next of the enabling factors, or therapeutic properties.

Sharing

Because the group is made up of several individuals who each has distinctive life experiences there is a wide variety of viewpoints available. The experience of some will differ greatly from others, but there will also be similarities. Both the similarities and the differences are important.

Many of the people who join a therapy group will have struggled for years believing that they are the only ones who have ever felt, or behaved, or responded in a particular way. They may feel, as Yalom (1970) puts it, 'unique in their wretchedness'. This feeling is often made worse by the isolation produced by problems with interpersonal relationships, it can become a lonely and frightening experience. Once the group has been together long enough for the members to begin to trust each other, it becomes possible to be more open so that sharing can begin. This sharing starts in the forming or parallel stage and initially will be focused on quite innocuous, or safe, subjects. For example, the group will ask questions about the names of each of the members, their jobs, their marital state, their children (are they boys or girls, what are their ages?), their hobbies and other interests.

This initial sharing has at least three purposes; the first is to diminish the anxiety of not knowing; the second is to begin the process of finding out; and the third is to establish a group norm of appropriate interest and of exploration.

As the trust in the group deepens so does the level at which it operates, consequently the group will be able to look at and deal with issues which are the cause of greater discomfort. Yalom called this factor *'universality'* and suggested that there are three main secrets which cause the greatest anxiety to individuals and which provide the greatest relief when they are shared. These are:

1. *Inadequacy*, which was expressed as a feeling that others would avoid the individual concerned as they would recognise the faults in the individual and disapprove of his character.

2. *Alienation*, which is experienced as a feeling that all one's emotions are shallow or unreal and that it is not really possible to love or care for another.

3. *Sexual secrets*. These may be of many kinds. Yalom reports that one of the most common is a fear that one has homosexual tendencies. Others may be to do with incest or other forms of sexual abuse or a variety of sexual practices.

The sharing of these and other 'secrets' again deepens the level at which the group can work. Much information will be made available during the earlier stages of the group which sets the scene for the sharing of secrets later. This earlier and less anxiety-provoking form of sharing begins in the parallel phase, enables the inclusion phase, where it deepens, and peaks during the mutuality phase, when sharing deepens still further.

Altruism

Altruism (Yalom, 1970) is another aspect of sharing. It may be understood as the discovery that one is of value to others, that one has a meaning in terms of a larger whole. It is more possible to struggle on if we can see that others can value us for what we are, for the unique and personal contribution we make, without making demands on us to give, or do, or be something else.

In the introduction to the Penguin edition of his book *The Informed Heart*, Bruno Bettelheim writes:

● The Nazis murdered the Jews of Europe and millions of others whom they considered undesirable. That nobody but the Jews cared for the Jews, and that even many Jews on the outside did not care very much, that the free world did not care – this was why the will to survive of so many European Jews became first weakened and then extinguished. One of the last messages from the Warsaw ghetto said: 'The world is silent; the world knows and stays silent. God's vicar in the Vatican is silent. There is silence in London and Washington. The American Jews are silent. This silence is incomprehensible and horrifying.' (1986, p. xvii)

We can see from this passage how very necessary it is that we should feel valued and cared for by others. If we do not have this sense of being accepted and the valued by others, then it becomes very difficult to maintain a sense of personal worth. As human beings it seems that personal worth is measured in terms of the esteem of others. When this breaks down then we may all too easily succumb to the destructive impulses of the dark side of our human nature, which Freud called the death drive, and give in to a downward spiral of self-loathing. In Hitler this found expression in the fantasy of a race of supermen, and in his attempts to exterminate the 'lower races'. It has many faces and may be expressed in many ways – in suicide, or through rape and so on, when it is in extreme ascendency.

In a sense this leads us to another aspect of sharing which is generally called feedback.

Feedback

This is the term we use to describe the process of being measured by others and of measuring ourselves against the responses of others. If we receive a negative response or responses then after a time we modify our behaviour until we meet different responses. In this way we find out what is acceptable and what is not, and we learn to allow ourselves to be appropriately influenced by others. The therapist may be relied upon to guard against anti-social norms being established, but in most groups there is a sufficiently wide spectrum of opinion and a sufficient concern for the regard of others to make this unnecessary.

We measure our social performance against both the internal values that we gained in infancy and which we imbided with our mother's milk. We also use as a measure the responses we provoke in others. This feedback will affect how we behave in other circumstances and on other occasions. If we stay with the example of Hitler, then we can see that he received apparently general approbation for himself and his policies at the Nuremburg and other rallies. He also surrounded himself with like-minded people who could be relied upon to support his points of view, or with self-seeking sycophants who would flatter rather than give reasonable opinion. Consequently, he did not get the feedback which could otherwise have curbed his wildest destructive impulses.

The group phenomenon we described as the see-saw is part of the feedback process. Through the swings of opinion the individual is quietly influenced towards modifying his own stance as he is affected by the regard which the group gives to the final balanced position of the see-saw.

Another way in which we might think about this is to recognise the relationship between the group situation and reality. There may be a thousand different views of the mountain, but the individual can see only one at a particular time. With the benefit of a group of people who may each have a slightly different view, it is possible for the individual to see more of the total view, so that he can separate common ground from individually held ground.

In the therapy group feedback may initially be fostered by the therapist who uses his early powerful position to encourage 'good' group behaviour in the members by giving positive feedback to behaviour and interventions which further the therapeutic aims of the group.

Identification

Another therapeutic property which may be included within the heading of sharing is *identification*. Yalom (1970) refers to this as *imitative behaviour*. This works at both a pre-conscious and a conscious level. Individuals will observe and emulate the behaviour of others within the group. In the early stages much of the imitative behaviour will be derived from the therapist, but as the group progresses towards the mutuality or established phase then individuals will identify with the attitudes and behaviour of the other members. The individual recognises in another something which he admires and, initially consciously, seeks to emulate the admired quality. He models himself on the target of his admiration and strives to be like him or her. This is often followed by a second stage when the individual absorbs the admired quality and it becomes part of his personality or character. In other words, it becomes *introjected*.

Corrective Emotional Experience

This was first described by Alexander (1946) and has since been confirmed by many others, including Yalom (1970), whose research identified patients who talked of 'turning points' in their therapy. Such experiences usually had the following characteristics:

1.   It usually involves another group member, rather than the therapist.

2.   The circumstances or the experience would be highly charged beyond the usual emotional limits.

3.   It would deal mainly with negative feelings such as anger or hatred. Much less frequently it may have to do with powerful positive feelings of tenderness or closeness.

4.   It would involve taking risks, with a concomitant fear of painful consequences, but this would be possible because secure boundaries would have been established

long before and the individual would know that both the group and the conductor could be trusted to maintain safe limits.

5.   Following upon the explosion of powerful feelings there would be a time when the group would help the individual to examine the incident and his feelings.

6.   This would enable him to feel validated, in other words, that his feelings were justified.

7.   It would provide a chance for the individual to acknowledge the inappropriate degree of his behaviour, of his feelings and of his reaction.

8.   This leads to more appropriate behaviour, to self-disclosure and subsequent greater involvement.

Re-experiencing

There are many experiences which may be usefully re-experienced within the group. The position an individual occupied within his family of origin and the feelings associated with this is an obvious one. (Yalom refers to this factor as *'the corrective recapitulation of the primary family group'*.) Other relationships from the present as well as the distant past may be re-experienced also, yet almost invariably these will have their origins in the family experience too, if we trace them back. When an individual joins any group he will bring with him expectations which are inherent; that is, they belong to an unconscious part of the self which influences him in ways he cannot know about. These inherent expectations may be to do with how he will be received by others, whether or not he will be treated fairly, whether or not he will be liked or respected, and whether or not he will be listened to. There are, of course, many other expectations which the individual carries within him and many of them are related to the treatment he received within his family of origin, or his perception of this.

The group situation offers the individual an opportunity to recognise how his expectations of relationships influence his behaviour. This occurs in the following way:

1.   A situation develops which has, or seems to have, similarities with circumstances from the individual's past.

2.   The original experience resonates with his current experience in the group, so that many of the feelings attached to the original experience become manifest in the present situation.

3.   Then the individual in question responds to those around him according to the feelings evoked in him by the resonating circumstances.

For example, in one group Mary was often cross and impatient with Colin. He was an annoying man who irritated many of the group's members, but none was so strongly affected as Mary. Her impatient remarks to or about him went on for weeks until it became obvious to the group that there was something more in this interaction than met the eye. Some of the other members of the group, who had given up on the idea that Colin could be expected to share much of himself, wondered why Mary was so upset by Colin's lack of openness. Mary, of course, behaved in quite a defensive way by saying that it wasn't her, it was Colin who was the problem, they should ask him why he never said anything. It was like getting blood out of a stone. She went on in this way for some time, becoming more and more cross whilst the group gently kept up the pressure. Eventually, almost beside herself with anger and loathing, she spat out: 'God! You're just like my father, he was just the same, he never responded to anything I did or said, and they all stuck up for him.'

So we can see that Mary was responding as if Colin was her father and the group were other members of her family. The difference was that the group neither victimised her nor allowed her to maintain a view of herself as being a victim. The group stayed with this incident and helped Mary to deal with it more effectively. Even the reviled Colin was able to help by offering his view of her, which was a far cry from how she imagined he saw her. In other words, as with the *corrective emotional experience* described earlier in this chapter, the 're-experiencing' was

Fig. 8.1 Therapeutic qualities

followed by a period of supportive reality testing and a validation of Mary as she was seen in the group, together with some recognition by her and others of what was appropriate or inappropriate in her view of Colin and the group (figure 8.1).

Group Cohesiveness

This property of the group is related to, dependent upon and also forms part of the other properties listed so far. It is the sense of commitment to the group which is possessed by each of its members. It is based on the establishment of a sense of trust in, and a commitment to, one another. Group cohesiveness is similar to the 'therapeutic alliance' (Greenson, 1967) of individual therapy. It is the good relationship which the individual establishes with his fellow members and with the therapist. It is based upon the qualities of non-possessive warmth, unconditional positive regard, empathy, trust and understanding. It has to do with the positive value which the members attach to the group and to the sense of security and support which is derived from it. This sense of belonging to something that one values and which is valued by others produces a sense of worth. Because an inherent sense of worth is established in each of the individuals it becomes more possible for them to face aspects of themselves which had previously been deeply hidden because they were felt to be so unattractive. A sense of increased worth diminishes the power of unwanted and unattractive parts of the person so that they are felt to be less threatening, less important, and can be faced more easily.

This bears similarities with *altruism* and returns us to the point that was made at the beginning of the chapter. All of the therapeutic properties are linked to each other and to the various other properties of the group, its development, the members, the group phenomena, and so on. Although it may be useful to consider the component parts of the group in sequence, as we have done throughout, it is imperative that we do not suppose that they exist in isolation in the living group. They weave in with each other, providing both the stimulus and the effect. Several strands of the group experience will coexist during each moment of the group, influencing and being influenced by one another (figure 8.2). In essence the group is a reciprocal and interactive, evolving forum. The therapist strives to remain aware of this, whilst not becoming overwhelmed by it.

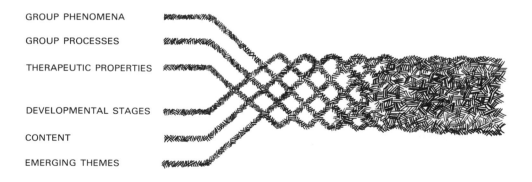

GROUP PHENOMENA

GROUP PROCESSES

THERAPEUTIC PROPERTIES

DEVELOPMENTAL STAGES

CONTENT

EMERGING THEMES

Fig. 8.2 Threads of group experience

References

Alexander F and French T (1946) *Psychoanalytic Therapy: Principles and Applications*. New York: Ronald Press.

Bettelheim B (1986) *The Informed Heart*. Harmondsworth: Penguin Books.

Bion W R (1970) *Attention and Interpretation*. London: Tavistock.

Foulkes S H (1975) *Group Analytic Psychotherapy. Method and Principles*. London: Gordon and Breach.

Foulkes S H and Anthony E J (1957) *Group Psychotherapy. The Psychoanalytic Approach*. London: Maresfield Reprints.

Greenson R R (1967) *The Technique and Practice of Psychoanalysis*. London: The Hogarth Press and The Institute of Psycho-Analysis.

Truax C B and Carkhuff R R (1967) *Toward Effective Counselling and Psychotherapy*. Chicago: Aldine Publishing Company.

Winnicott D W (1974) *Playing and Reality*. Harmondsworth: Penguin Books.

Yalom I D (1970) *The Theory and Practice of Group Psychotherapy*. New York: Basic Books.

9

The Role of the Conductor

The heading of this chapter needs some explanation before we proceed any further. The title *conductor* has been given for a specific purpose. Although it is in many ways synonymous with *therapist*, it identifies the role more clearly. The person who is responsible for running the group is given many titles by those who work with groups. They include:

1. *Group Convenor* which indicates part of the overall responsibility which is to bring the group together, or to convene it;

2. *Group Leader* which acknowledges the early relationship between the group and the therapist through the group's early identification of him with the leadership role within the group;

3. *Group Therapist* which highlights the responsibility of those working with groups to establish the group as a therapeutic organism; and lastly

4. *Group Conductor* which illustrates the function of his role with the group in every aspect. The conductor has a similar task to that of the conductor of an orchestra. He brings the group together in one place to work towards a harmonious conclusion. On the way there will be much disharmony and many themes which run counter to the therapeutic aims of the group, but also there will be themes composed of shared issues and anxieties to which each member will contibute some understanding, so that a rounded whole eventually emerges. S H Foulkes is regarded as the first to have suggested the title conductor, and he used many musical terms to define various factors in the life of the group. It is said that he would describe the actions and interventions of the conductor as being very like those of the orchestral conductor, but more of this later.

For our purposes here we may divide the role of the conductor into two parts – the conductor as administrator and the conductor as therapist. It might be tempting to suppose that the second of these – the conductor as therapist – is the more important, but this is not so. If the conductor gets the basic administration of the group wrong then it is likely that he will have great difficulty in providing it with a therapeutic experience. In other words, whilst it is possible and helpful for our purposes to define these two aspects of the role of the conductor separately, they are inextricably interwoven, mutually influential and interdependent.

THE CONDUCTOR AS ADMINISTRATOR

In this aspect of his role he is responsible for: the selection of group members, the setting of the group, the boundaries of the group, breaks and cancellations, the duration of the group, and keeping a register.

Selection

Generally speaking, his responsibility is to establish a group membership who, at the outset, are able to work together. A useful size for a therapy group is between five and eight members, although this is not mandatory. A well-established, successfully constituted, larger group of, say, twelve to fifteen members may work better than a smaller, poorly constituted group of badly motivated members. If we think about this in more specific detail we will note that the conductor will need to bring together a group of people who are able to relate to each other. This means that the group needs to be comprised of people with some similarities of experience and background. However, the conductor also needs to provide a broad span of experience within the group so that a variety of views and experiences become available to the members in order that they might be influenced by new ideas and new experiences (see p. 93).

To achieve a reasonably balanced group he will need to ensure that there is a mix of men and women in the group. It would be unfair and unhelpful if there were to be only one man or one woman; there would be no one with whom to share gender-linked issues, and the consequent quality of support or understanding within the group would be impaired.

The same applies to other groupings. For example, if the conductor is considering admitting a depressed person to the group, then he would do well to admit two people suffering from depression. Any single such person would find it difficult to share in the experience of *universality* (see p. 93) as the group would not be able to comprehend the depth of despair experienced by this individual. Similarly, if one of the group members happens to be homosexual, or a single parent, or phobic, then it would be helpful to try to ensure that he, or she, is not alone. Any individual may become the focus of a scapegoating attack (see pp. 85–6), but it is more likely if he or she is distinguishable from the rest of the group in some way. In this event, if the individual is unsupported by another group member, it is more likely that the scapegoating will result in his feeling thoroughly unwanted and then leaving the group.

The Setting

As we shall be discussing the setting in a great deal more detail in chapter 10, we shall confine ourselves here to thinking about the immediate setting for the group.

The circle is part of this setting and its purpose is to allow the group to see each other, to be in visual as well as audible contact. Its purpose is also to establish the group as a forum of equals; no one is above another, the distances between each is the same for all. In this sense the circle enables a sense of equality to develop.

Very often the circle will have a small, round table at its centre. This table is a helpful addition to any group setting; it is symbolic of the matrix, or the core of the group, in which the sum of all of the members resides. In visual terms it represents the notion that the group has a centre; it represents the mutual influence that each member has on the others and illustrates the notion that each group has an identity which is greater than the sum of its members. It is placed neither to one side nor to the other, and therefore information to be shared by the whole group is placed or 'tabled' upon it. It may also provide a greater feeling of security as it provides a barrier against primitive, 'acting out' behaviour, whence feelings become translated into action. It encourages talk rather than action.

Boundaries

These too come within the general heading of 'The Setting'. The first boundary we need to consider is the 'Time Boundary'.

Time

The conductor should expect punctuality and regularity of attendance from the group members and in order to achieve this he must adhere to these principles himself. He begins the group by entering the room in which it is to be held promptly at the time the group is due to start, and he ends the group promptly at the time it is set to finish. In general it may be considered reasonable for the group to continue for two or three minutes beyond the set time if the conductor sees this as necessary, helpful or appropriate. The duration of each session should be consistent but, as has been said, some flexibility at the end of the session is acceptable within the above guidelines.

The purpose of the time boundary is to enhance the establishment of group cohesiveness and to instil a feeling of safety within the group. Its purpose is also to make available transference issues which occur at the beginning and the end of the group. If the time boundaries are not monitored, or are monitored inadequately by the conductor, then many transference issues will be missed.

In one group, which had been functioning for over a year, the co-therapists left the room promptly at the end of the session. The next session began with an angry outburst from two or three of the members which focused on how bad-mannered the therapists were considered to have been to have left the group without making the social niceties usual when parting from company. One of the therapists acknowledged the angry feelings and the appropriateness of them in social situations, but went on to point out the fact that the group was a treatment rather than a social situation, that the group knew this, and also knew the time that the group would finish. He said that it seemed that there was something else happening.

The group became more angry and continued to berate the co-therapists for their 'ill-mannered and insensitive' behaviour until eventually one of the more vociferous of the group members exploded: 'Damn! You lot are worse than my father.'

The therapists took this up and, with the help of the group, enabled the individual concerned to see that her depth of feeling, her fury, had more to do with the unresolved feelings of anger and loss which had been provoked originally by her father, who would frequently disappear without a word for weeks or months at a time, than with the therapists whose behaviour had sparked off painful, if not immediately conscious, memories of her father.

There were other resonances for other group members, with experiences that held the same quality of feeling. The important thing to note is that, if the therapists had observed the usual rules of social engagement and if they had extricated themselves from the group in a way which left everyone feeling comfortable, (perhaps by letting the group run on a little in the pretence that it was a gathering of friends) then they would have prevented some useful work from taking place.

The Duration of the Group

This is another feature of 'The Setting' which may be included within the sub-heading of 'Boundaries'.

Quite simply it refers to the principle that, if the group is to be time-limited, each member should be told of this at the assessment interview. If it is to be an open group – that is, planned to continue over a number of years – then each candidate for membership should be told of this too at his assessment. If the group is to begin as an open group until its membership is established, then each prospective member should be told this also.

There are a number of types of group which are defined by their duration.

1.   An *open group* is one which usually has a fairly rapid turnover of members. Groups held in the admission units of hospitals are often like this because of the constraints to admit and to return patients to the community as rapidly as possible.

2.   A *slow-open* group is one which, as its name implies, remains with a stable membership for long periods until one of its number leaves. After a suitable time a new member will be admitted, and so on. These are mostly treatment groups.

3.   A *closed group* is one which begins and ends with the same membership and usually lasts for an agreed period of time. Some treatment and many training groups are closed groups.

In practice, many treatment groups begin their life as slow-open groups until a satisfactory membership has been established and then are closed for an established period of time, as people frequently drop out in the early stages.

Breaks and Cancellations

Once again this is included within the boundary-keeping role of the conductor who expects the members to inform the group, as far as possible, of any cancellations and absences. He models this himself by informing the group of any holidays or other breaks right at the beginning so that the members may fix their own accordingly. There is an expectation that, again as far as is possible, the members will try to avoid taking holidays during the time the group would normally meet. To facilitate this the conductor strives to fix holidays at times when others might reasonably be expected to take theirs anyway, such as Christmas and Easter and regular summer holiday periods. This, as with his management of the time boundary, enables the establishment of group cohesiveness and a feeling of safety within the group. It is related to the early maternal relationship when the baby is helped to feel safe by the comforting continuing presence and predictability of his mother. For this reason, it is important to any treatment situation that the practitioner does what he says he will do, when he says he will do it.

Drugs and Other Treatments

Strictly speaking it is a useful general guideline that drugs should not be given to patients undergoing psychotherapy. This is because many of the drugs administered by psychiatrists alter the way in which an individual experiences himself and his social relationships; they alter and distort levels of anxiety and reduce the impact of other feelings on the individual. As the individual or group therapist aims to work with the feelings and whole-life experiences of the patient these distortions interfere with the quality of the work that can be undertaken.

In practice and for many reasons it is not always possible for the group convenor to abide by this guideline. He may be a nurse or a social worker on an admission unit with a traditional medical bias towards treatment, with the consequence that all his patients may well be taking medication as part of their prescribed treatment. Whilst it is not always the best option to offer an individual, the practice of treating all sorts of human emotional difficulties with psychotropic medication is widespread. One should not deny that in many cases the administration of medication is necessary to the continuing functioning of the individual in society. Consequently it has to be accepted that whilst it is preferable in most situations that group members be free of medication, in many circumstances the group conductor will work with patients who are undergoing other forms of treatment, including drugs and physical treatments.

This being the case the conductor should try to ensure that any medication is prescribed and administered by practitioners other than himself. The conductor may be a doctor on the ward or unit who carries responsibility for prescribing medication to patients himself. He should try to make sure that a colleague prescribes (if this is necessary) for the members of his group, just as the nurse should ensure that he does not administer medication to the members of his group. If this is not possible then it becomes very difficult to work with the material of the group as the therapeutic field will have become tainted by the many other transactions in which the conductor has become involved with his patients. Or, as one trainee put it:

● How can you possibly work as a group conductor with someone who fears being taken over or intruded upon, when in your other role as charge nurse you are expected to inject him with powerful drugs and prevent him from leaving the ward?

It is imperative that the group conductor establishes and maintains a good, open-minded relationship with his prescribing colleagues. If he does not, then it will become possible for the patient or the group to become involved in 'splitting' manoeuvres intended to set one against the other in an attempt to externalise their own bad feelings. It would be better to have no contact at all between the group conductor and the prescribing doctor than for them to become involved in a collusion about splitting.

The Register

The conductor keeps a register of the group, it is an attendance record which is expanded to include other useful information. There are many ways of doing this. Foulkes (1975) presents a 'Record of Group Analytic Sessions' (figure 9.1) which is very similar to the classroom register used in schools, but which offers the option of adding brief notes.

Cox (1973) developed a Group Interaction Chronogram (figure 9.2) which is essentially a clock face divided in two along an axis between 3 and 9 o'clock with the topmost section bisected by a line running between 12 and 6 o'clock and ending at the axis. Each group member is represented by one of these 'clock faces' so it is possible to make a note of the seating arrangements of each group. The conductor uses the Chronogram by making notes of the individuals' behaviour during the beginning (the first quarter of the clock), the middle (the second, larger portion representing one half of the session time), and the end (the last quarter of the clock).

There are many different styles of recording the group. Some try to keep a verbatim record in written form, whilst others keep a record of the main themes and events that occurred during the group. Others still will keep a record of the group process (see p. 91), or will attempt to chart the direction of the flow of communication between members and between members and the conductor in the session. Some may use a structural map to highlight the hierarchical system within each group session.

The recording of each group session is important as it is an aid to memory – so many colleagues speak of how often much of a group session is lost to memory after the first 12 to 24 hours. If the group conductor has the wisdom and foresight to record each group session and takes the time to review his records, he will find some themes and issues that he had missed during the session and which only become apparent over a period of time. For example, he might notice the absence of a particular member and relate it to events from the immediate life of the group, but he would not remember, unless he looked at his records, that the member in question had been absent immediately prior to every break the group had had. This has much more relevance and would carry more impact than merely pointing out the coincidental relationship between one absence and one group break.

Keeping the register marks the last of the administrative duties of the conductor, we now move on to discussing the conductor's clinical or therapeutic role. The first of these is 'Conducting'.

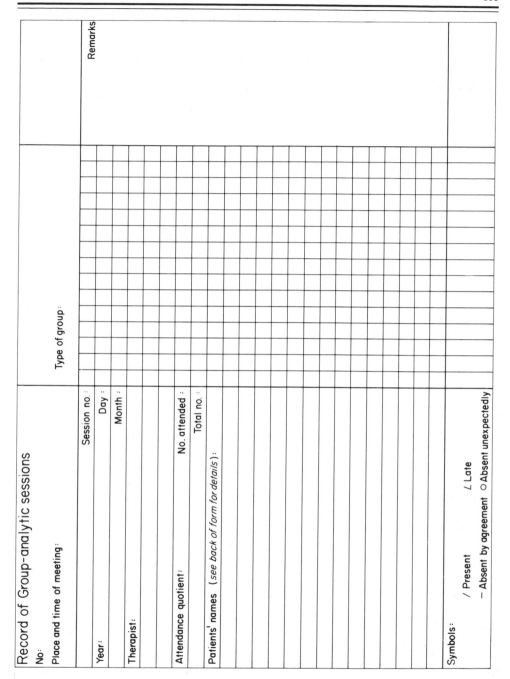

Fig. 9.1 Foulke's register (from Karnac, 1984. Reproduced with kind permission of the Group Analytic Society)

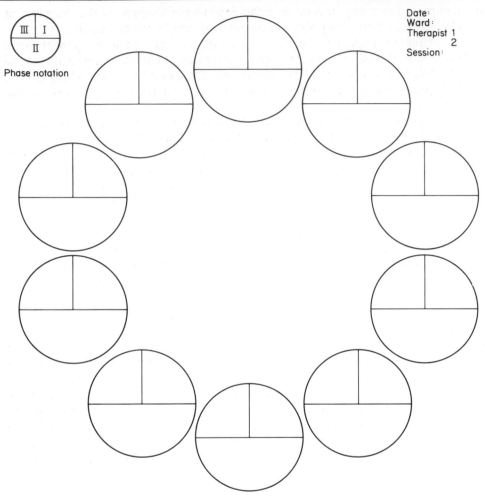

Fig. 9.2 Murray Cox group interaction chronogram (reproduced with kind permission of the *British Journal of Social Work*, **3(2)**: 243–256).

THE CONDUCTOR AS THERAPIST

Conducting

As we have already noted, the conductor will work in some ways that are similar to an orchestral conductor, using gestures to encourage or discourage behaviour. A simple example of this would be the sort of gesture he might use to encourage the group to talk to each other at the start of a series of groups. At this stage in the life of the group the members will defer to the group conductor, asking him questions and addressing most of their remarks to him. It is exceptionally easy to be drawn in to giving answers in this situation, but to do so would be to agree with the group that the conductor has all the answers and must be deferred to. This, of course, is not true and is a denigration which leaves the group bereft of certain of its abilities.

It encourages the group to remain in the dependency position of the 'forming' or 'parallel' phase of the group's development, and would not be healthy.

The conductor might say: 'Well . . . what do . . .' and perhaps open his arms wide to encompass the whole group, giving the message clearly that he is interested and involved but would really like to hear what the group has to say. He might use his body position to include or to exclude certain of the members from a particular situation.

A colleague tells of one session with a long-standing closed group which had been struggling to help one member in particular to recognise, let alone deal with, his destructive feelings of jealousy and envy. He had not been able to recognise it at all and was extremely heavily defended against acknowledging this part of himself. During the session in question a young woman in the group had aroused a great deal of sympathy, and appropriately so, because she had been describing her grief and rage and her dreadful sorrow at having miscarried a much-wanted child. The jealous patient, although sympathetic to the young woman, could not contain his jealous feelings for any longer, and tried to draw the group's attention to himself. He could not bear that anyone should have what he felt he missed. He was sitting to one side of the conductor who had the young woman some chairs away on his other side.

The conductor turned slightly in his chair so that he was presenting a part of his back to the jealous patient and was facing the young woman more directly. In this way he gave space to the young woman in which to experience her grief and helped the group to continue to work with her whilst emphasising to the jealous patient that his behaviour was unacceptable and hurtfully intrusive. It also had the effect of raising the temperature of the jealous patient's feelings, so that he became so full that he could not control them at all. He exploded at the conductor for his 'bad manners' in turning his back on him. The conductor remained calm and agreed that he had turned his back on the patient but that, on the contrary, it had been done because the patient had been bad-mannered and had wanted to intrude on the young woman's grief. With this the conductor again turned to the young woman whereupon the jealous patient angrily vented his feeling that he was being deliberately excluded, that no one liked him and that he never got a fair share of anything. The conductor was at last able, with the help of the group, to show him how jealous he was as he could no longer deny it; he was full to bursting with jealous feeling.

As indicated earlier the conductor may use incomplete phrases to indicate his preparedness to be involved, whilst encouraging others to take on their own responsibilities within the group. He might also use incomplete phrases to help the group to deepen the emotional level at which it is currently working. For example, he might say something like:

'I keep feeling that perhaps . . . it seems a little sad to be talking about, yet I can't help but believe . . . but what do others . . . ?'

If he does this whilst sitting lower, or less upright in his chair, then it often has the effect of lowering the mood of the group. This can be useful at times when the group is resorting to excited behaviour to avoid some painful emotional experience.

Alternatively he may use complete phrases and a brisk manner, whilst adopting a more upright posture to lighten the mood; it can sometimes be useful to lighten the mood at the end of the group to help the members to leave the difficult feelings in the group room so that they might free themselves to face the outside world. There are many other ways in which the conductor conducts the group. He might nod encouragingly to one member to help him to say what is in his mind, or he might gesticulate to two or more others in a way which encourages them to continue with and pursue further the topic under discussion. Each conductor eventually finds or develops a personal style of conducting with which he is comfortable.

Modelling

The conductor helps the group to develop an ability to work with difficult issues through his personal commitment to acknowledging feelings, recognising symbols, observing the process, and so on. He does this by displaying a personal willingness to face honestly any of the areas of conflict that present themselves within the group. In practice this would mean that he would notice, for example, how the group might turn away from anything that causes discomfort – an expression of hostility perhaps, or the beginnings of a disagreement.

In one group the conductor noticed that Janet had responded to Phil by asking in a quietly angry way what he had meant by a particular remark. Phil chose to say that he had meant nothing by it and Madge joined in to say something about how uncertain she was about her ability to work in the group. Very soon the group members were jokingly talking about how they felt it was silly to examine everything they did to establish its true meaning.

Eventually the conductor reminded them that they had avoided dealing with Janet's feelings and were, perhaps feeling defensive about it through suggesting that many things did not have a meaning. The conductor did this in a non-threatening way, his attitude being one of acceptance and of enquiry. Phil was able to admit that he had been feeling guilty for having avoided facing up to Janet's question and said that he felt he had left her with some of his own discomfort.

Through his willingness to listen, to tolerate anxiety, sadness and hostility (along with a host of other feelings) the conductor instils in the group a similar attentive, accepting and questioning attitude. Through his willingness to accept his mistakes, or his opinions, he models an attitude of honesty for the group which enables them to feel that it is safe to be honest with oneself and others too.

Following

The conductor should follow the group, which means that he does not try to force an issue to come to the attention of the group. In an earlier example we saw how one conductor used the positioning of his body to emphasise the jealous feelings of a male patient. He did not decide that it was about time that the patient was confronted by his jealousy, but he recognised a situation in which the patient was feeling jealous and behaved in a way that allowed it to build up until it reached such a peak that the patient could no longer avoid facing it in himelf. He was conducting the group in a way which followed the events in the life of the group.

The conductor waits to interpret until he is sure that the group has almost discovered what is happening, what the underlying issues are. Even then he might wait for the group to make the discovery itself; we know from Yalom and other researchers that insights gained within the group from other members have more impact than interpretations offered by the conductor (see p. 90).

A story is told about Foulkes that he would tell his students that in any group there would come a time when they felt they knew what was happening. His advice would be that they should wait to seek further clarification from the group. After a time they would become certain that they understood what the group was dealing with. It was then he would tell them that they should wait. After a little more time they would find themselves almost bursting with understanding; he would tell them that it was most important at this time that they should take the bull by the horns and . . . that they should say nothing.

Only after the steam has gone from your personal need to make an interpretation and when you feel that the group is almost there and not able to make the last connection, or if it is stuck, should you interpret.

In order to follow the group in this way the conductor proceeds from what is manifest, that is, what is consciously presented in the group, to what is latent, that is, information which is concealed but revealed in the symbols used by the group.

For example, in one community meeting on an acute admission unit, the group complained about the lack of wastebins, then when several were pointed out in the room by the staff, the group complained that they were not all the same, some were more attractive than others as they were newer and had been bought at the same time as the ward's new furniture.

It is imperative that the conductor recognises and deals with the manifest content, that is, in this situation he should note the complaints and investigate them seriously. He should also pay attention to the underlying concerns that were being expressed through the medium of the wastebins. The conductor knew that the ward had been having a difficult time lately, many very disturbed patients had been admitted, several student nurses had left having completed their placements, whilst only one or two new students had arrived to replace them. The ward was down on its establishment of nurses and the senior, permanent staff were hard-pressed to keep up with demands.

The wastebins stood not only as real containers, but also as symbolic containers for the bad, damaged or messy feelings of the patient group. If we refer to chapter 1 (see also chapter 8, p. 92) we can remind ourselves that, amongst other important functions, the mother is used by her baby as a container for unwanted bad feelings. In other words, he imagines that it is possible for him to dump his rubbish into her.

Bearing this in mind, if we return to the example, the patients were complaining of the lack of bins and they moaned about the old ones. It does not take too vivid an imagination to recognise that it is likely that the patients were feeling unsupported and were responding to a sense of having lost important relationships with the students who had left the ward. They were also attacking the senior staff (perhaps as transference 'parents') for not giving them enough time by moaning about the old bins (the senior staff) and praising the new ones (the new students). This behaviour can be understood as a re-enactment of relationships from the patient's past which have been triggered by events on the ward in the present.

This leads us on to another of the conductor's therapeutic responsibilities, that of interpreting in the group.

Interpreting

Whilst Foulkes (1975) acknowledges that there are many interpretations which occur in the group at all times (he writes of unconsciously-made interpretations in word or actions) we are concerned here with the consciously-made interpretations of the conductor.

A consciously-made interpretation is given to the group by the conductor to draw to the group's attention a piece of behaviour, or a verbal communication, which contains a meaning of which the group is unaware. The purpose of interpretation is to bring to the conscious mind material which was previously unavailable and communicated in unconscious ways. The focus is mainly on the group process, that is, the activity being undertaken by the group, the action of the group and the effect of the action on or in the group. For example the conductor might say: 'The group seems to be very excited today [i.e. the activity being undertaken], perhaps it is easier to do this [i.e. avoidance is the action of the group] than to face the residue of the angry feelings from the end of the last session, but already it appears that there is some frustration or disappointment [the effect of the activity and the result of the action].'

Interpretations can cover the whole of the life of the group and should generally be brief. However there are some exceptions to this guiding rule. Where the interpretation is a summarising statement then it can perhaps be a little longer and would need to include examples from the material of the group. Also where there have been incidents around the group's boundaries such as lateness, absenteeism or a member leaving early or coming and going in the group the conductor may feel that a fuller interpretation is required. This is because the boundaries of the group are the particular responsibility of the conductor. The quality of his management of the group's boundaries will always effect the ability of the group to feel secure and consequently cannot fail to affect the group's ability to work.

Where there is a crisis in the group the conductor may need to give the group a complete interpretation of their behaviour, otherwise the group may not be able to cope entirely alone with the degree of stress the crisis evokes. The conductor has somehow to balance between allowing the group enough room to feel they have the strength to deal with difficult issues alone and leaving the group floundering and overwhelmed by the anxiety that the crisis has produced. Any interpretation should be related to, or based on, the experience of the moment and as near as possible to the emotional level which seems most prevalent in the group. In other words, interpretations should be emotionally as well as intellectually appropriate.

Foulkes (1975) warns us that we should be wary of making interpretations which are premature and at an inappropriately deep level, it is better, as we saw earlier, to allow the group time and to wait for the group to make discoveries for themselves. At times it will fall to the conductor to make the final connection, but on the whole, he only needs to do this when it is clear that the group is stuck. In the early stages of the group he may need to help the group to develop awareness by making observations and interpretations more frequently, but even then he will only interpret at the level with which the group are comfortable and upon which they are currently operating. In some ways it may be compared to unpeeling an onion layer by layer – as each layer is removed it exposes another, and so on.

We are also warned against making interpretations which 'catch people out', for example:

'But this is different from what you just said . . .'

This sort of interpretation is unhelpful and sets a critical tone. It raises the possibility of the recipient feeling that he must defend his position rather than work with the issue, and it runs the risk of tilting the group into Basic Assumption *fight/flight* (see p. 66 above).

Linking and transference interpretations should also be avoided (Foulkes, 1975) as it is better to allow the group to make discoveries for itself. There are two reasons for this. First, research has indicated that the group learns more from its members than from the conductor; and secondly, if the conductor does this work for the group he is denigrating the group by denying its strengths and abilities in this area. In some senses the conductor who does this may be defending against his own anxieties and inadequacies by investing (projecting) them into the group. It is important to remember that understanding, or insight, follows change rather than precedes it. That is, the group may come to understand the reasons behind a piece of behaviour or some feelings and attitudes once they have been experienced and worked through in the group over a period of time. If something is deeply hidden and defended against it is not possible for the individual to know about it until preparatory work has been done to make it more accessible. This is a gradual process of working deeper whilst maintaining a feeling of safety.

The Analysing Attitude

It is basic to the analysing attitude that the conductor approaches the group with integrity and honesty. This means that he openly faces the worries and anxieties that he brings to the group and recognises them as his own. Having recognised his own concerns, which must be a continuous process, he is able to become receptive to communications at many levels, including the emotional, from within the group. He 'holds' these communications within himself and allows himself to reflect on their meanings. He pays them what others have termed 'a free-floating attention', which means that as well as thinking about the stated communications, he becomes aware of the many nuances of meaning and feeling which any comment contains. He also allows himself to reflect upon the associations and linked impressions that the group evokes in him through their behaviour and conversation. Bringing these multiple facets together he is then more able to understand some of the events occurring in the group. This process is part of the process of *containment* (see p. 91).

The conductor fulfils the other responsibilities of his analysing role by paying attention to the following:

1. He receives all communications and reflects on them as described above, yet he uses his understanding prudently, little by little. He does not force the group to take more than they want, nor does he give them too rich a diet. In this way he is like the 'good enough mother'.

2. He is non-directive and respects the ability of the group to do the work themselves. He helps by clarifying and interpreting (Foulkes, 1975). He uses verbal means that lead to the group eventually gaining insight.

3.   The relationships that the members of the group and the group as a whole make with him and with each other become the object of communication and analysis.

4.   He uses his powerful position with care and with respect for the group and its members. He does not submit to the temptation to manipulate the group, but points to current action and the consequences of that action.

5.   Using his position thoughtfully and judiciously, he helps the group's members to fulfil their potential.

6.   He treats relationships as transference situations in which resonances and repetitions can be thought about and understood.

7.   As well as being aware of transferences, he also pays attention to resistances, defences and the group as a system (see pp. 29–32). He is sensitive to the unconscious nature of all these processes and to the importance of symbolic communication.

8.   He is able to listen, which is sometimes harder than it might seem. He has a taste for the truth which he cultivates in others through the lead he gives, and he is non-judgemental, maintaining an inner honesty in the face of conflict.

Because the conductor is human it is almost impossible that he will possess all of these qualities. Consequently he is likely to make mistakes from time to time and it is important that he admits to them. In order to be able to work towards attaining the attributes of the good conductor, and to recognise his mistakes and oversights, he will need to seek regular supervision with an experienced and qualified colleague.

This chapter concludes part II, which has been mainly concerned with the life of the group and the role of the conductor within it. We now move on to part III to consider the practical considerations that are an integral part of group work, beginning with the setting and its influence on the group.

References

Cox M (1973) The group therapy interaction chronogram. *British Journal of Social Work*, **3(2)**: 243–256.
Foulkes S H (1975) *Group Analytic Psychotherapy, Method and Principles*. London: Gordon and Breach.
Karnac A (1984) *Therapeutic Group Analysis*. London: Allen and Unwin.

PART III
Practical Considerations

10

Settings

We begin part III with an examination of the practical considerations that must be borne in mind when establishing or working with groups, In order to achieve this task we have to focus our attention on two main areas – the *broader setting* and the *narrower setting*. The broader setting includes those aspects that are influenced by the management of the ward, unit, department or hostel, and by the outside world, whilst the narrower setting deals with those areas which are the direct responsibility of the conductor.

THE BROADER SETTING

Before the conductor can establish a group he will have to take into account and work on many factors that will affect his group. The first of these is his own role within the organisation.

The Role of the Conductor

Before he takes on the task of establishing a group the conductor must consider whether or not his role as conductor is discrete or complex. If his role is discrete then matters become a little more simplified than if his role is complex. By discrete we mean that his only function in the ward, hostel or unit is that of group conductor. If his role is complex – for example, he may be the nurse in charge of a ward, the director of a hostel, or a ward doctor – then he has to recognise that the other functions he performs in the department affect, or have an impact on, his work as a group conductor. Even if he is fortunate enough to have a discrete role, he will need to take account of many or most of the issues discussed in this chapter. His discrete role would free him from needing to take into account those issues that follow immediately under the heading of:

The Complex Role

We shall take as our example the influences which would affect the work of a staff nurse or ward sister who has responsibility for the management of an acute admission ward of a psychiatric hospital and who wishes to begin group work on her ward. Many of the dilemmas posed for her will correspond to similar problems for other professional disciplines.

In this setting the ward sister has a varied function. She is responsible for the day-to-day running of the ward, for supervising the work of the nurses on her ward, for maintaining high standards of nursing practice, for providing nurses in training with a teaching programme that is appropriate to their needs, and for implementing the decisions of management in the area of planned developments. Also, she has to inform management of the specific requirements of her own ward and to advise her senior nurses and unit administrator of new practices and developments within the field, and keep them in touch with the impact on the ward of management decisions. She has to liaise with the medical staff, social services, the patients' relations, occupational therapy departments, catering staff, and many others. She is responsible for the fabric of the ward, for basic nursing care and for programmes of nursing treatment.

She is also responsible for ensuring that the decisions of the staff team are implemented, which means that she has to make sure that patients receive their medication and are supervised if this is necessary, even if this means a temporary deprivation of liberty. The role of the ward sister is so complex that we would need to devote more space to it than we can afford in order to do it justice, but the above brief description is sufficient for our purposes here.

In terms of *field theory* (Lewin, 1951) she is the *gatekeeper* of many *gate regions*. According to Lewin a gate region is a point at which many different fields converge. In our example the fields are areas which influence what eventually occurs on the ward. They include the impact of the doctors upon the treatment of the patients on the ward; the ideas and attitudes of the nurses; the wishes and needs of the patients; and the impact of higher levels of management on the ward.

If the ward sister is to take on the responsibility of running a treatment group herself this introduces an added dimension, or several other fields which she must consider before embarking upon her work as a group conductor. As the group conductor she is the keeper of many other gate regions (Whiteley and Gordon, 1979). These include the junctions between the inner worlds of the group members and external reality, the structure of the individual's psyche, the individual and the group, the group and the ward, the ward and the whole institution, and the institution and society. In particular, she must consider whether or not her role as ward sister makes it impossible to work as a group conductor. She should weigh in the balance whether or not her primary role as ward sister would intrude too much upon her work as conductor. Would she have to administer medication, for example (see p. 105), or restrict the freedom of any members of her group? If the answer to either of these questions is yes, then she should not begin a therapy group which includes these patients. If she believes that her work as a ward sister is incompatible with running a group for other reasons (such as implying preference for some patients over others, or detracting from her responsibility to see the ward as a whole), then she must give serious consideration to these concerns and permit them to influence her final decision.

This need not mean that she should forget the idea of becoming involved in group work altogether. She might consider it more appropriate, for example, to establish community meetings which would be attended by all of the patients and most of the staff involved with the ward. It would be ridiculous to suppose that it is possible to recommend a complete range of alternatives from which the ward sister could choose: the variety of situations and the range of individual experiences is limitless. Consequently it is for each of us to decide for ourselves what seems appropriate to the circumstances in which we work. The information given here might help form such decisions, but they remain the responsibility of each conductor to make for herself, and, provided this is done honestly with due regard for personal skill, experience and training, and with respect for the society of the ward she can be confident of a degree of success.

The conductor whose role is discrete is not hampered by having to consider the group and its members in terms of any other relationship that she has with them, for she has none. However, she does need to take into account many other factors, including personal skill, training, experience and the society of the ward.

The Society of the Ward

We can further subdivide this heading into political and cultural considerations.

The Political Setting

By this we mean the relationships that exist between the various professional disciplines that are involved with the ward, the ward and the rest of the unit, the ward and other wards or departments, the ward and the institution as a whole, and the ward and the outside world. The outside world may be experienced through contact with the friends and relations of patients, through the attitude of the local community, or through contact with colleagues working in the community.

If the medical staff on the ward are hostile to, or suspicious of, the idea of a nurse running groups then the conductor must address himself to their worries in an attempt to establish a state of tolerance of, if not goodwill for, the endeavour. The same would be true if the conductor were a doctor, a social worker or an occupational therapist and the nurses were opposed to the idea. Whenever something new is introduced in any situation there is usually, and often inevitably, a period of opposition to it from many quarters, which may not be consciously felt or stated. Such opposition can often successfully sabotage any new developments, so the successful conductor will negotiate his position with his colleagues before setting up the group and will continue to maintain good relationships throughout its life. The failure of the first 'Northfield Experiment' can be attributed in large measure to Bion's neglect of this area.

Northfield was a military psychiatric hospital which, during and shortly after World War II, was the location of some early experiments in group work (Bion, 1961; Main, 1983; de Maré, 1983). The first of these experiments was conducted by Bion, who, after a very short time, fell foul of the military hierarchy which ran the hospital as his methods seemed to run counter to the military ethic. Subsequently S H Foulkes established many small psychotherapy groups within Northfield, but it was not until Tom Main arrived at the hospital that proper attention was paid to what he termed the *higher-system tensions* (Main, 1983), by which he meant the issues referred to above as the political setting.

The Cultural Setting

There are many cultural influences which have an impact on the group. Perhaps the most straightforward are the obvious differences which can be seen between different locations. It has been suggested (Temperley, 1984) that it is often easier for the psychotherapist, whether group or individual, to work with patients in certain areas of North London where the idea of psychotherapy has been accepted by many of the local populace. Even if the ideas are not accepted then at least they are familiar. It can be considerably more difficult to work in a setting which is remote, both geographically and in terms of the ease of access to established centres of psychotherapy. Jane Temperley acknowledges that the therapist who works in a remote setting may often have qualities that the therapist who works in a centre of psychotherapy does not possess. She argues that this is because these individuals have been forged in the fires of criticism and resistance; they have had to explain and justify their methods to sceptical colleagues and an unsophisticated patient population. Consequently they often possess a confidence and strength that those working in North London, for example, cannot aspire to. On the other hand, she also warns of the likelihood that those who work in remote settings are more vulnerable to their skills and the rigour of the method being undermined by the continuous challenges to which they are subjected in the absence of the supportive presence of therapist colleagues. Those who work in such settings are more at risk of committing heresies and of finding that their work is diluted.

Other colleagues are also concerned with the impact that the cultural group to which the patient belongs has upon the therapist's method. The conductor of any group must be able to take into account the influence which the patient's ethnic or cultural grouping has upon his relationship with his own inner world, with the group, and with the outside world. For example, it may be difficult for Asian partners in a relationship to take part in a couples group as inevitably there would be a clash between gender roles in Eastern and Western cultures. A group being run in a rural setting would experience difficulties with confidentiality and with keeping the rule of no contact outside the group, as inevitably many people would know each other anyway and would have already established relationships.

Where cultural influences have an impact then the conductor may need to spend some time in modelling for the group the purpose of the group, how to use the group, or how to become psychologically minded. He may need to work with many doubts and preconceptions which are culturally based and which need to be understood and acknowledged as part of the therapeutic situation. He must also respect the cultural heritage of the group's members and must not try to inculcate his own point of view, or his own cultural bias. It is the role of the therapist to follow the group, to recognise and value cultural differences, as they enrich the group and the conductor.

THE INSTITUTIONAL SETTING

We have already paid some attention to the institution when we looked at the role of the conductor and whether this was discrete or complex. Even if the conductor's role is discrete, the institution is bound to have an impact upon the group, its conductor and its members. If the institution is sympathetic to group work then the task of the conductor is made much easier, yet there is still an impact to be felt from the institution. In this favourable situation the conductor's work will be enhanced as it is supported by the institution. He will be helped by the holding function of the organisation and by the transferences which take place from the individual to the institution, which is experienced as being supportive.

If, on the other hand, the institution is hostile to group work then it will have a negative effect on the life of the group and its potential for success. The unconscious resistances to any form of psychotherapeutic work are extremely powerful and can militate strongly against a group becoming established.

On one acute admission ward the sister in charge and several of the staff nurses had completed an introductory course in group work and wished to begin working with groups on the ward. Their intentions were viewed with much concern by other nurses on the ward, by the senior nurse and by the medical staff. Consequently their plans to establish groups which would focus on the here and now of the patients' interpersonal relationships became extremely diluted. Instead of tackling a variety of different styles of group work, which were not intended to involve 'deep' interpretations, they were forced to restrain their reasonable ambitions and confine their group work to whole-ward community meetings which would be limited to working with the problems caused by institutional living.

Even when they did this there were considerable difficulties to be overcome. Because group work was regarded as innovative it was not felt to have a place in the established treatment structure and the nurses were only able to hold the meetings after 5 o'clock in the evening, once the 'real' work of the day had been completed. All the other treatment programmes ran between 9 a.m. and 5 p.m., so there was a covert implication from various colleagues that the group or community meeting was not 'work'. With this as the unspoken attitude of many on the staff team it is not surprising to find that many of the patients did not value it either. In addition, the team meetings would occasionally run over time, thus intruding across group time boundaries although there was an agreement that this would not happen. Once again, this may be understood as a statement which is unconsciously intended to subvert the group. Eventually these small and niggling attacks took a negative toll; it became more trouble than it was worth to the exhausted and previously enthusiastic nurses and they stopped running the community meetings. They had found the institution's commitment to the status quo more than a match for them.

The institution affects the group in other and perhaps more mundane, though still important ways too. It is responsible for the facilities available to the group.

The type and size of the room is as important as its location. In one hospital the large unit meeting is held in a room that is used by patients from other wards as a corridor. It is not surprising to find that this group is not felt to be safe. This is because there are established associations with the room as being without boundaries, a place that is not private. If the room is hard by another room, has poor sound insulation, or is vulnerable to outside observation then it will impede the development of the group as it creates an atmosphere of uncertainty and the suspicion of being overheard or watched, which may well be real. The physical properties of the boundaries of the room are important. Membership of a group in a quiet setting that has been especially created for work with groups is more likely to be a solid, secure experience than membership of a group that has to make do with rooms with partition walls, with walls that are largely glazed, and a setting that is unused to group work. The experience is far more unsettling in the latter case and the conductor has to work very hard to help his group feel safe in such circumstances.

If the room is too large then the space may overwhelm the group and leave it feeling unheld or uncontained. Too small a room produces a sense of being stifled or in a forced situation where it is not possible to have some space between oneself and the other members of the group. It can feel intrusive and may lead to the dissolution of the group if the anxieties to do with loss of individuality and identity are not successfully addressed.

The type of seating is important too; comfort encourages a deeper quality of thought and attention whilst discomfort discourages it. It is difficult for the individual to locate himself in the inner world and to pay attention to associative links when all he can think of is how cramped and uncomfortable the seats are.

Heating is another such consideration. If it is too hot then the group will become drowsy and less able to work; if it is too cold then the group will not be able to think for shivering. These considerations may seem obvious and very small beer indeed, but it would be a foolish conductor who paid them no heed at all, for their effects are far greater than the importance that is usually attached to them.

The conductor must ensure that he can maintain the privacy that encourages private thought and establishes the possibility of self-revelation in the group. When a group is intruded upon it will usually withdraw from any reasonably deep exploration of personal difficulties and either fall silent or talk only about safe subjects that do not touch the core. One of the problems with the institution is that any member of staff is likely to feel that his business is sufficiently urgent for him to ignore the engaged sign on the door and walk into the group room without any thought for the group. After all, it's only talk anyway. If the conductor does not deal with interruptions effectively then the group will eventually dissolve into chaos. The conductor should make sure, before establishing the group, that all staff know that on no account is the room to be entered when the sign says 'engaged'. If he is interrupted anyway he should not allow the intruder into the room but should find a way of firmly and politely excluding him without becoming involved in a lengthy conversation.

Increasingly over the last few pages we have been moving from a focus which influences the conductor to a focus in which it is the conductor's influence that matters. It is time to look at the narrower setting, which deals more precisely with the conductor – his style, skill, experience and method as the setting.

THE NARROWER SETTING

Boundaries as Setting or Setting Boundaries

The group is like a diamond, it has several facets which may be seen separately, but which when viewed together make up a whole. If we regard the face of the diamond from one position we see a number of planes and angles. If we view the same face from another vantage point we see different angles and planes. It is the same with the group; we can look at one aspect of group life from the viewpoint of the conductor's responsibilities and see one thing, whilst when we look at the same aspect of the life of the group with settings in mind we still see the group, but in an altered perspective. We have already examined some of the following areas with other interests in mind. Here it is important that we review them in terms of their relationship to the setting. The main subheading within this section of the chapter is concerned with boundaries and, although there are other headings to follow, all of the matters under discussion refer to boundaries in some way.

The following list illustrates the relationship between each of the areas, to acknowledge the influence that they have on each other and to suggest the partly sequential nature of the boundaries which affect the setting. It is a useful checklist; before the conductor can even think about interpretive work he will have to consider points 1–8; before he can think about group mix he will need to have a clear idea of the numbers which will make up the group; before he can decide on the numbers he must be sure of his aims with the group.

We shall take each of the points and examine them in greater detail as we go along, but the full list is as follows:

1. The aims of the group
2. Group numbers
3. Group mix
4. Privacy
5. Time
6. The agenda
7. Confidentiality
8. Inside/outside
9. Containment
10. Trust
11. Timing

1. *The aims of the group*

This is a basic consideration. The type of work undertaken by the therapist will be influenced by the group aims. If the group is a community meeting then the conductor will know that it should focus on the here and now. He will confine his work to enabling the group to communicate at the appropriate level and will refrain from making interpretations at any depth. Because a community meeting is likely to be a large group he would possibly help the group to deal with some of the primitive defences inherent in such situations by speaking directly of his own feelings as they are evoked in the group situation. In this way he deliberately circumvents the defences of splitting and projection which are present in all large groups (Main, 1974; Menzies, 1976. See also p. 82 above). If he were to interpret as he would for a small group then it is likely that he would increase the anxieties of those present as the interpretations would inevitably enhance the propensity to split off uncomfortable feelings in a defensive way.

For instance he might say: 'It seems that the group is experiencing some difficulty in getting started today, perhaps there is some anxiety which gets in the way of talking?' This is quite an innocuous interpretation, but in a large group where people are feeling anxious and a little wary anyway, it can quite easily be felt as a criticism. It can sound to the group as if the conductor is saying:

'I can think rationally and still find my own voice, I am not anxious but the rest of you are and you're allowing that to prevent us from working.'

In other words, it may be experienced as ridicule and as blame. He can help to prevent these splits from occurring by speaking for himself in the large group setting, for example:

'I can't speak for the rest of you, but I've been finding it very difficult to talk. I've been feeling really anxious and wondering why that is. Does anyone else feel the same?'

He has addressed the same issues but in a way that encourages others to admit their own feelings (he has declared it safe to do so through his example) and to respond to each other.

If the group is a training rather than a treatment group then this would also influence the conductor. He might feel that he could establish his training group with slightly higher numbers than his treatment group, on the assumption that the motivation of his trainees would be higher than that of his patients. Both groups might be ambivalent, but he may be justified in feeling that his trainees would be more highly motivated than his patients. However, this is not always necessarily the case; the conductor should weigh all such notions carefully before committing himself.

If the group were to focus on social skills (in a sense a training group) or on offering techniques to help with a variety of anxiety states, then this would also influence the conductor's decision about group size.

2. Group Numbers

The number of people in a group affects the ambience. There are differences of course, but as suggested above, the larger a group is, the more difficult it becomes to think, and the easier it is to feel and to react primitively to group pressures. With smaller groups it becomes more possible to think. Indeed, the ability to think in small groups sometimes gets in the way of the group being able to feel anything. In other words, thinking can be used as a defence against painful feelings. So the conductor needs to address his aims for the group before deciding upon the numbers he will invite to the group as the numbers will affect the sort of work the group can do. Both the aims of the group and its size will influence group mix.

3. Group Mix

The way in which a group is constituted will affect the work its members can do. If there were to be only one woman in the group it would become very difficult for the group to tackle, for example, the attitude to women in our society, or the subjugation of women by men. The lone woman would be out on a limb, having no others for support or for sharing. However, it might be considered better in a training situation to admit a solitary woman (or man) to the group and to keep the fact of her potential isolation in mind than to exclude her from training altogether. Although it is clear that staff are often as well defended as patients, those who seek out further training may be a little more ready than most to work on those defences. The conductor has a responsibility to manage many such considerations as the group that he brings together should be balanced in favour of the work group (see p. 66 above).

4. Privacy

The conductor protects the group from intrusion by outside influences. Initially, he addresses this when he talks with colleagues about starting the group, he gains their recognition that the group is private and should not be interrupted. Later on, when the group is running, he might need to exclude the occasional person who interrupts either because he didn't know about the group or because he forgot. The conductor will also have to guard the group against breaches of privacy from within. The group's members may well have been members of other groups too and from time to time they will introduce episodes from other groups into the life of the current group. Normally this is not much of a problem; it can be regarded as a communication which must be understood, just like any other. However, there are times when it will need to be dealt with by the conductor. One example that comes to mind concerns a training group which had been meeting for nearly a year.

One of the group members was very obviously angry and began to berate another of the members. The conductor allowed this to occur; there is nothing inherently wrong with the healthy expression of feeling, and waited to see the group's reaction. The angry complainant said, 'You were just like this in the psychodrama group . . .'

That is where the conductor intervened because he knew that the psychodrama group applied the same rules of confidentiality as the training group and the irate member was about to breach those rules. Had he allowed it to continue he would have set a double standard. He chose to emphasise the importance of maintaining confidentiality in *all* groups, and also suggested that any comments the members might make about each other should be confined to what they knew of each other within the group. Had he failed to see and act on this breach of confidentiality then he would have been a party to establishing a growing feeling of insecurity in the group, and an uncertainty about trusting anyone.

5. Time

Once again we refer to the time boundary but on this occasion it is as part of the setting which the conductor provides. We have already looked at the importance of the time boundary in chapter 9 (see pp. 103–5), so we shall confine ourselves here to the reminder that they are of vital importance as many transference issues occur around, or are about, the beginning and ending of the session, holidays, other breaks and cancellations.

6. *The Agenda*

In the therapy group, which intends to help the members to examine and to work through the difficulties which bring them to the group, it is helpful not to have any kind of agenda. In fact, this is essential for this type of group as otherwise it becomes very difficult to look at what happens naturally and spontaneously in the group. This freedom of expression is the bread and butter of psychotherapeutic treatments; without it the group is disabled as the associative links with the unconscious are made impossible. The agenda may help the group and the conductor to feel relief by taking away their anxiety. If it is full enough it will take all of the group's time to work through it. The group and the conductor may feel relaxed, they might even enjoy the group and feel as if they are achieving something. In a sense they are; they are managing to deal with an agenda, but it is not therapy. In this sense the agenda becomes a defence against the work of the group as sticking to it precludes other work from taking place.

There are some groups, however, where an agenda is appropriate – some community meetings, for example, where there are day-to-day issues of management, of cleaning and cooking, of shopping and so on to discuss. These sorts of group are, or can be, therapeutic too; they go a long way towards preventing the institutionalisation of the patient and personal boundaries are healthily maintained through dealing with rights and responsibilities in the 'here and now'.

Social skills groups, anxiety management and other sorts of focused group may have an agenda. This type of group may be beneficial to the individual, and does not aim to deal with basic issues which lie at the heart of the problem. In these situations having an agenda can be positively helpful. Once again we can see how all of the many facets of the group touch and affect each other; before he decides if the group should have an agenda to work from, the conductor must first know what the aims of the group are and whether an agenda would hinder or aid those aims.

7. *Confidentiality*

The conductor maintains the rule of confidentiality (as described in point 4 above), for without it there can be no trust, without trust there can be no self-revelation and without trust there is no group. Confidentiality is not simply a matter of keeping secrets, it is also a matter of having confidence in the other group members to be prepared to do some very difficult work over an extended period of time.

8. *Inside/outside*

Part of the setting that the conductor provides is the group and the regular meetings in which many problems are explored. He keeps the group as the place where people meet to work hard on very personal matters. A friend or relative cannot give the individual the sort of help the group can and the group can only give such help because it occupies clearly-defined boundaries whose limits are known to all its members. It is important to be able to feel that private matters, which are problematic, stay in the group. For these reasons the conductor discourages individuals from meeting outside the group, and if this does happen he encourages them to report to the group the contact that they have had.

9. Containment

This is another of the settings that the conductor provides. Clearly it is related to the matters discussed above. (For a fuller discussion of containment see pp. 91–2.) Unless the group feels safely held or contained by the conductor, which requires him to maintain the various boundaries we have discussed and to receive, understand and interpret all communications, then the group will not proceed very far beyond failing adequately to resolve the conflict between trust and mistrust. Even if the group does move into later developmental stages, unless it is 'contained', it will only be able to work at a fairly shallow level.

10. Trust

This obviously depends on the conductor's ability to maintain privacy, to require confidentiality, to protect the group's boundaries and to contain the group. The conductor's management of these considerations will directly affect the level of trust achieved by the group. If he manages the boundaries successfully he is well on the way to helping the group to feel contained. As the group matures the basic conflict between trust and mistrust is worked and reworked at an ever-deeper level.

11. Timing

There is often great difficulty in knowing when to make interpretations. Suffice it to say here that this is part of the setting that is provided by the conductor and he has a responsibility to make interpretations at the correct time and at the appropriate level. He ascertains that he interprets what the group is ready to hear; he is of no use to the group if he makes interpretations that are way over the heads of all except himself, he might be correct, but his effort is wasted and the group bemused (see pp. 90–1, 110–11, 112–13).

Part of the setting that the conductor provides is himself. How he holds himself and his responsiveness or otherwise are vitally important. We shall look at the conductor as part of the setting under the next subheading.

Responsiveness v. Blank Screen

The conductor must place himself in a relationship with the group which furthers the aims of treatment. The treatment situation is not the same as a social situation, although there are apparent similarities between them. In social circumstances the conductor becomes just another person and reacts and responds as such, as do the rest of the group. The group has special qualities, it intends to examine and to

understand issues which are otherwise avoided or acted out in the patients'
relationships. Consequently the behaviour of the conductor is governed by the
central need to provide a therapeutic environment. He cannot do this if he
responds to the group in a social way. Friends or neighbours cannot help in the way
that the conductor of a group can, with the appropriate distance he maintains from
the group's members.

The conductor must resist invitations from the group to behave and respond as
an ordinary person would to the communications taking place. If he fails in this
then he would become useless to the group who need him to be able to take a
different, analysing attitude (see pp. 113–14) in which he pays attention to symbolic
or latent communications. If he responds to the group in an ordinary way he loses
the particular qualities that are valuable to the group. In therapy it is useful for the
group to have no notion of the conductor's life circumstances. This enables the
group to enage in unconscious fantasies in which he might be regarded as a saint or
a sinner, a lover of all women or a homosexual, and so on. The fantasies are
numberless and are useful because they allow the conductor and therefore the
group a glimpse of the unconscious life of the group. If the group know the
conductor to be married with four children then the type of fantasy that they might
have about him is limited or otherwise modified.

It is also of tremendous benefit to the group not to know why the conductor has,
for example, had to cancel the group. It enables unconscious concerns to surface as
ideas (fantasies) about what he is doing instead, and why he is doing it. The
conductor understands that these fantasies may reveal important formative
elements, impulses and experiences in the lives of the individuals in the group. If he
related to the group in a social manner (see also pp. 103–4) then he would miss
most of these covert and unconscious communications. Yet the group also needs to
feel that he is there in a supportive way that encourages hard work. If he were felt
as a hostile, critical or punitive person then the group would eventually be unable
to work with him. The conductor has to bear both the need for the distance that
allows him to work and the group's need for a supportive presence in mind. He is
faced with effecting a balancing act between being responsive (with other qualities
of unconditional positive regard, warmth and empathy) and being a blank screen,
which enables him to be in touch with the sub-plots and unconscious concerns from
within the group.

Supervision

The work of interpreting the group process and the symbolic content of the group's
communications is difficult, so it is important that the conductor, particularly when
inexperienced, is supervised by a more experienced, trained colleague. This too is
part of the setting that the conductor provides. We shall be looking at this in more
detail in a later chapter.

In chapter 11 we shall take a closer look at selection, one of the first concerns of
the conductor when he considers the setting, as his skill in selecting will directly
influence the group's ability to become a cohesive unit and to face the work task.

References

Bion W R (1961) *Experiences in Groups*. London: Tavistock.

de Maré P (1983) Michael Foulkes and the Northfield experiment. In: *The Evolution of Group Analysis*. London: Routledge and Kegan Paul.

Lewin K (1951) *Field Theory in Social Science*. New York: Harper Bros.

Main T F (1974) Some psychodynamics of large groups. In: *The Large Group, Dynamics and Therapy*. London: Constable.

Main T F (1983) The concept of the therapeutic community: variations and vicissitudes. In: *The Evolution of Group Analysis*. London: Routledge and Kegan Paul.

Menzies I E P (1976) *The Functioning of Social Systems as a Defence Against Anxiety*. London: Tavistock Publications.

Temperley J (1984) Settings for psychotherapy. *British Journal of Psychotherapy*, **1 (2)**: 101–111.

Whiteley J S and Gordon J (1979) *Group Approaches in Psychiatry*. London: Routledge and Kegan Paul.

11

Selecting For The Group

This chapter is concerned with the need to build a picture of each potential group member so that his suitability for group work can be assessed. This can be done by conducting a formal interview which will give the information asked for and by subjecting the interviewee to a barrage of psychological tests. In some circumstances, for example when there is doubt about an individual's ability to cope with an intensive group experience without breaking down completely or decompensating into a frankly psychotic state, such methods are positively helpful. However, when the referer and the conductor, together with other relevant colleagues, are reasonably sure that the individual has sufficient personal resources (ego strengths, or a clear sense of personal identity), such formal methods can hinder the assessment process.

Before we even get to this stage we should remember that many people find the prospect of joining a group very frightening and would prefer to work in a one-to-one relationship. If the candidate is a patient in a hospital or other institution he may find it less of a worry as it is probable that he will participate in ward and other meetings as a matter of course. In addition he will be in touch with others on the ward who may already be members of the group he is to join and who will be able to allay some of his fears. Obviously it is more of a problem for the candidate from an outpatient group. In this case the manner in which the first contact is made and the interview conducted is of particular importance. The conductor will be able to ease the worries that the candidate has by paying attention to the emotional as well as the verbal levels of communication, thereby helping the candidate to feel that he is recognised as an individual and will be understood. The relationship that the conductor establishes goes a long way in reassuring the candidate and lessening his anxieties about joining a group as the processes of containment and instillation of hope have already begun (see chapter 7).

THE ASSESSMENT PROCESS

The process of assessment is undertaken at several different levels. The first of these is the patient himself. He (or she) has to decide to seek treatment, or at least agree to the recommendations of others that he needs it. Then the referer – often the GP in the first instance, although increasingly it may be a Health Visitor, a social worker or a community psychiatric nurse – decides that some form of psychodynamic intervention is called for. Having reached this conclusion a referral is made to the appropriate clinic or person. The referral will usually be accompanied by a letter which will normally contain information about the individual. Sometimes this information is very helpful and the clinic or the conductor can make an initial assessment on the basis of it. Occasionally it will be clear that the subject of the referral is eminently suitable for group work, at other times it will be equally clear that he is not. In either case the wise conductor will offer an assessment appointment in order to reach his own conclusions, based upon his observations and informed by his experience before arriving at a decision. From time to time the referer may become caught up in his own feelings about the patient and it is not unheard of for a referral to be couched in glowing or negative terms.

Judging the content of referral letters is a complicated business. There can be an element of gamesmanship with the referer writing of his patient in very positive terms and in a way that flatters the conductor or his ability. Beware: all that glisters is not gold. Every conductor occasionally receives such glowing references, often from a colleague who has worked extremely hard to help the subject of the reference, has failed and now is desperate. Main (1957) called such persons special patients. On the other hand, a patient may be heavily criticised by the referer when this is not deserved. Consequently it is very important that each referral is considered independently of the referer's judgement. Sometimes, even when the referer's negative remarks are accurate, the conductor will admit the subject to his group. This will depend on a number of factors, such as individual motivation, personal honesty, the state of the group and the confidence of the conductor. This confidence should be based on an accurate assessment of personal skill, training and experience, together with an equally careful appraisal of the group's strengths and abilities.

Much of the information that the conductor receives may be regarded as material from the external level of experience. If he works in a team he will have his colleagues' views and opinions to help him form a picture of the suitability of any individual. This is information that he can consider at an intellectual level. In other words, he thinks carefully about the data and measures it against other variables such as his own abilities and those of the group.

He will also have other information that he will pick up during his interview with the patient. Some of this too will be the sort of information that he will think about as above. Other than this there will be the impressions he gains from being with the patient which may not be based on anything the patient has said. This may be regarded as material from an internal level of experience. The conductor intuits (Bion, 1970), that is, he uses his intuition to help him sense the patient's difficulties, just as the physician uses sight, touch and smell to aid him in making a diagnosis. The conductor combines these various strands of experience – that is, his intellectual and feeling responses – to help him build as rounded a picture as possible of each applicant for the group. This is a complex procedure and we shall examine it in greater depth by presenting an assessment interview in order to clarify how it may be done.

THE ASSESSMENT SITUATION

First Considerations

Therapists from many different schools of thought will interview candidates for treatment without reference to a list of questions or a format. They choose instead to listen to what the patient has to say, in the knowledge that he will reveal more than if the interview is hampered by lists. For if we listen to what people have to say and pay attention to the emotional content, we gain a far greater understanding than if we were to follow a more structured method.

Whilst a formally structured interview may be particularly helpful in establishing certain facts, such as the duration of the problem, areas of difficulty, previous treatment and so on, because it follows a line of enquiry which is established by the interviewer such techniques may leave the patient feeling that his point of view is excluded from consideration. It is important to recognise that this first contact may be the beginning of a therapeutic relationship and that it is an inter-view. This means that it is an activity engaged in by two or more people together. The patient is expected to make a decision about his preparedness to work in a particular way and he should have the chance to assess whether or not he wishes to work with a particular person.

In earlier chapters we have seen that change, when it occurs, takes place within established relationships (see chapters 6 and 7). Consequently we need to be aware that the relationship begins during the assessment interview and in this sense is part of the therapeutic process. Bearing this in mind it is clear that the person who is to conduct the group should participate in assessing each prospective group member himself.

Occasionally an instant antipathy develops between the patient and the conductor, or it may be one-sided on the part of either. In either case it would be unfair to insist that these people work together since they would be seeing a lot of each other over a lengthy period of time. In some circumstances such initial difficulties may be worked through within the group when it starts, but the conductor should be careful to recognise and manage his own hostility and that of the patient.

When the prospective conductor is inexperienced he may need the help of a more qualified colleague to assist him in making an assessment. In this situation it should be made clear to each candidate that the more experienced colleague will not be participating in the group (Foulkes, 1975). He should also be careful to be as opaque as it is reasonable to be in order to discourage the candidate from beginning to establish a relationship with him, rather than with the conductor. The assessment interview is a chance for the conductor to begin to establish a therapeutic alliance with the candidate. To achieve this he needs to help the candidate to feel that someone has heard him and may already understand a little.

If the conductor follows a rigidly defined and formally structured interview he will have lost a valuable opportunity to begin this work. If the clinic or the team do not respect the importance of staying with one person throughout the assessment and treatment process, and the candidate is passed from one to another, then he is likely to begin to feel rather like a package or a bundle of interesting symptoms but that no one is interested in him as an individual.

Unfortunately many of our hospitals and out patient departments are like this, with concerns about the patient coming second to other considerations, such as the training needs of the clinic staff and the unconscious desire of the staff to defend themselves against painful contact with their patients by keeping them at a distance (Menzies 1976), or through establishing procedures that make it impossible to develop relationships at any depth (see p. 48). We should not blame others for this state of affairs, for we all utilise these unconscious processes. We should try to be alert to the defences that we have installed as individuals and as contributing members of our particular social system (e.g. hospital, social security department, or hostel).

THE ASSESSMENT INTERVIEW

During the assessment interview the conductor aims to help the candidate to supply the information needed to make an informed decision about his suitability for the group. He also wants to form some idea of the sort of difficulty that the patient is in and to begin to understand why. At the same time he needs to put the candidate at ease and allow him to feel that someone has truly heard him.

Very often candidates for group treatment come to us having been involved with the psychiatric services for some years. They are used to giving an account of themselves and usually have a predetermined notion of what the conductor wants to know. This is because they have been asked the same questions many times at different interviews by several interviewers over the years and each of the interviews has followed a particular pattern. There is a sort of standard psychiatric interview which is intended to help the psychiatrist make a diagnosis which then suggests the sort of treatment the patient will receive. This will usually mean some form of drug-based treatment. This procedure fails to acknowledge the individual and to offer self-motivated change.

The conductor is not seeking to make a diagnosis but to gain a working impression of the candidate – his difficulties, his motivation, his capacity for long-term commitment to facing painful issues, and his willingness and ability to work in a group with other people towards personal change and growth. Consequently, the way he takes the interview will be different.

The following account is taken from notes made by a student of groups whilst interviewing a candidate for group work. The candidate was a middle-aged man who was a patient on an admission unit at the time. He had several previous admissions to various psychiatric hospitals over a period of years. He was therefore very familiar with the psychiatric services and with their procedures.

The conductor is identified by the abbreviation *Th.* and the candidate by the abbreviation *Pt.* The conductor's uncommunicated thoughts are noted in **bold** when this is appropriate or helpful.

Th. Hello, come in and take a seat. I'm . . . (*here the conductor gave his name*). Your doctor has suggested we meet to discuss the possibility of you joining the group that I am running.
Pt. Yes . . . he thought it might help . . .
Th. Did you have any ideas yourself or is it too . . . ?

I wonder if he's here under duress, does he want the group or is it his doctor . . . or is it too soon to know?

Pt. Well . . . I . . . It's been going on for so long and I . . . I thought it wouldn't harm to see you.
Th. Perhaps we can think about that together . . . you don't have to make up your mind now and it's up to you to say if you want to or not . . .
Pt. Well . . . I thought . . . I mean I can't go on like this.
Th. I've heard a little from your doctor but not really much . . . perhaps you could tell me what . . . could you say something about yourself . . . ?
Pt. It's all in the notes.
Th. Yes . . . I'm sorry . . . it must be . . . it can't be easy to repeat it all the time . . . but I . . . it would help me to hear . . . in your own words . . . something of the sort of thing that is difficult for you.

It seems he might be expecting another session going over old ground uselessly and it can't be pleasant to be expected to tell strangers about your intimate life, even if they are professionals and are supposed to help you.

Pt. What do you want to know?
Th. Anything that comes to mind about how you find yourself in difficulty . . . What's happening in your life at the moment . . . ?
Pt. I've been . . . for years now . . . I always feel so tense . . . and I get depressed . . . I feel unsafe everywhere.
Th. Has it always been like that?
Pt. It's worse since my wife . . . she left me . . . and . . . last year . . .

I wonder if there are any other associated problem separations?

Th. Were you close before that . . . before things started to go wrong?
Pt. We were never . . . we were miserable together. It was an ill-advised union . . . she was very puritanical . . . she . . . she accused me of treating her like a whore. (*laughs bitterly*) We didn't consummate the marriage for years. . . .
Th. Was that . . . did you have any problem managing . . . ?
Pt. No there was nothing . . . not until later . . . she was frigid . . . I didn't want to hurt her.

I wonder if he worries about hurting other people? Where does this start?

Th. Were you close to . . . who would you say you were closest to Mum or Dad?
Pt. My mother died when I was little . . . about four months I think . . . she had polio . . . she was only twenty-five.

It seems there may be something here, there *is* a very early tragic separation, and perhaps there is some residual infantile worry that he hurt his mother too . . . Children often do blame themselves for everything that goes wrong, and that feeling often continues into adult life as an unconscious concern.

Th. Who looked after you?

Pt. I was passed around from one aunt to another . . . I mean they would keep me for six months to a year and then . . .

Th. You'd be sent to the next one . . .

Pt. That's right.

Th. Can you remember what that was like . . . I . . . how long did that go on for? I guess that was very . . . difficult . . . perhaps that has something to do with what you said earlier about being unsafe?

Pt. It was very unsettling . . . They were very kind . . . looking back they were only girls really . . . but I liked them . . . I used to hope that they would keep me but . . .

Th. They didn't . . .

Pt. Yes.

Th. It seems a bit like what happened to you with your treatment . . . you know . . . being in one place then another . . . and now being passed on to me . . .

Pt. It's very unsettling . . . (*laughs, a short, harsh sound*)

That's what he said about his aunts . . . it seems that it is relevant. It seems that there might be a sort of compulsion to repeat experiences from infancy in his later life. I wonder . . .

Th. Does anything come to mind about that . . . about being passed on?

Pt. Not really . . . I . . . the only thing is my job . . . I move about the country a lot . . . from one place to another . . . it's company policy . . . keeps you on your toes.

I wonder if that is still likely to happen . . . will he stay around long enough for the group to have an impact? Why did he choose that company . . . that job? Is this based upon an unconscious need to repeat his childhood experiences until something turns out right?

Th. Is that still likely . . . will you be moved again?

Pt. Not now . . . I'm on probation . . . they are monitoring my work and want me to work with one person . . .

Th. I was thinking that it's very difficult with your background . . . having to move around like you did when you were little . . . and about the group because it . . ., this sort of thing takes time . . . You've had these problems for years and you have found that it doesn't change . . . it can't change overnight.

Pt. I was used to it . . . do you mean that . . . I'd have thought that it would be easier for me because I was so used to moving around as a child . . .

Th. Yes . . . I was thinking that maybe your problems had something to do with feeling so unsettled . . . with losing your mother . . . and having no one who was really a sort of mother to you for any helpful length of time . . .

Pt. I . . . I knew the psychiatrists . . . the doctors thought it was interesting . . . but you know as a sort of case . . . a kind of syndrome . . . but I never thought of it that way . . . I'd have thought it would have made me tougher . . . someone who could take a lot . . . (*Here he broke off and seemed very thoughtful rather than questioning. After a short silence he continued*.) I . . . when my dad remarried he . . . I was living with him and my grandfather, his dad then . . . they wanted to move out and I was happy there . . . I didn't want to go . . . and they took me . . . it caused bad feeling . . . my grandad took my side . . .

> I have an idea that he feels responsible for the deterioration in the relationship between dad and grandad. Perhaps there *is* something in the idea that he fears he hurts the people he gets close to . . . has he ever had a close relationship, is he capable of making them? It would affect his ability to tolerate the group experience.

Th. You sounded quite sad . . . was that a sad time?

Pt. I was worried all the time but it had been a happy time and I missed my grandfather.

Th. So you were unhappy to leave and it makes you unhappy remembering that time?

Pt. That's true . . . he was a warm man . . . not like my dad . . . he didn't understand children . . .

Th. And grandad did . . . ?

Pt. Yes.

Th. Was there anyone else that you . . . that cared for you . . . that you got close to?

Pt. There was a vicar . . . he was a good man . . . he was good with children and he kind of gave me self-esteem.

> It's unusual how he uses language in such a stilted way at times, it's quite formal . . . First of all he did not say we didn't have sex or make love, he said consummate our marriage, and he spoke of his marriage as an ill-advised union. Now he talks of self-esteem. I wonder if this is a form of language that he's learned from being a patient, or is it his way of distancing himself from what he feels like when he thinks of these things?

Th. They were fatherly men . . . your grandad and the vicar?

Pt. Yes. Much more than my real dad . . . I resent him for that . . . he used to open my letters and would ridicule me for things I wanted to do . . . I tried acting for a while . . . it's still like that now. They're both contemptuous of things that are important to me.

> Perhaps there is a sense of needing to protect the things that matter, to keep his important feelings to himself unless others ridicule him like he says his father did. This might explain why he uses such formal words to describe emotive issues.

Th. Does that make you angry?

Pt. Yes . . . I have felt that . . . they still treat me like a child . . . unlike Mum, she would have encouraged me.

Th. Who are you angry with?

Pt. God . . .

> If he did feel that his mother's death was somehow his fault then he would feel potentially powerfully dangerous. I wonder if he directs his anger against God because he feels it could overwhelm anyone else . . . is it too frightening for him to contemplate?

Th. What about people closer . . . ?

Pt. I was never angry with Mum . . . I could never be angry with her.

> That's not what I asked, it seems he *is* anxious about feeling that he could be angry with his dead mother. I was wondering whether or not he was ever angry with his father, or his

employers, or his wife, whom he didn't want to hurt. I begin to feel that a lot of his aggression and assertiveness is denied and that this may be because he is fearful of its potency, its destructive potential.

Th. It sounded as if you felt it was unthinkable . . . to feel angry with your mother . . . it seemed as if you might be worried about having been angry with her as a baby . . .

Pt. My wife said I was her fourth child . . . that made me angry . . . she didn't understand me or my job . . .

Th. Perhaps that's a bit like it's been for you for a while . . . feeling that no one understands. I mean here too . . . and with other doctors and so on . . .

Pt. I have felt that . . . all they want to know is have you been sleeping and do you ever have suicidal thoughts . . . but it was different once . . . with grandad and later when I'd been married for seven years . . .

Th. What changed . . . ?

Pt. It was one of the best times of my life . . . I felt accepted as a candidate for this job . . . I'd always wanted to do it. I felt fulfilled . . . confident . . . the future looked good. My relationship with my wife improved . . . became more tender . . . more intimate.

Th. What about your failure to consummate the marriage?

Pt. That changed . . . we could . . . we made love . . . but for a long time I couldn't . . . It was a problem to ejaculate.

Th. Yet you have children . . .

Pt. Yes . . . I managed to overcome that after a while . . . my wife was so puritanical . . . I fantasised about other women who were more disinhibited than my wife and imagined I was with them . . . then I could do it.

> It seems that the thread of worrying about his aggressive impulses continues through this into his marital relations. There is also a feeling of not ever having been fully accepted, occasionally and for a short time yes, but never entirely. Being accepted seems so important to him that when he's accepted for a job his other relationships improve too. I suspect that in an unconscious way moving about in his job made him feel somehow unaccepted and unwanted. If this is so then it would tend to confirm his fear that his angry feelings are potentially destructive, he would see this as why he was moved on by his aunts . . . again in an unconscious way.

Th. Was it to do with disinhibition or were you worried what you might do if you let go?

Pt. The latter . . . yes . . . I always used to worry that I might injure her.

> It is clear that there is a great anxiety about his destructive potential. He was so worried he might somehow injure his wife that for a long time he could not make love to her. When things changed and they became closer he was unable to ejaculate, *as he says himself*, because he used to worry that he might injure her. If I think about his stated complaints at the beginning of this meeting he was worried and anxious wherever he was. That is evidently based upon his childhood experiences of being moved around and the loss of his mother during infancy, but it seems that he has grown up feeling that he is somehow dangerous and potentially destructive. He worried about injuring his wife and was very anxiously defensive about the idea that he could be angry with his mother. Again that was his idea not mine, it was a notion that was in his mind and therefore is quite likely a continuing concern for him. I wonder if all these internal anxieties and worries become identified with the outside world so that they add to the discomfort he already feels from having been moved from pillar to post?

Th. I think that you have given me quite a lot to think about . . . I'd like a little time to go over in my own mind some of the things we've talked about . . . if that's all right with you . . . and perhaps we could get together again to have another talk and to think some things over in a few days time or perhaps a week . . . Do you have anything you would like to ask me? No? Well maybe next time . . . if you think of anything in the meantime we can look at it when we next meet. I think that it is too soon for both of us to be able to make a decision about the group just yet, and I'm sure there will be lots you want to know about it before you commit yourself to a decision.

The conductor closed the interview at this point and arranged another meeting later in the same week.

The above example gives a good idea of the way in which issues of primary importance will come into focus if we pay attention to what the patient is saying, and what may influence what the patient is saying, along with the emotional content of the communication. In the next section of this chapter we shall examine what took place, what the conductor was thinking and why, and we will think about the appropriateness of group work for this candidate.

PAYING ATTENTION

The conductor did have a lot to think about, but how did he manage to elicit the information in the first place? What were his aims in the assessment interview and how did he set about fulfilling them? The first positive thing that he did was *not* to read the patient's notes. He had decided not to for the very sound reason that he wanted to get to know the individual rather than his diagnosis, and he wanted his own views to be unbiased by the views and opinions of others. Furthermore, he wanted to begin a relationship with this man on an even footing. The patient did not have any access to notes on him, so it would be unhelpful to begin by reading notes on the patient. There can be an element of dehumanising, no matter how unintentional, if we take our information from the contact that others have had with our patients. They somehow become less relevant than their notes, they can be locked in a drawer and filed away, the views of others wrongly take on the consistency of fact.

As the heading implies, the conductor paid attention to what was taking place, he listened with an ear that was attuned to the nuances of the unstated and the symbolic, and he noticed the apparent resonances between the past and the present. For example, when the candidate spoke of his aunts – 'I used to hope that they would keep me but . . .' – the conductor was able to notice a possible link between that wish and the patient's relationship with his current carers, the psychiatric hospital: *Th.* 'It seems a bit like what has happened with your treatment . . . you know . . . being in one place then another . . . and now being passed on to me . . .' The patient's reply was quite telling: 'It's very unsettling . . .'

The conductor had thought the following at this time: 'That's what he said about his aunts . . . it seems that it is relevant. It seems that there might be a sort of compulsion to repeat experiences from infancy in his later life. I wonder . . .'

It was exactly how he had described what it was like being passed from aunt to aunt as a child. So we can see that the conductor was very probably right to think that the patient was feeling passed on as he had when he was small and that he wished that someone would keep him.

It is profoundly important to be influenced in one's thinking by the impression that the candidate makes. This is another reason for not reading the notes beforehand as one can never be certain that the impression gained belongs to the impact made by the patient or by the feelings of others as set out in the notes.

From the beginning of the interview the conductor followed the candidate, not to where he might consciously have wanted to lead the conductor, but to where his communications actually led. These communications included his verbal statements and their symbolic components as well as the non-verbal communications of his tone of voice and his body language, his facial expressions, his gestures and so on. In addition, the conductor, as has been said, related information from the candidate's past to his present circumstances.

The conductor listened to what the patient had to say, he tried not to prescribe what he should say or to tell the patient what he, the conductor, wanted to hear. He tried to make it plain that he was interested in the patient's experience, that he would try to understand and begin to make some sense of it which he would share with the patient. He did this by allowing the patient time to think, or to reflect on his thoughts and feelings, and by noticing and reporting on the emotional content of the interview. For example, at the very beginning of the interview the conductor had explained the purpose of the meeting and the candidate/patient had responded with: 'Yes . . . he thought it might help . . .'

The conductor had noticed that the patient identified his doctor as the one who thought it might help and that his reply had been noncommital and slightly hostile. He chose to respond to this in a sympathetic way by saying: 'Did you have any ideas yourself or is it too . . . ?' He then paused to allow the patient time to think and to respond, whilst he considered what the patient might have been thinking and feeling as the following shows:

'I wonder if he's here under duress, does he want the group or is it his doctor . . . or is it too soon to know?'

A little later when he had asked the patient to tell him something about himself, the response had again been a little hostile and wary. The patient had said: 'It's all in the notes'.

The conductor had thought the following: 'It seems he might be expecting another session going over old ground uselessly and it can't be pleasant to be expected to tell strangers about your intimate life, even if they are professionals and are supposed to help you.'

The conductor also links the past with the present. This helps the candidate to begin to believe that someone can understand him and it is the start of the therapeutic alliance. We can see that the patient began to feel understood if we look at the following example, the conductor had been thinking as follows:

'That's not what I asked. It seems he is anxious about feeling that he could be angry with his dead mother. I was wondering whether or not he was ever angry with his father, or his employers, or his wife, whom he didn't want to hurt. I begin to feel that a lot of his aggression and assertiveness is denied and that this may be because he is fearful of its potency, its destructive potential.'

He said: 'It sounded as if you felt it was unthinkable . . . to feel angry with your mother . . . it seemed as if you might be worried about having been angry with her as a baby . . .'

The patient made the association himself to the recent past: 'My wife said that I was her fourth child . . . that made me angry . . . she didn't understand me or my job . . .'

The conductor continued this linking process into the present with the following interpretation: 'Perhaps that's a bit like it's been for you for a while . . . feeling that no one understands. I mean here too . . . and with other doctors and so on . . .'

The patient responded with a criticism of his previous doctors and a memory from a time when things had been a little better. He spoke warmly of his grandfather and of his wife. It is reasonable to consider that he may have begun to entertain the hope that the conductor might turn out to be a little like his understanding and loyal grandfather and that this hope had been stimulated by the feeling, gained via the above interpretations, that the conductor understood him a little, just as his grandfather had.

The conductor must also remember that the purpose of the interview is to select for the group. To this end he pays attention to the patient's communications and sets them alongside his knowledge of the group, its current state and the patient's background. For example, this patient had appeared wary and a little hostile at the beginning of the interview, as we have seen:

Th. I've heard a little from your doctor but not really much . . . perhaps you could tell me what . . . could you say something about yourself?
Pt. It's all in the notes.
Th. Yes . . . I'm sorry . . . it must be . . . it can't be easy to repeat it all the time . . . but I . . . it would help me to hear . . . in your own words . . . something of the sort of thing that is difficult for you.

We have already looked at this example from another point of view. Here it serves to show that the same piece of information can and should be considered from a variety of viewpoints. In this case we have already examined it and learned that it illustrated a possible hostile antipathy to the psychiatric profession at large and the conductor in particular as yet another person to whom the patient was being passed. It also alerted the conductor to the patient's feeling that he could never really hope that someone could understand him, or that all he could expect was to be considered as an interesting but unhelpable case. We focus on it now to see if we can glean from it some idea about whether or not this patient would survive in, contribute to, or benefit from group therapy.

The conductor pondered upon this piece of information and thought that it could be understood in several ways. The terse and wary reply (for this is how the conductor remembered it) that it was 'all in the notes' could mean that the patient was weary of repeating himself to unhelpful strangers, an appropriate reluctance to share personal and intimate details with a stranger, or an unwillingness to do any of the work himself. Consequently the conductor needed clarification and listened for it during the rest of the interview. Later on the following exchange occurred:

Th. Who looked after you . . . ?
Pt. I was passed around from one aunt to another . . . I mean they would keep me for six months to a year and then . . .
Th. You'd be sent to the next one . . .
Pt. That's right.

The conductor was able to see that the patient's earlier chary response was probably rooted in unsettling and disturbing childhood experiences and that it was appropriate behaviour in these terms as well as being an ordinary cautiousness with a stranger. This led the conductor to think about the patient's ability to tolerate the lengthy time commitment that intensive group work demands. With this in mind he continued with the session and listened for other clues. A little later this happened:

Th. It seems a bit like what has happened to you with your treatment . . . you know . . . being in one place then another . . . and now being passed on to me . . .
Pt. It's very unsettling . . . (laughs, a short, harsh sound)

That's what he said about his aunts . . . it seems that it is relevant. It seems that there might be a sort of compulsion to repeat experiences from infancy in his later life. I wonder . . .

Th. Does anything come to mind about that . . . about being passed on?
Pt. Not really . . . I . . . the only thing is my job . . . I move about the country a lot . . . from one place to another . . . it's company policy . . . keeps you on your toes.

I wonder if that is still likely to happen . . . will he stay around long enough for the group to have an impact? Why did he choose that company . . . that job? Is this based upon an unconscious need to repeat his childhood experiences until something turns out right?

We can see from the above that the conductor's concerns are supported or at least given emphasis by the patient's responses. However, he is not convinced that this patient is an unsuitable candidate for the group and persists with the interview. At this juncture he is listening for some evidence that will either convince him that the patient would fail in a group, or give him hope that the patient is able to find the sort of value in relationships that will enable him to engage in other helpful relationships within a group. The interview proceeded in this way:

Th. Is that still likely . . . will you be moved again?

This is an obvious and important question to ask directly as the conductor needs to know if the patient is able to stay in the vicinity long enough to have a sound group experience. The following reply reassures him:

Pt. Not now . . . I'm on probation . . . they are monitoring my work and want me to work with one person . . .

The conductor makes the following remark to test the temperature of the water. He wants to know if the patient can respond to insight-promoting interpretations and he wants to help the patient to feel that working in this way might help him:

Th. I was thinking that it's very difficult with your background . . . having to move around like you did when you were little . . . and about the group because it . . ., this sort of thing takes time . . . You've had these problems for years and you have found that it doesn't change . . . it can't change overnight.
Pt. I was used to it . . . do you mean that . . . I'd have thought that it would be easier for me because I was so used to moving around as a child . . .
Th. Yes . . . I was thinking that maybe your problems had something to do with feeling so unsettled . . . with losing your mother . . . and having no one who was really a sort of mother to you for any helpful length of time . . .
Pt. I . . . I knew the psychiatrists . . . the doctors thought it was interesting . . . but you know as a sort of case . . . a kind of syndrome . . . but I never thought of it that way . . . I'd have thought it would have made me tougher . . . someone who could take a lot . . . (*Here he broke off and seemed very thoughtful rather than questioning.*)

It seemed that this was a new way of thinking for this patient and that it was possible that he could find a value in it, yet he is still sticking with the defensive notion that his experiences toughened him, until after a short silence he said:

I . . . when my dad remarried he . . . I was living with him and my grandfather, his dad then . . . they wanted to move out and I was happy there . . . I didn't want to go . . . and they took me . . . it caused bad feeling . . . my grandad took my side . . .

The conductor was reassured by the above remark. It showed that the patient could let current experience resonate with his past and allow the product of this resonance to surface in his conscious mind when he felt acknowledged and that his experience was valid. The conductor pursued this because he wanted to be sure that the patient could, given the right help, be in touch with his feelings and because he wanted to develop the fledgling therapeutic alliance still further:

Th. So you were unhappy to leave and it makes you unhappy remembering that time?
Pt. That's true . . . he was a warm man . . . not like my dad . . . he didn't understand children . . .
Th. And grandad did . . . ?
Pt. Yes.
Th. Was there anyone else that you . . . that cared for you . . . that you got close to?
Pt. There was a vicar . . . he was a good man . . . he was good with children and he kind of gave me self-esteem.

The conductor began to feel really hopeful at this point, the patient had been able to value his grandfather and a local vicar, finding something in them that he could respond to. The conductor decided to take this up:

Th. They were fatherly men . . . your grandad and the vicar?
Pt. Yes. Much more than my real dad . . . I resent him for that . . . he used to open

my letters and would ridicule me for things I wanted to do . . . I tried acting for a while . . . it's still like that now. They're both contemptuous of things that are important to me.

The conductor now felt that the patient could very probably become a successful member of the group as he was able to express both positive and negative feelings. He had little doubt that much of the patient's story was true, that he had been neglected in some ways by his father or misunderstood by him. He kept in mind, however, that there was an element of splitting apparent with his grandfather and the vicar being only good and his father and stepmother being entirely bad. He realised it was quite likely that the patient would involve himself in many other splitting manoeuvres in the group once he had joined. It was a realistic possibility that this patient would seek to split the staff in a similar way too, with the conductor being seen as helpful and the previous doctors as being useless, at least for a time.

The problem of motivation was still a consideration. The patient had come because his doctor had sent him and because he thought it 'couldn't hurt'. He had no questions to ask, probably because his point of view had seldom been asked for by his carers and because he had held no hope for himself before the interview. The conductor decided that the patient needed to think about his experience of the interview and to consider what it might mean for him to join the group. The conductor had intimated that it would be a lengthy commitment in terms of time and an intensive commitment in terms of his emotional involvement with the group.

They met a few days later because the conductor was alert to the patient's earlier experiences of being offered help and then apparently being dumped or passed on. At this interview he was much more positive, though still anxious, and said that he had thought about little else since the first interview and had decided he would like to know a lot more about the group with a view to joining it if the conductor agreed.

The outcome was that the patient joined the group a couple of weeks later and, despite some early problems of attendance (which the conductor had half-expected as the patient's way of unconsciously testing out his and the group's commitment) he has stayed with the group. Although his treatment continues he is much less anxious, tense and depressed, and it is likely that he will eventually manage a full life without support or medication once he has completed his group therapy.

Although we have followed the assessment of a candidate who was a patient in hospital, the assessment procedure is the same for both in-patients and out-patients. One must still pay particular attention to the personal motivation of each candidate individually, and have a regard for group mix, confidentiality, and so forth. In some areas, particularly rural districts, which have a relatively small and stable population, it may be difficult to ensure that the members of the group are strangers, for obvious reasons. It is still possible to establish groups in such settings, but the conductor must take into account the very natural worries that people may have in revealing themselves to family, friends or neighbours, and he must be careful to maintain confidentiality in the group. Where possible it is better to run groups that are made up of people who are strangers to one another at the outset.

Once the conductor is sure that he will accept a candidate into the group then he must ensure that the candidate knows that promptness and regularity of attendance are expected. The new group member will also need to know about planned holidays, breaks, confidentiality and the meeting-place of the group. Beyond these considerations it is quite helpful to allow the new member to have some doubts, concerns or questions. He might want them answered now, or they may keep until he attends the group. It would be a breach of confidentiality if the conductor were to speak about the group in anything more than general terms. If the new member wants to know any details then he should be encouraged to take his questions to the group when he joins.

In the next chapter we stay with many of the points raised here, particularly with the need to pay a particular kind of attention, this time in a group setting.

References

Bion W R (1970) *Attention and Interpretation*. London: Tavistock.

Foulkes S H (1975) *Group-Analytic Psychotherapy*. London: Gordon and Breach.

Main T F (1957) The ailment. *British Journal of Medical Psychology*, **30**: 129–145

Menzies I E P (1976) *The Functioning of Social Systems as a Defence against Anxiety*. London: Tavistock.

12

Understanding Latent

and

Symbolic Communication

Following the precedent set in the last chapter we shall look at a verbatim record of one session, but this time it is taken from the life of a group. Before we do so we need to establish some ground-rules which may help us to understand where the conductor places the focus of his attention and why.

The group session presented here has been chosen because it is very typical of many such sessions. Most of life is concerned with the commonplace and the ordinary and for this reason amongst others the group should be concerned with the commonplace too. Much of the life of any group is taken up with ordinary matters from the daily life of its members, their hopes and aspirations and their fears and failures. Most groups will make discoveries of a profound nature, but these are not the bread and butter of group work and only occur, or have real impact and meaning, when the commonplace has been consistently understood and unflinchingly faced over time. New lives are not built on earthshattering discoveries, but on patient commitment to open and honest inquiry over time. They are built on the continuing constancy of presence and purpose that the conductor or therapist brings and which is adopted by the group. It is important to remember that the task of the conductor is to establish and maintain the conditions necessary for the group to make its own discoveries. This is one of the most difficult tasks that the conductor undertakes, and in order to fulfil his obligation in this matter, he pays attention to a number of factors which will help him to understand the material that the group reveals. These factors include the following:

HELPFUL FACTORS

The Stage of the Group

If we look at what was discussed in chapter 6 on group development (see pp. 68–9) we see that four distinct phases were identified: the parallel phase, the inclusion phase, the mutuality phase and the termination phase, in order of their appearance in the life of the group. During each of these phases it is possible to identify a series of crises, or concerns, which preoccupy the group. The first of these, the authority crisis, marks the end of the parallel phase and the beginning of the inclusion phase. It is characterised by the group challenging the power and authority of the conductor. The parallel phase is the first stage of development and the activity of the group is focused on avoiding anxiety, on establishing relationships, on dealing with issues of trust and mistrust, and on forming as a group

The inclusion phase is marked by an increase in communications between group members, with more individuals taking part in each topic, and a decrease in direct communications to the conductor. It proceeds from pairing and sub-groupings (a legacy of the parallel phase) to a more complete pattern of relationships between all members of the group, Again, trust remains a key issue.

The second crisis is the intimacy crisis which underlies the ending of the inclusion phase and the beginning of the mutuality phase. Many issues which surface during this time have to do with what may be dealt with by the group and what must be excluded. There is an ambivalence, sometimes conscious, sometimes not, about which members, which thoughts, which ideas, which feelings, which memories, impulses, hopes, wishes and desires may be brought to or included in the group and those which should be barred. The mutuality phase grows from a satisfactory, partial resolution of these conflicting concerns and brings a capacity for intimate relationships. This is the operating phase of the group.

The separation crisis is the third crisis and it may happen at any time in the life of the group. It is provoked by absences, departures, breaks and other losses or separations. When circumstances are severe enough, or if the group is fragile in anyway, the separation crisis may precipitate the group into the termination phase. During this phase the group returns to dealing with issues it first faced in the inclusion phase.

If the conductor uses the knowledge that all groups develop in this way as a background to what the group is discussing, how it is behaving and so forth, it will help him to understand where he should focus his attention. He will know, for example, that during the first few weeks the group will be feeling anxious and vulnerable, that it will be trying to avoid dealing with any real issues, and that this is appropriate. He will also be aware that the group is gradually working at finding out about one another and is slowly establishing the trust that is essential to the work of the group. Consequently he will be able to help the group task by gently pointing out their appropriate lack of trust, subsequent anxiety and so on, as these feelings become revealed in the material. He will know that the group will turn to him as the expert and he will be able to further the aims of the group by returning their questions and encouraging them to work things out for themselves.

The next of the factors which helps the conductor is:

The Process as Group Material

This process includes the relationships between members and the behaviour that they provoke or invoke in each other. We shall take our example from a group which had only recently been established at the time the reported occurrences took place.

One group member, Janet, offered an explanation for her absence from the previous week's group. Chris acknowledged it but in a way which disallowed further comment and discussion and the rest of the group colluded to talk about matters from the previous week's group in such a way that Janet was easily excluded. She had nothing to offer as she had not been there. The group also talked in such a way as to make it difficult for Janet to know what had happened the previous week, leaving her doubly excluded. This is *process material* and as such it is a form of communication which the conductor strives to understand.

The essence of the process in this example is of absence and exclusion. Janet was absent one week and was excluded the next. The next thing that the conductor might note is that much of the talk is between couples or small sub-groups within the group. This part of the process interaction would alert him to the fact that the group was behaving in a way that was prevalent in groups in the inclusion phase, or of groups in the termination phase. If this is the case then his thoughts are given direction. The process of absence and subsequent exclusion are features of the inclusion and termination phases. These phases both include anxieties about loss, about personal disclosure and about membership. They are often related to powerful negative feelings. The conductor might observe the process for the group: 'It seems that the group is excluding Janet from this week's group. Perhaps this has something to do with her absence last week.'

If the conductor observes the process he is helped to recognise the developmental stage of the group; this in turn helps him to understand what the underlying concerns of the group may be. Closer attention to the content of the material will enable him to identify more precisely where the largest part of the group's concerns lie. Before we look at the content as one of the helpful factors we should examine the role of another such factor – emerging themes.

Emerging Themes

Over a number of sessions or weeks of sessions it may become apparent that the group is preoccupied with a particular topic, group of topics or experiences. He may be able to notice this happening because he can remember much of the detail of the previous three or four groups, but it is more likely that he will remember if he has made notes of the previous sessions.

If we stay with the example we have been developing we would find that the conductor discovered from his notes that the group has spent a lot of time talking about failed marriages, divorce, death, loss and separation. When this has happened over a period of weeks he can be certain that he has a developing theme which is of paramount importance to the group and its members. This awareness would put the group's behaviour towards Janet in a new light. It may then be seen as a hostile response to her and also as a demonstration of the group's need to defend against some powerful concerns about other personal losses. The group do this by treating her as they feel she treated them. It is important to remember transference phenomena here. It is quite likely that some of the responses of individuals in the group will be enhanced by past relationships and other experiences of separation.

Breaks and Holidays

If the conductor keeps in mind the relationship between group material and the position of the group in regard to holidays and other breaks he has more information which helps the accuracy of his interventions. If, as was the case in the example, the group faced a break for Christmas, then he would be able to understand that the attack on Janet for her absence from the group for one week was also a deflected attack on him (see Scapegoating, pp. 85–6), for abandoning the group, or excluding it, or for being absent from it himself. This separation would reverberate with other important separations from the pasts of individual group members and the powerful feelings which are thus promoted will often be directed against the conductor and deflected toward a scapegoat who is more manageable than he is. In this sense we can understand scapegoating as a displacement activity. It is a familiar notion to most of us and is often cruelly referred to as 'kicking the cat'. What happens is something like this.

Someone makes us angry, perhaps our boss upon whom we depend for continuing employment. Because of this it is impossible to vent our feelings on him, but they need to be released. The consequence is that the office boy might get a forceful ticking off for some minor mistake or omission. In other words, the anger which was provoked by the boss has been deflected onto the office boy because he is less threatening and powerful.

Content

The last of the factors which we might discuss here as being helpful to the conductor in his attempt to focus his interventions accurately, is that of the content of the session. This includes the subjects under discussion and their relationship with the other factors that have been enumerated. It would be helpful here to move on to presenting a verbatim record from a group so that we might discover the interrelationship of these factors.

The reader might consider it helpful to place himself in the role of the conductor and to make a note of the various factors he identifies or the observations and interpretations he would wish to make as the group unfolds. It might also be helpful to note his perceptions of what is happening in the group throughout, as there will be a chance for him to compare his findings with those of the conductor of this particular group later in the chapter.

We shall continue with the group we have been discussing throughout this chapter, beginning with a little background information from meetings which immediately preceded the group session in question. This group has also been referred to in chapter 9, (p. 110), so this is a chance to see it at a later stage of development.

Background Information

This group meets weekly and has five members. It had begun with six but one member had left after only one week because, she said, of a lack of time to give the group the commitment it deserved. The session in question was the thirteenth time the group had met and, four weeks previously, Phil had been absent without explanation for two weeks. He had sent his apologies, but had given no information about why he would not be present. In short:

On week 1 there were six members.

By week 2 one member had left, leaving five.

On weeks 9 and 10 Phil had been absent with apologies but no explanation.

On week 11 the whole group of five had been present.

When week 12 came Janet was absent and during the group neither the members nor the conductor had any idea that she would not be coming or why. After the group had ended it received a message that she could not get to the group for some unspecified reason.

She returned on week 13, the week of the session to be presented.

On week 11 Phil had returned to the group and explained in a manner that was devoid of emotion that he knew that he should have attended the group but had not because his wife had left him a fortnight ago and he had not been able to face anything. That he was in great distress was evidenced by his need to speak about his loss for the whole of the time available to the group, but his feelings were not apparent in the way that he spoke. His loss was echoed in the group by others who had recently experienced similar hardship.

Elaine had cried quietly and explained that her relationship of many years was in the process of ending. Madge had sat in silence throughout the session looking very miserable and only spoke when the conductor pointed out that the group had not noticed her distress or her tears. She had recently lost her lover, whom she had expected to marry, to another woman. Phil had seemed so self-absorbed and out of touch with his own feelings and the feelings of others that he had interrrupted Madge whilst she was struggling to find her voice through her tears. Elaine had waited for a moment and then said to Madge that Phil had interrupted her, encouraging her to continue and gently pointing out to Phil his self-centred behaviour.

On week 12 Janet had not been present at the group and her absence was unexpected. It may be considered relevant that she was the one group member who most clearly stated her wish to see the group develop an ability to work with deep and difficult feelings. Whilst Phil had been absent she had identified him as the member who did most to prohibit this happening. The atmosphere in the group this week was very much more open than it had been the previous week. Phil still seemed to need to speak almost continuously about his wife leaving him, but this time there was more of a quality of sadness and a feeling of anger to his words and this was acknowledged by others in the group.

The theme of anger had been denied by Phil but later, after Elaine had told of angrily kicking a chair and ending up with a bruised face as a direct result of this action, Phil had been able to acknowledge some of his anger, which he felt to be completely out of character. He told of having been so angry that he had driven his car recklessly early one icy morning so that he had nearly turned it over on a sharp bend in the road. He also recounted an incident from his youth when he had, he said, been driven beyond ordinary limits by three louts who had tried to beat him up one night in the city centre. He had laid the three of them out with a vicious release of explosive violence, injuring one so badly that he had thought he had killed him.

It had seemed to the conductor that several important issues were beginning to be dealt with in an honest way, Madge went on to say that she was unable to express angry feelings and somehow felt she turned them against herself. She followed up this statement by saying she had broken out in cold sores over the last week. Phil said he had a rash of pimples and Elaine said she had irisitis which she thought was a largely psychosomatic complaint. The conductor felt that the group was beginning to own angry feelings and their defences against them.

The Group Session

This session came immediately before a planned break, which was to last for two weeks. The group usually gathered in an anteroom prior to moving into the group room at the start of the session. The beginning of the session was signalled by the conductor walking through the anteroom and entering the group room at precisely the time the meeting was due to commence. Normally he was the first to enter, but this time Elaine preceded him and sat in a chair at the far side of the group after the conductor took his seat near the door. Chris came in next and sat immediately to his left, then Phil who sat to Elaine's right. Janet arrived and sat to the right immediately beside the conductor and Madge took the remaining chair to the right of Phil and the left of Chris (Figure 12.1)

The members will be identified by the initials of their first names and the conductor, to save possible confusion with Chris, by Th. Once again some of the conductor's thoughts will be noted in **bold** when this might be helpful or relevant.

There was a fair amount of smiling with most of the group looking towards the conductor.

E. Hello (This was addressed to the conductor.)
Th. Hello . . .

I wonder why they are all smiling at me? Is it anxiety? Why does E. say hello to me and not to the whole group?

J. Did you get my message . . . ?
C. Yes . . . but what happened?
J. I was stuck outside of London with a broken-down car.
E. It's not very pleasant to break down when you're driving . . .
J. No . . . the garage . . . It was in the garage for repair and they said it would be ready by an agreed time but it wasn't . . . it was their fault really . . .
C. Did you think of us . . . Did you miss us . . . ?
J. Well I thought of what you might be doing . . . but I don't think I missed you. It was more like wondering what you would be talking about . . .
C. You thought we might be talking about you . . . *(he was smiling as he said this)*
J. (frowning) No . . . I don't think I was concerned about that . . . more like just thinking the group will be meeting now and generally wondering what would be happening . . . why . . . did you speak about me?
C. No . . . I mean we wondered where you were . . .
J. Oh. . .

Fig. 12.1 The group entering the meeting room

But they did speak of her and expressed some concern about her absence . . . and the message wasn't recieved until after the group . . . I'm not sure that all of them got it either . . . What's going on? Also only three of the group have spoken and mostly it's been Chris and Janet . . . is this significant . . . ?

There was a short silence broken by Phil.

P. I tell you what . . . this is a terrible business . . . I don't know what I'm doing half the time . . . I'm like a man possessed . . . I'm obsessed with her and I don't know what I can do to stop myself from seeking her out all the time . . . It's a dreadful thing when this happens at Christmastime and you have to pretend to be jolly . . . I can't try any more . . .

The group sat and looked at the floor. No one responded to Phil's remarks and they tailed off into another silence which lasted for another four or five minutes. Again it was broken by Phil.

P. You know . . . and I don't mind telling you this . . . I can't deny it . . . there'd be no point . . . but I have to do my best to stay away from her . . . An old flame has been very helpful to me . . . to be honest . . . and I know she'd have me back at the drop of a hat . . . She's said as much . . . and it would be so very easy . . . but it wouldn't be fair . . . no, not fair at all . . . I was honest with her . . . and she understood . . . I can't be making any commitment until I sort myself out . . . She sorted me out . . . my wife did. I was a right scallywag with my drinking and I wouldn't deal with anything . . . I'd do anything for a bit of fun . . . never count the cost . . . but not anymore. I want to do this properly . . . but I can't stay at home . . .

Again the group failed to respond and returned to floor-gazing. This time the silence was considerably longer, lasting about nine minutes. Eventually Chris spoke and addressed himself to Phil.

C. You want to make a clean break . . . ?

> **The group are avoiding looking at each other and responding to each other. There is something dishonest happening. Instead of allowing themselves to respond by being in touch with Phil through allowing themselves to be touched by their own feelings they seem to be relying on him to fill the silences for them and Chris is encouraging Phil to expose himself more in a way that he seems reluctant to do himself . . . as do the others, they're all silent.**

Th. The group is spending a lot of time looking at the floor, perhaps to avoid making contact with anyone else, and Phil is being encouraged to say more and more.

Several members of the group nodded in agreement and looked up and around the group.

E. That's right, but I'm not feeling as fragile as I did last week and I don't want to end up dealing with things here . . . it doesn't seem appropriate . . . we have to leave here and face up to life outside . . .

> **I wonder if Elaine is voicing a wish on behalf of the group? She is saying it is not appropriate to deal with things in the group, and I know she means she doesn't find the group safe yet, but I think she may also be referring to the break . . .**

M. Has he left . . . ?
E. No not yet . . . you can't just throw someone out after so long, even if it was a destructive relationship all the way through . . .
J. *(crisply)* How long was it?
E. It was about six years . . . *(slightly frosty)* about as long as you Phil . . .
P. Yes six or maybe seven . . .
C. Have you seen him since . . . are you still together . . . ? *(asked of Madge)*
M. No . . . I haven't seen him for two weeks now . . . *(trailing off wistfully).*
C. When I came in tonight I was feeling on a high . . . I've had a good day.
J. Are you feeling a bit more doubtful now . . . questioning the stability of your

relationships more?

C. *(defensively patient)* No . . . I was just feeling that I have a good relationship with a colleague who is also a friend and valuing that . . . I sort of . . . I felt sorry for Phil and Madge . . . but I guess I am questioning whether or not I'm denying something . . . I'm wondering if my relationships are as healthy as I would like to think.

J. You didn't mention your wife once . . . is that important . . . am I the only one who noticed that . . . ?

C. I felt closer to my friend today than to my wife . . . *(guarded)*

P. I had to be angry with her the other day. It's no good you know, I was going to a private party and she was in the pub all solicitous of me . . . wanting to be friends . . . to have everything nice and I know she'd come back if I asked her . . . I need it to be a clean break . . . it's against the grain but I had to get angry with her. I told her to piss off and leave me alone . . . just to stay away from me . . . Completely out of character for me . . . She's lost so much weight, she could be anorexic . . . and her moods are all over the place . . . not like your relationship Elaine, it was fine and I trusted her, it was so out of the blue . . .

E. I've known mine was destructive from the start, but I'm of an age now when I want to know why I do it . . . why do I always get into these destructive relationships?

> It seems to me that Janet is being excluded by the others in the group. They are warmly responsive to each other, but reply to her in an intolerant and variously hostile way. She is being a trifle combative, but she always is and has not met with this kind of response before. The content of the material is all to do with separation too . . . perhaps in resonance with the coming break and the themes of earlier meetings . . . Phil is clearly trying to lay the blame for his failed relationship at his wife's door and is extricating himself from responsibility by suggesting she has a mental illness, he doesn't see her response as a grief reaction. The group opinion swings quite a bit between Phil who wants to put the blame outside himself so he doesn't have to examine any personal issues and Elaine who wants to find out why she makes a mess of things. I wonder why the group is so angry with Janet? She's not being tolerated well at all. She's very thin too . . . is Phil expressing some feeling about her for the group in an unconscious way whilst talking of his wife . . . ?

J. Why should any relationship be destructive? Isn't it more to do with people trying to get something from each other . . . I mean . . .

E. I feel this is like an inquisition . . . what does it matter how long it lasted and why must you try and tell me different to what I know? Believe me, it was destructive right from the start, and why should you challenge Chris about his relationship with his wife? Why make problems where there are none?

C. I thought you were very hostile to Phil, if you're interested you don't have to behave so antagonistically . . .

J. Well I have feelings you know . . . if you can't manage them I don't see what you have to gain here . . .

> Janet is giving voice again to some anxiety that it isn't safe to bring feelings to the group. This is clearly related to all the absences, can she trust others . . . ? But it is also related to the break. No one wants to open themselves up when there is no chance of following things through . . . a termination issue from a separation crisis.

Th. Ever since the beginning today the group has placed Janet on the outside.

When she offered an explanation of her absence and expressed an interest in last week's meeting the group did not respond and said that there had been no talk about her . . . well there was . . . there was some concern about why she was not here . . . The group knows that there is a lot of angry feeling . . . we talked last week of Phil's near-accident in the car, Elaine's bruised face and Madge's cold sores as anger turned against oneself . . . it is clear that the group is avoiding something, certainly anger . . . but perhaps other things too, for which Janet becomes the focus . . .

C. We mentioned Janet but that was all . . . we certainly didn't talk a lot about her as you say . . .

> There was a short silence of something like a minute.

I didn't say that the group talked a lot about Janet . . . merely that there had been some concern about her . . . yet the group is leaving Chris's statement to stand . . . they are rewriting the group to suit a need to avoid something . . . I really do wonder if the anger which is being expressed is to do with the ensuing break . . . Janet's absence would reinforce a separation crisis and her sitting beside me, with the group's refusal to acknowledge the concern they felt for her last week would all support the notion that she is being scapegoated . . . that feelings about me in regard to the break are being displaced onto her . . .

Th. The group has not challenged what it knows to be false . . . I didn't suggest that Janet had been talked about a lot . . . so perhaps there is some feeling to do with me? It occurs to me that this is the last group before the break and that has not been mentioned . . . I wonder if there is some feeling about that which is being left with Janet . . . as a sort of response to her absence last week?

E. I knew you'd mention the break . . . (initially said in an exasperated, impatient way, but then with a mixture of relief, realisation and a continuing attempt to deny it any importance). It's funny, I was thinking about it driving here . . . (thoughtfully) . . . I thought it was three weeks not two . . .

Th. Then . . . perhaps . . . ?

E. I was looking forward to the break with relief . . .

Th. But perhaps there were other feelings too . . .

E. No . . . you're right come to think of it . . . I have found the group useful over the past few weeks . . . it has seemed different . . .

J. Well I was hoping that we could behave with feeling . . . we can't sit here pretending to deal with real issues if we don't feel anything . . . I am who I am and that includes feelings . . .

E. That's one of the things we talked about last week . . . I don't feel I can bring my feelings here . . . I want help with things . . . but I don't see it is appropriate here . . .

J. But where is appropriate if not here? Where else is there? You could say that about anywhere . . .

P. I wish I'd come to the group during those first two weeks . . . but there you are . . . I'll know differently next time . . . it helps to talk . . . I've had a lot of help . . . I wish I'd had it when my father died . . . I never thought I'd cry again after that, but by damn I have these last weeks. . . I never thought I'd trust again either . . . and now I don't know if I'll ever get back the kind of trust I had with my wife . . . six weeks ago tonight it was . . .

C. I don't know I sort of . . . don't know what I feel that's a problem for me
. . . it'd be all right if I knew . . . but it's . . . I just find it so hard to identify what
I'm feeling . . . I . . . it troubled me a week or two ago when I felt something quite
deeply . . . I don't know what it was . . . it worried me . . .
J. I want to believe that someone, somewhere will be able to tolerate my feelings
. . . but I just don't know if the group can . . .
M. I'm feeling much better really . . . I'm looking forward to my holiday with my
sister . . .

It was time for the group to end and the conductor chose to make a closing
statement as there was a break and feelings had been running so high.

Th. There is a lot of uncertainty in the group at the moment . . . there is both a
wish to open up more and a fear that to do so would be inappropriate. The group
has faced a lot of separations with individual members and now faces another with
the break. It seems that there is a resonance between personal losses and the break
from the group and there are mixed feelings of relief and regret about the group
holiday . . . as there are with other separations. There is a wish to blame others for
individual dissatisfactions . . . Phil blames his wife . . . Elaine blames Janet
. . . Janet blames the group . . . the group blames me . . . but perhaps displaces
this onto Janet . . . and so on. No doubt these are issues which we will face again,
but for now it is time to end the group.

This report of part of one session in the life of a group is helpful as it illustrates a
number of the points that we need to consider. In the next section of this chapter
we shall review the session from the point of view of the conductor and how he
understood what was taking place and was assisted in this by the four helpful factors
identified earlier. They were: the stage or phase the group occupies, breaks and
holidays, emerging themes and the group process as material.

Understanding Communication in the Group

The conductor began thinking about the group at the beginning. He noted how the
members arrived and what they said or did. The group begins at the time arranged
for it to begin whether or not there are any members there. That can seem a little
odd. How is it possible to have a group without any members? The simple answer is
that it isn't possible, but if the group is due to start at a certain time and the
members know this and are not there, then this is a communication in group terms.
Everything that happens at times when the group is expected to meet is material for
consideration, so the conductor notices as much as he can. As we can see from the
following the conductor noted the seating arrangements:

This session came immediately before a planned break, which was to last for two
weeks. The group usually gathered in an anteroom prior to moving into the group
room at the start of the session. The beginning of the session was signalled by the
conductor walking through the ante-room and entering the group room at precisely
the time the meeting was due to commence. Normally he was the first to enter, but
this time Elaine preceded him and sat in a chair at the far side of the group after the
conductor took his seat near the door. Chris came in next and sat immediately to

his left, then Phil who sat to Elaine's right. Janet arrived and sat to the right immediately beside the conductor and Madge took the remaining chair to the right of Phil and the left of Chris.

There was a fair amount of smiling with most of the group looking towards the conductor.

E. Hello. *(This was addressed to the conductor).*

The conductor had taken his seat before Elaine sat opposite him. This is possibly significant as it is easier to express hostility when seated opposite someone than it is if one is seated in an adjacent position. Janet took a seat beside him even though there was another vacant chair, Chris had already taken the other adjacent chair. This could be significant too as it may convey a need for closeness or support, or a sense of something shared. Phil had seated himself beside Elaine and Madge had taken the last chair. As we shall see, these early considerations had some relevance. They are part of the process of the group and as such may be considered as material for the group's understanding.

Let us take a look at the early part of the session:

J. Did you get my message . . .
C. Yes . . . but what happened?
J. I was stuck outside of London with a broken-down car.
E. It's not very pleasant to break down when you're driving . . .
J. No . . . the garage . . . It was in the garage for repair and they said it would be ready by an agreed time but it wasn't . . . it was their fault really . . .
C. Did you think of us . . . Did you miss us . . . ?
J. Well I thought of what you might be doing . . . but I don't think I missed you. It was more like wondering what you would be taking about.

Janet has denied any responsibility for her absence and that she missed the group. This could be understood as providing the spark to the group's hostility later. It was followed with an assumption that she would have thought the group had talked about her, and then a denial of the concern the group had felt for her the previous week:

C. You thought we might be talking about you . . . *(he was smiling as he said this)*
J. (frowning) No . . . I don't think I was concerned about that . . . more like just thinking the group will be meeting now and generally wondering what would be happening . . . Why . . . did you speak about me?
C. No . . . I mean we wondered where you were . . .
J. Oh . . .

The conductor had some valuable information at this point. The group and Janet had been affected by her absence and were not prepared to take it any further. He also knew that this was the last group before a break and that Janet had been absent the previous week. He was able to reflect upon this in terms of how it might affect the development stage of the group. Before Phil's absences it had certainly moved from the early parallel phase and into the inclusion phase, but had been hampered in its ability to move into the mutuality phase because of the series of absences. The conductor would have expected a return to the issues of the inclusion phase anyway with the break on the horizon, and this was made more likely by Janet's absence. The group had briefly gained access to some of the benefits of the mutuality phase (the working phase) during the session which preceded Janet's absence when the group had seemed to have a clarity of purpose which was shared by all, together with a determination to face painful issues. Consequently, the conductor was able to see that the group had returned to the inclusion phase with its preoccupations with safety and anxieties about trust. There was an early indication that an honest determination to face the real issues was to be one of the first things to be excluded, as were feelings of concern and support. Remember, Chris had failed to acknowledge the group's concern for Janet.

Later on in the group, after Phil had spoken at length about the break-up of his marriage, he had been met by a number of silences and the following then took place:

C. You want to make a clean break . . . ?

The group are avoiding looking at each other and responding to each other. There is something dishonest happening. Instead of allowing themselves to respond by being in touch with Phil through allowing themselves to be touched by their own feelings they seem to be relying on him to fill the silences for them and Chris is encouraging Phil to expose himself more in a way that he seems reluctant to do himself . . . as do the others, they're all silent.

Th. The group is spending a lot of time looking at the floor, perhaps to avoid making contact with anyone else, Phil is being encouraged to say more and more.

Several members of the group nodded in agreement and looked up and around the group.

The conductor had evidently freed the group by his interpretation of the group process. You will note that he did not say anything that was terribly deep, but it was something that was almost available to the group which the group had not been able to deal with. A burst of feelingful activity followed on from this interpretation:

E. That's right, but I'm not feeling as fragile as I did last week and I don't want to end up dealing with things here . . . it doesn't seem appropriate . . . we have to leave here and face up to life outside . . .
M. Has he left . . . ?
E. No not yet . . . you can't just throw someone out after so long, even if it was a destructive relationship all the way through . . .

The content of the material here has to do with anxieties about self-revelation in the group (as is to be expected from a group in the inclusion phase) and whilst it is clearly and most immediately relevent to Elaine's experience of her personal life, it also could be considered to reveal some of the group's feelings about the impending break. There is a reluctance to deal with anything in the session and attention is drawn to the fact of leaving the group and living in the outside world. There is often this sort of resonance between individual experience and the life of the group which is revealed in information about individual matters.

J. (crisply) How long was it?
E. It was about six years . . . *(slightly frosty)* about as long as yours Phil . . .

P. Yes six or maybe seven . . .
C. Have you seen him since . . . are you still together? *(asked of Madge)*
M. No . . . I haven't seen him for two weeks now . . . *(trailing off wistfully)*.

The group's antagonism towards Janet is firming up at this point, the response to her is very different from the response given to the others. The group swiftly act to take the conversation away from her. Again this is part of the group process which informs the conductor, but she fights back:

C. When I came in tonight I was feeling on a high . . . I've had a good day.
J. Are you feeling a bit more doubtful now . . . questioning the stability of your relationship more?
C. (defensively patient) No . . . I was just feeling that I have a good relationship with a colleague who is also a friend and valuing that . . . I sort of . . . I felt sorry for Phil and Madge . . . but I guess I am questioning whether or not I'm denying something . . . I'm wondering if my relationships are as healthy as I would like to think.
J. You didn't mention your wife once . . . is that important . . . am I the only one who noticed that . . . ?

Again the content of the material is important. Janet is the one who is being excluded from her relationships with the rest of the group and is perhaps feeling a little doubtful. She is the one who notices that Chris has not mentioned his wife, that the wife is 'excluded'. Perhaps she is expressing her own feeling of exclusion and the group's overriding concern with such feelings at the moment? The exchange continued:

J. Why should any relationship be destructive? Isn't it more to do with people trying to get something from each other . . . I mean . . . ?
E. I feel this is like an inquistion . . . what does it matter how long it lasted and why must you try and tell me different to what I know? Believe me, it was destructive right from the start, and why should you challenge Chris about his relationship with his wife . . . why make problems where there are none?

Perhaps Janet *was* making problems where there was none, but Elaine knew that the purpose of the group was to enquire and to work with problems, so perhaps she was expressing a group wish to avoid difficult areas especially as the group would not be meeting to continue its work the next week. If we apply Elaine's statement to the group it could certainly be understood to mean as much. After a short time the conductor decided to do something about this:

Th. Ever since the beginning today the group has placed Janet on the outside. When she offered an explanation of her absence and expressed an interest in last week's meeting the group did not respond and said that there had been no talk about her . . . well there was . . . there was some concern about why she was not here . . . The group knows that there is a lot of angry feeling . . . we talked last week of Phil's near-accident in the car, Elaine's bruised face and Madge's cold sores as anger turned against oneself . . . it is clear that the group is avoiding something, certainly anger . . . but perhaps other things too for which Janet becomes the focus . . .

He acknowledges the destructive feelings and the group's avoidance and is helped in his ability to do this by his knowledge of the group over months. One of the emerging themes in the group has been to do with the denial of angry feeling and another has been to do with separations. Feelings of anger towards lost partners are avoided or denied and for some time the conductor has felt that there may well be some painful losses in the lives of the members of the group. However, he knows that these can only surface safely when the group is ready. He points to the possibility that the group is turning angry feelings against Janet rather than facing them individually, but without saying so in a definite way. He allows room for the group to discover this for themselves, or to find another meaning.

C. We mentioned Janet but that was all . . . we certainly didn't talk a lot about her as you say . . .

This denial is a confirmation that the conductor is on the right lines as it is not true, and it puts words into the conductor's mouth that he did not speak. The conductor draws the group's attention to it:

Th. The group has not challenged what it knows to be false . . . I didn't suggest that Janet had been talked about a lot . . . so perhaps there is some feeling to do with me? It occurs to me that this is the last group before the break and that has not been mentioned . . . I wonder if there is some feeling about that which is being left with Janet . . . as a sort of response to her absence last week?
E. I knew you'd mention the break . . . (initially said in an exasperated, impatient way, but then with a mixture of relief, realisation and a continuing attempt to deny it any importance) It's funny I was thinking about it driving here . . . *(thoughtfully)* . . . I thought it was three weeks not two . . .
Th. Then . . . perhaps?
E. I was looking forward to the break with relief . . .
Th. But perhaps there were other feelings too . . .
E. No . . . you're right come to think of it . . . I have found the group useful over the past few weeks . . . it has seemed different . . .

This confirms a return to the inclusion phase and a move away from the mutuality phase, Elaine had noticed a helpful difference wherein it was possible to feel helped and safe in the group. The following remarks tend to confirm the ambivalence to do with sharing and vulnerability in the group and the return to working on the issues of the inclusion phase once more:

J. Well, I was hoping that we could behave with feeling . . . we can't sit here pretending to deal with real issues if we don't feel anything . . . I am who I am and that includes feelings . . .
E. That's one of the things we talked about last week . . . I don't feel I can bring my feelings here . . . I want help with things . . . but I don't see it is appropriate here . . .
J. But where is appropriate if not here? Where else is there . . . you can say that about anywhere?
P. I wish I'd come to the group during those first two weeks . . . but there you are . . . I'll know differently next time . . . it helps to talk . . . I've had a lot of help

. . . I wish I'd had it when my father died . . . I never thought I'd cry again after that . . . but by damn I have these last weeks . . . I never thought I'd trust again either . . . and now I don't know if I'll ever get back the kind of trust I had with my wife . . . six weeks ago tonight it was . . .

C. I don't know, I sort of . . . don't know what I feel. That's a problem for me . . . it'd be all right if I knew . . . but it's . . . I just find it so hard to identify what I'm feeling . . . I . . . it troubled me a week or two ago when I felt something quite deeply . . . I don't know what it was . . . it worried me . . .

It is possible to understand Phil's remarks about trust and Chris's agony of uncertainty in terms of the group experience. It is difficult to find the kind of trust that the group seeks when the group is not going to meet for a while. It is sometimes safer to be confused about one's feelings than it is to own them.

There are other important points to consider. The first is that Phil talked about the death of his father for the first time, but no one took this up. The conductor allowed this to ride as he did not feel that the group could help Phil to handle deeply sorrowful feelings in their current state. The second is that on many occasions in other sessions, Phil had mentioned that his wife had left him on a group night, but no one had taken this up either. Thirdly, no one contested Phil's repeated claim that anger was out of character for him, despite all the evidence there was to the contrary. This was further evidence of the group's wish to avoid painful areas. However, this thought did not occur to the conductor until after the meeting when it was too late to take it up. The conductor made this closing statement:

Th. There is a lot of uncertainty in the group at the moment . . . there is both a wish to open up more and a fear that to do so would be inappropriate. The group has faced a lot of separations with individual members and now faces another with the break. It seems that there is a resonance between personal losses and the break from the group and there are mixed feelings of relief and regret about the group holiday . . . as there are with other separations. There is a wish to avoid angry feelings and to blame others for individual dissatisfactions . . . Phil blames his wife. . . Elaine blames Janet . . . Janet blames the group . . . the group blames me . . . but perhaps displaces this onto Janet . . . and so on. No doubt these are issues which we will face again, but for now it is time to end the group.

The conductor felt that this was a necessary interpretation to make. The group had been scapegoating Janet and unless he acted to recognise this and the attack she sustained on his behalf there was a risk that she would feel so battered and excluded that she would not return after the break. It would also have been unhelpful to others in the group if he had failed to indicate their projected and avoided feelings of loss and anger. To fail in this would have been to imply that they really were unmanageable.

This group continues to meet and Janet did return from the break. They have their ups and downs, but have managed to deal with anger, loss and vulnerable as well as destructive feelings in a more open way. Phil has managed to cry about the sad loss of his father when he was a small boy and there is a sense of mutual trust and respect for one another in the group.

The skills that the conductor showed in his management of this group only come with experience. It is not really possible to gain this sort of experience in isolation. We all need help and support in recognising our mistakes and in rectifying them. In the next chapter we shall therefore look at supervision and other related issues.

13

Supervision and Training

As we have seen in previous chapters, group work is a multilayered and complex undertaking. There are many considerations that the conductor needs to keep in mind – the stage of the group, breaks, information from last week's group and those that went before, the manifest or consciously available content of the conversation, its unconscious components and concealed meanings, the interpretation of these, the purpose of the group, other forms of communication and their meaning, group defences and other unconscious phenomena. The list continues and is long.

It would be unreasonable to expect anyone to accept the mantle of responsibility for such a serious and difficult undertaking without proper training and support, but this is often the case. Unfortunately, health care professionals, particularly those who work in the mental health sector, are frequently required to take on groups of many kinds without any training in group work whatsoever. All too often the very few lectures on group work that they receive as part of their basic training for a profession are regarded by managers as sufficient to meet the novice conductor's needs.

There is an ambivalence in our attitude towards groups. It is generally agreed that they are a good thing, and that they are therapeutic. They are regarded as intricate structures which are responsive to dynamic forces, they are living organisms which are susceptible to and provoke change. Yet we ask someone who is young and inexperienced (in life as well as in group work) to 'run the group this week'. This sort of unrealistic expectation reveals at best an ignorance of groups and at worst a sloppy attitude to the care and trust invested in us as professionals. Unfortunately, we all have our own examples of ignorance and negligence. We should also remember that senior staff sometimes relinquish their responsibility to junior staff because they have no group skills either. It is difficult to admit to shortcomings, and the sad consquence is that helpful practices become devalued in order to protect the fragile self-images of some senior staff.

Junior staff may be given unwarranted responsibility for many reasons, one of the most important, which is linked to the final comment of the last paragraph, is that the organism, whether it is an institution, an outpatient setting, hostel or society at large, will often resist change in order to maintain the comparative comfort of the status quo. When you don't want a scheme to succeed it should be given to the person least qualified to complete it, so the newly qualified staff nurse will be given the opportunity to establish group treatment on the ward. What has happened in the past is that the new conductor, who begins with such enthusiasm and hope, gradually becomes discouraged and disillusioned, eventually joining the ranks of those who distrust group's and practitioners' group work. The institution can say 'Group work? We tried it and found it wanting, unhelpful and at times harmful to staff and patients.'

Currently there is a new hopefulness, an increased understanding amongst nurses, social workers and other professionals of the value of groups and a greater commitment to successful group work. There is a willingness to learn and a determination to confront shortcomings. Those junior staff who have been charged with the responsibility of running groups are more likely nowadays to deal with the lack of support, supervision and training from within their own institution by looking for it outside, or by forming special interest groups within the employing organisation to give each other peer-group support.

Whilst this is a tremendous help where there has been none before, it is not sufficient to meet all the needs of new conductors. There is such a variety of experiences to be understood within the group that it would be unfair to expect them to be recognised without proper training and continuing supervision. There is much that would be missed by a seminar of peers that would be picked up by a trained or experienced conductor.

One of the biggest problems that new conductors find is that of making sense of the unconscious life of the group. It is difficult to know how to make sense of verbal and other clues which reveal the unconscious component. We have seen in chapters 11 and 12 how this may be done by following links and associations whilst paying attention to what is current in the group's life. It is hard to get the hang of this process if one is attempting it without training and support, it is easy to make mistakes because we place too much or too little attention in one place or another. Where there is supervision from an experienced and trained colleague then it becomes much easier to know whether an observation was right or wrong, timed well or badly, was complete or incomplete, and so on. Exposure to this sort of continuing scrutiny allows the new conductor to build confidence in his developing skills. As time passes he will know more and more than he is making reasonable observations as he has learned more about groups from his supervisor.

It is even better if the new conductor has an experience of training for himself. Such a training, at a reasonable level, would last for about a year and would include a requirement that the trainee become a member of a training group for the duration of the course. A full training as a group worker will take much longer, something like a total of three or more years of intensive experience and learning.

In this way the new conductor has the chance to experience at first hand what the client or patient may feel, and will have the opportunity to recognise and deal with some of the personal problems which might otherwise interfere with or cloud his judgement as a conductor. As a member of the group he will have an invaluable chance to see at first hand how the conductor deals with transference issues, interpretation, the group process, and so on. It would be difficult to lay too much stress on the need for training and the way it may enhance the conductor's skill. All those who work in groups should have sufficient training for their needs and the demands of the task. Even when someone has been offered or has completed a good training, there is no guarantee that he will be a good group worker. It is all too easy for people to become complacent and to believe too much in their own views and skills. For these reasons amongst others it is important for group workers to have regular supervision. Even when trained, it is possible to fall into bad or unhelpful practices.

UNHELPFUL PRACTICES

It would be impossible to give examples of all such practices that can occur: we do not have sufficient space. What we shall do is to take an example from a real situation, embellish it and present it to highlight some of the difficulties which people get into without support or when there is insufficient regard for the value of training.

The following example is taken from the account of a group that was being run in a newly established day hospital. The nurse in charge was a ward sister who had attended a one-year training course, but who had been unable to accept either the teaching that was offered or the group experience part of the training. Because she had attended a training course her managers regarded her as having some expertise in group work. She believed herself to be a skilled practitioner and had been unable to value her teachers or the other members of the training group. She established a group for outpatients that met after lunch every Wednesday.

One of the patients who joined the group after it had been established for a little time was a woman who had struggled for years to manage her difficulties without help and who had recently sought help from her family doctor. He had referred her to the group and she was accepted after an interview. During the assessment process it had been stressed that she should attend regularly and promptly each week.

The woman had attended for the first two weeks and the conductor had been delayed both times by staff meetings which ended late. At the end of the second meeting the group was told that the day hospital would be closed during the following fortnight as all of the staff would be on holdiay. The woman decided that she would go ahead and take the holiday that previously she had considered cancelling in order to attend the group. She did not discuss this in the group as her holidays ran consecutively to the staff holiday.

Whilst she was away the conductor raised the question of her absence with the group and they concluded together that her failure to attend was due to a lack of commitment on her part. The conductor shared with the group information that he had gained from her during her interview, that she had a history of failed relationships. It was on the basis of this information and her unexplained absence that the group reached its decision to exclude her.

Let's take a look at the mistakes that were made, taking it from the beginning. In one sense the first mistake was a management responsibility. An appointment was made because the managers did not understand the skills required of group work practitioners. Managers need and should possess some skills in working with groups, after all they are dealing with staff and with patients as groups throughout the working day. Most managers do not have the opportunity to develop these skills so it would be sensible, when appointments are to be made which call for some particular skill, for the managers to include a recognised practitioner of merit on the interviewing panel.

The conductor was a very confident person who found it hard to listen to the recommendations and advice of others, or to accept offers of supervision from a skilled and experienced conductor. This was a mistake, an example of poor practice. One of the qualities of a good conductor is his ability to recognise his fallibility. He is ready to seek help when it is needed, and is able to recognise when it is necessary. This conductor was unfortunately unable to do this.

During the interview the conductor rightly stressed the importance of promptness and of commitment to the group as a prerequisite of membership, but then was late for the first two group meetings that the new patient attended. The patients were told that it was because of staff meetings running late.

This statement established a number of things. First, that the conductor is a busy person. Secondly, that she has important and (implied) confidential matters to deal with. Thirdly, that patients can wait but that staff can't. Fourthly, that the group members are required to have a commitment to the group which the conductor doesn't share as they have to be prompt and she does not. Whether it was consciously intended or not, whether or not the conductor was aware of her own negative feelings towards the group, she got it wrong. She broke the basic requirement of any therapeutic endeavour. She was inconsistent and inconstant.

The conductor gives a lead to the group for its future behaviour and relationships, she owns the hope and belief which the beginning group cannot feel as yet and holds it in her safe-keeping. This conductor established instead an unhelpful arena of carelessness and disrespect. In many non-verbal ways the group was given the message that they were not as important as the staff, nor were they to be taken seriously.

The next mistake that the conductor made was that she failed to inform the group in advance of any planned holidays and breaks, even though it was a requirement that the patients should take holidays to coincide with the staff holidays and that they should give early notice of any absences outside of these times. The group had neither the opportunity to discuss the break nor the chance to organise their own holidays around the staff break. The woman patient had not been told at interview of the impending break and was not familiar with the expectations of the group. Those she knew were readily breached by the conductor and so she did not take them seriously. It is easy to see that the new patient would feel that she was doing nothing wrong in taking a break that she had neither planned nor discussed with the group. After all, she was only taking her cue from the conductor, who had done exactly the same thing.

The conductor had set an example which undermined trust, prevented the establishment of a quality of containment, and inhibited the development of a sense of group cohesiveness. She had also missed a chance to work on some of the separation issues which undoubtedly would ensue from the announcement of the break. The group's response was pre-empted when it reconvened after the break as the group theme was not allowed to emerge; the conductor focused the group's attention on the absent member. In this way she unconsciously drew away from herself and placed onto the new patient any negative feelings that may have been provoked by the break itself and the manner of its introduction. She sided with the defensive, Basic Assumption aspect of the group and provoked or at least supported a scapegoating attack upon the absent member.

This last mistake had serious repercussions, as it led to the exclusion of the new group member, which were compounded by the disclosure of privileged information that the conductor had gained at interview and which the new patient had not shared with the group herself. It was information from outside the group and as such it was a breach of confidentiality and a further blow to the establishment of trust within the group. In addition to this there had been no attempt to seek information from the new patient about her reasons for her absence. Consequently it was not possible to make an informed decision about the most appropriate response to her behaviour.

The group was invited to make a decision which was really the responsibility of the conductor. The conductor manages many of the boundaries of the group, including and especially membership. When the conductor invited the group to decide upon the new patient's future with the group she breached this boundary and the group consequently became a less safe place.

The conductor should try hard to help the members of the group feel that it is safe to say or feel anything within the group. He has a responsibility to foster honesty, openness and freedom of thought, feeling and communication. This time the conductor failed in that duty and the group tried to fulfill what it thought to be her wishes.

The conductor was perhaps right to conclude that this patient's absence was related to her disturbed pattern of relationships, but she excluded the example established by herself and her staff from her consideration of events. The communication itself may be seen in part as a response to separation, which could be worked with if identified correctly. In other words, it is likely that the new patient thought that it would be all right to take unannounced leave as the precedent had been set by the conductor and her staff. It is also possible that her absence was a response of a different order to the fact of another separation or separations earlier in her life.

Quite often we find when working with emotionally disturbed people that the absence of the therapist or the conductor will provoke an absence or series of absences on the part of the patient. This is related to the feelings of loss and sadness, anger and other negative feelings as well as a sense of need, which the small child may experience when a parent is away or otherwise unavailable for any length of time. The child is not able fully to express his feelings through the medium of spoken language, so he will resort to behaviour in order to evoke in the parent feelings akin to those which he has felt left with.

Observe any small child who has been kept apart from his mother for a number of days and you will see his uncertainty when his mother returns. He may have cried, bereft with loss and anxious for her return since her departure, only to turn his back on her for a time and ignore her or pull away from her when she attempts to comfort him on her return. After a time he will return to her with affection, but only if she remains constant for him and tolerates his abandonment of her. This process is both a communication of feeling (through his behaviour the child evokes in his mother feelings akin to those with which he has struggled during her absence) and a testing-out of his mother's commitment. The child has to be reassured that his mother is not about to abandon him again, so he withholds his affection until he is certain of his mother's continuing affection for him.

In our example the conductor missed these possibilities and assumed that the absence meant a lack of commitment on behalf of the patient. If we think a little more about this we can see that the conductor perhaps was projecting onto the patient her own lack of commitment. This unconscious lack of commitment was made evident by her refusal to accept supervision when it was offered, by her frequent lateness for the group and by her attitude to the group in giving no notice about the break. If we follow this example through we can add that the purpose of the projection was for the conductor to rid herself of an unwanted aspect (lack of commitment) by identifying it with the patient and then excluding the patient along with the unwanted, projected part of herself.

There are a couple of points that need emphasis here. The first is that training is immensely important and that an essential part of the training for psychotherapeutic work, whether with groups or individuals, is for the trainee to have an experience of therapy himself. In this way the would-be therapist can deal with personal problems which could otherwise interfere with his ability to see group or individual processes clearly. Consequently he would be less likely to act out his personal problems in the group as the conductor in the example did.

The second is that, as is obvious from the example, training is not enough. If the training course had been longer there is a possibility that the nurse in question would have dropped out, or that she would have been brought along by the others in the group and would not have been able to keep up her defences against her negative self. In either case this is mere conjecture. The fact remains that she attended a course which her managers thought equipped her for group work. The old adage remains as true as ever: 'You can lead a horse to water but you cannot make it drink.' In this case you can lead anyone towards discovery but you cannot make them think . . . or feel.

In a perfect world only experienced practitioners would find themselves in the position of running groups, but that is not this world. In the real world people with no training at all are asked to take on the responsibility for group work.

Whilst it is not possible to counter entirely the effects of no training or resistances to personal change, they may be alleviated by regular supervision. In the case in point, if the nurse who conducted the group had been required to have regular supervision then many of the mistakes she made and the poor practices she established would not have occurred. The supervising conductor would have noted the group conductor's lateness and would have required her to announce the break in advance. He would have been able to counsel the group conductor to follow the group's lead. Surely, she should draw the attention of the group to the absent member, but only as part of the group process if this is something that they had been avoiding. She should not introduce it as a subject that the group should talk about and decide upon.

The example that we have just looked at identifies many unhelpful practices which, on this occasion flowed from the shortcomings of a conductor. They illustrate the need for training and for supervision, whilst showing that training is not the whole of the sum, the suitability of the trainee is an inevitable part of the equation too. Many of the pitfalls which we discovered through this example may also occur for other reasons, they are not always due to the inability of the conductor to own his or her personal problems. Lack of experience and the powerful nature of group dynamics may also provoke the same practices. The new conductor will find that his ability to work with the more complex aspects of the group is enhanced if he pays attention to the basics.

Many of the faults that we saw in the management of the group stemmed from the conductor's poor grasp of the requirements, basic to group work, of constancy and consistency. The conductor was often late for the group and did not give advance notice of breaks, and she involved the group in decisions about group membership. These are all boundary issues, the management of which, when given proper attention and respect, will go a long way towards enabling the group to build a sense of trust, of group cohesiveness and a feeling of being safely held.

New conductors commonly fail to pay sufficient attention to these important basics in their eagerness to deal with 'significant' issues and in their anxiety that they might miss something of importance.

If the conductor has been patient enough to deal with the basics effectively then it is more likely that these 'significant' issues will arise in the group later in its life. Groups are reasonably tolerant organisms. If the conductor has missed an important piece of information in the welter of communications which he must process, then they will return to the missed theme time and again until it has been successfully dealt with, provided they feel safe in doing so. It is more likely that the group will feel safe in dealing with significant or problematic issues if the conductor has been able to manage successfully the group's boundaries. It is more likely that the new conductor will do this well if he is made aware of the need for and value of these boundaries through his training and through continuing supervision.

THE STRUCTURE OF THE SUPERVISION SEMINAR

It would be as well to state as clearly as possible what is meant by supervision as there is occasionally some confusion. In certain areas the word has become synonymous with the giving and receiving of orders and instructions, or with the service monitoring function of management. There may also be a feeling that there is an implied slight, that the offer is being made because there is covert criticism about the quality of work being undertaken in a particular area or by a particular team. (Sometimes this may be so, but it would be better if concern were openly expressed.) Usually this is not the case. It is more likely that an offer of help will come from an experienced and skilled practitioner if the work being undertaken has already aroused his interest and admiration.

Some who want to seek help may find it hard to request supervision because it might seem like an admission of failure. Nothing could be further from the truth. It is heartening to find those who think enough about their work to want to learn more or to find out if they are doing things well or badly. The willingness to examine oneself through one's work shows a degree of maturity and responsibility which many do not possess. It can be a hard decision to make. The individual exposes himself to the scrutiny of others as he is revealed through his work, when he enters into a supervision arrangement. The conductor in the example is a good illustration of this. If she had sought supervision for her work with this group then her supervisor might have recognised that she was dealing with unacknowledged parts of herself through projection and denial. In seeking supervision she would have risked her supervisor knowing about this aspect of her, but her real concern was more probably to do with finding out about and dealing with these unacceptable facets herself.

Some would-be seminar members are extremely anxious and fear that they will be torn to shreads by the criticisms of others, or that their work will compare unfavourably with everyone else's. These are common worries – we all have them about this sort of thing. When we stop to think about it, aren't they the same as the sort of anxieties that we discussed when talking about the developmental stages of the group? The early concerns of the group are to do with trust and with the management of self-revelation. There is also a preoccupation with uniqueness, usually in some negative area (such as being the worst group conductor ever) which is eventually addressed through the experience of universality that the group offers.

These are some of the preconceptions and worries that people have about supervision, but what is it really? In its simplest form it is a meeting between two people who have a declared purpose in examining a piece of work. Either one or the other may present the work and together they will think about what was happening and why, what was done or said, how it was handled – could it have been handled better or differently, and if so how?

Usually a supervision seminar will be made up of a number of people, perhaps up to eight or nine including the convenor or conductor of the seminar. Supervision for individual work will usually be given individually or in very small groups of two or three. Supervision for group work is given in small groups which compare in size with treatment groups. We will confine ourselves to thinking about supervision seminars for groups.

The first thing to remember is that it is a group, and as such it is governed by the same principles as treatment groups. The seminar convenor has to establish his criteria for membership quite clearly and he has to select the members to ensure compatibility. To some extent there will be a certain amount of self-selection, only those who have an interest in and commitment to group work are likely to want membership.

The convenor's duties in establishing the seminar are the same as those of the group conductor. He has to ensure that the meeting room is private, secure and safe from intrusion. The seminar group will be doing work which is just as important and as confidential as the work of the treatment group. Much of the work done will touch upon the members as they stand as professionals, so confidentiality is equally important.

The seminar convenor has a responsibility to establish the basic guidelines for the seminar, just as he does with the treatment group. These are to do with expectations of constancy of commitment, advanced notification of any breaks or absences, and so on. The reasons for this are the same as they are for the treatment group. If individual members are erratic in their attendance it inhibits the ability of the seminar group to establish the trust and commitment to one another that is necessary before any of them can feel safe in revealing themselves in their work. Consequently, it inhibits the work of the seminar. If members were to be absent regularly then the seminar would be limited in terms of the depth at which it could work; it would be confined more to the surface and the superficial.

The same characteristics that prove helpful to treatment groups prove helpful in the seminar group. There is the instillation of hope, a developing group cohesiveness, a sense of containment, feedback, identification and all the positive benefits that one would expect from the group experience. There is an important difference and that is in the role of the convenor or conductor.

Whereas it is the role of the group conductor to observe the group and to draw to its attention anything in its behaviour or relationships that it might have missed, it is the role of the seminar conductor to help the group to share its knowledge and experience and to keep the seminar focused on the task of examining the group session being presented.

It is usual for seminar groups to be held weekly. This is regarded as being a useful interval, it allows the seminar members to keep in regular contact and thereby establish good working relationships. If the seminar takes place any less frequently than fortnightly then its value becomes severely restricted. In the first place the work rate is considerably reduced and in the second place it is no longer possible to present a series of group sessions, or to see any immediate results in the seminar of the hard work that its members contribute. When a seminar meets weekly it is possible to follow one group over a series of meetings for a number of weeks. If this happens then the seminar can see how the understandings gained or conclusions reached have influenced the work of the presenting conductor and how this may have affected the group.

When the seminar meets it is usually for something like an hour to an hour and a half. One person will present a session from his work with one of the groups that he conducts. Each seminar group will make its own decisions about how this is arranged. Some seminars prefer to arrange a rota so that everyone has a regular opportunity to present. Some prefer to leave it open-ended and to allow the member with the greatest need to use the time by working on a difficult situation. Still others prefer to follow a series of three or more groups with one conductor in order to get a better perspective on the developing themes of the group and of its developmental stage, whilst watching for the influence of the seminar in the presenting conductor's interpretations and observations.

The presenting member will usually speak for a time, giving an account of the group. Again there is a variety of possibilities here. Some seminars require that the contributing member should have prepared a verbatim account of the session immediately after the session took place, in order to aim for accuracy and completeness. Others prefer it if the presenting member does not prepare a written report as the absence of a written report frees him to focus on the issues which were most important or problematic as these will influence his memory.

Usually the seminar members will feel free to interrupt a presentation to ask for more information or clarification about one thing or another. In all seminars it is usual for the members to talk freely amongst themselves about what they think is happening, once the presentation is finished and they are encouraged in this by the seminar convenor. The seminar will often look to the convenor for opinion and advice. In this it is no different from the treatment group that looks to the conductor for his wisdom. It is part and parcel of the group process to make identifications with the conductor. Again, the wise seminar convenor will encourage the seminar to make its own discoveries, but also will work hard at striking the balance between encouraging independent thought and withholding information the seminar needs to be able to make progress in its understanding. The convenor will not let the seminar jump to wrong conclusions but will help it to find its way towards a fuller understanding of the life of groups. No convenor would have stood by and let the conductor in the example make such a mess of her group, but would have intervened as gently as possible and as forcefully as necessary to prevent the worst of her mistakes.

The supervision seminar is an invaluable aid to the work of any clinician and, once the initial anxieties mentioned earlier have been overcome, it is usually a comfortable and supportive meeting for all involved. It is an inspiring way of working as it is possible to see people grow in ability and stature throughout the life of the seminar.

This chapter marks the end of Part III and reintroduces the notion that . . . a group, is a group, is a group. That is, any small gathering of people constitutes a group and all groups are subject to the same principles of development and process, as we have seen with the seminar group. Bearing this in mind, in Part IV we shall look at the application of our knowledge of groups to a number of practical situations.

PART IV
The Group in Context

Introduction to
Part IV

In the first three parts of this book we have followed the development of the individual from the early maternal relationship, through his involvement with the family and into his membership of groups in the outside world. We have seen how these early experiences influence the pattern of his relationships in later life and we have learned how he might work through incomplete and unsatisfactory formative experiences in a group situation. In addition, we have seen that group development is similar to the development of both the individual and the family. We have examined group processes and phenomena, and learned how to use the knowledge gained from this study to understand the concerns that underpin group behaviour. We have discovered how such understanding can free the group to experiment with new and more healthy ways of relating.

The underlying theme has been that *all* groups are governed by the processes described throughout the book and exhibit similar phenomena, whether they are therapy groups, informal gatherings of friends, or formal committees.

In part IV we shall expand this theme by enquiring into the patterns that can be seen in more fluid groupings than we have observed so far. In chapter 14, the links that exist between a number of groups with an ever-changing membership (naturally occurring groups) will be reviewed, as will the interplay between them and other events. Special attention will be given to the unconscious concerns that are thus demonstrated.

Chapter 15 will continue our investigation into interrelating groups by looking at a variety of management styles, the unconscious processes that promote them and the distinctive responses that they produce. In order to achieve this we shall make use of both an analytic and a systems perspective.

In chapter 16 our discussion will be concluded by reviewing the positive properties inherent in one of these management styles and relating them to the form of institutional living that is identified as the therapeutic community (Main, 1946).

A final chapter on beginning in groups has been included in the hope that the student of groups will find some comfort from any anxieties he may have about starting in groups, by reading of the anxieties that others have faced and overcome when in the same position.

14

Naturally Occurring Groups:

A Definition

In order to explore group phenomena, process and development we have largely used examples from therapy or training groups. This is because such groups are reasonably well defined by time and duration and, as most are comprised of groups of strangers, there is a minimum of external influences to muddy the waters of our understanding. Consequently this has helped us to clarify quite complex issues without becoming bogged down in a swamp of outside concerns. The risk has been that, despite repeated statements to the contrary, some readers may have gained the impression that groups are only for the purpose of therapy and that other gatherings of people cannot be therapeutic nor used to understand and work through unconscious difficulties or emotional problems. If this has happened it is to be hoped that such misunderstandings can be corrected in this chapter.

Naturally occuring groups are gatherings of people which take place spontaneously. They are unplanned and fluid. The membership of such groups can have a rapid turnover, or it can remain static for quite lengthy periods of time.

The examples that have been chosen are taken from the acute admission unit of a psychiatric hospital and they are placed in relationship to the events that occurred within a twenty-four hour period and to the other groups that took place on the unit during that time.

One manifestation of naturally occurring groups is the gatherings that will come together and change as people walk from one meeting to another. Five or six people will briefly congregate together to exchange a few words and then move on to form other short-lived groupings, make a comment or two and then move on again. Another configuration is the sort of group that takes place, often with a solid core membership and a peripheral fluctuating membership, such as a handover meeting between staff members. The multidisciplinary team will gather and remain for the duration of the handover and there may often be other staff members who will join for a short while before moving on to fulfil other commitments. A further example might be the patients who come together for breakfast and then move on to form other groups to chat or to perform shared tasks such as washing up, and so on.

So that we can deepen our understanding of naturally occurring groups and their place in the wider picture of institutions, we shall present a number of meetings and related occurrences in chronological order. As we have already said, they are taken from a twenty-four hour period in one psychiatric admission unit.

THE HANDOVER

This meeting is a regular feature of all residential communities providing care for a client or patient group. There will often be at least three 'handovers' in a twenty-four hour period: an early morning meeting between night and day staff, a mid-day meeting between morning and afternoon staff, and an evening meeting between day and night staff. This was a morning meeting which was held to pass information from the night staff to the day staff. The senior nurse on the ward would meet early in the morning with nurses who were finishing their night duty and would then discuss the information received from them with the multidisciplinary team when its members arrived at 9 o'clock.

On this occasion the senior nurse was a staff nurse of considerable skill and experience. It is pertinent to our discussion to note that she was a petite, slimly built woman in her mid-twenties. The charge nurse, a mature man who had been responsible for the ward for over ten years, was on leave and the ward sister was acting as administrative senior nurse to the whole unit. The main focus of attention was upon a series of disturbances which had happened late the previous evening and which involved a tall, middle-aged patient of strong build. The staff nurse reported that this patient had behaved in a consistently violent way for a considerable time. He had thrown chairs about the room, broken windows and thrown heavy ashtrays through the glass in the ward's doors. One of the consultant psychiatrists asked if the patient had been confronted with his behaviour as he believed there could be no excuse for it. The man was his patient and it was his opinion that there was no evidence of any psychotic illness which might otherwise have explained the outburst.

The staff nurse said that he had not been challenged, the patients on the ward were cowed and the staff had decided to let the matter rest until other members of the team had arrived before deciding on a course of action. The consultant's response is significant to later events. He said that it was a pity that the charge nurse was on leave as it was certain that he would have confronted this patient about his behaviour. Some of the staff present left at this moment because they had to attend a community meeting which was due to begin.

THE COMMUNITY MEETING

This was a large meeting that took place four times each week at 9.30 a.m. and was attended by all the patients; there was a firm expectation of attendance as it was part of the programme of treatment. Many of the nurses also attended. In fact, it was usual for all nurses to be present unless pressing matters required that they be elsewhere. They were joined by the occupational therapist for the ward, some of the junior doctors, a psychologist and the social worker. The consultants would each attend at least once each week. On this occasion only the patients, the nurses, the occupational therapist and the junior doctors were present.

The meeting began with a complaint from the patients that the ward washing maching was broken, the door could not be opened and two or three patients had washing in it having decided to share a wash. The patients spoke sullenly and blamed the staff for the broken machine. They said that they could not do anything about it, the staff should set matters to rights; after all they were responsible for what went on in the unit. They asked in a rather petulant way if the staff could make alternative arrangements for them until the machine was repaired and that the staff should find a way of returning the clothes that were still locked in the machine. A staff nurse agreed to do what she could and spelled out what was possible, but the patients continued to talk about the machine as if they had not heard her.

This discussion continued for a little while until a student nurse wondered aloud if the patients might be talking about the machine instead of addressing the violence that had frightened them all the previous night. One of the patients declared that she would rather talk about the washing machine as that was a more pressing problem and several other patients agreed with her. Other nurses supported the student nurse and expressed some concern for the fear that many patients had experienced during the violent outburst and for the fact that they were unwilling to deal with the events, their feelings about them, or the male patient who had terrorised them the previous evening. There was a brief pause and the patient group then mounted a sustained, collective verbal attack upon the perpetrator of the violence.

This was quite a sudden switch and was undertaken with great excitement and, apart from allowing the patient group to ventilate their feelings, was unhelpful and potentially destructive. Mindful of this, the staff nurse who had intervened before spoke up again. She said that she could understand the anger and fear that the patients experienced and their wish to give voice to some of their feelings but that the reaction seemed very extreme, particularly as some of those who were most vociferous in their condemnation had done similar things themselves only recently.

The patient group tried to justify their vehement attack by suggesting that there was a difference as the earlier acts of violence had been committed by women. The nurses questioned this, clearly not taking such denials seriously. The patients continued to attempt to deny any culpability by suggesting that, as they were patients in a psychiatric hospital, they must be either mad or ill and could therefore not be held responsible for their actions. They maintained that their behaviour was beyond their control as individuals.

Another nurse intervened to say that, whilst it was true that they were patients in a psychiatric unit, this did not mean that they had no sense of right or wrong, and that they were there to look at and try to understand their difficulties. He said that acting on impulse prevented, or at least got in the way of, any such understanding being reached. There were general murmurs of agreement amongst the patients and the staff, and one patient thanked the male nurse for what she called his 'wise' contribution. With this the meeting ended.

Once a week the staff on this ward had a meeting of their own to look at any issues that may have arisen between colleagues which would need addressing and to give each other some support and recognition for the stressful work that they were engaged in. It was a time to share and air feelings and to think about the effect of their work upon each of them.

THE STAFF GROUP

This meeting was composed of all the clinical staff involved with the ward and took place at a time when two shifts of nurses overlapped. The consequence of this was that the meeting was a rather large one and was governed by the same processes that bind all large groups. As one would expect, the meeting began slowly, there were many small sub-groupings and pairings evident in the room before the members settled down to work, and there was an initial atmosphere of tension and anxiety. Gradually the conversations that abounded in the room (and which focused on the previous night's violent incidents and upon the consultant's remarks to the staff nurse) diminished until there was a short period of silence. Many members looked around the room but avoided making eye contact with the staff nurse who had been in charge of the ward during the morning shift, although they were perfectly able to make contact with each other. One member of staff, who had more experience of working in groups than many of his colleauges, was able to break the silence:

'It's been a terrible twenty-four hours, I feel as if I've been trampled emotionally speaking, and I don't have to be here for the whole of my working day like some of you do . . . I don't know how you cope'

This remark seemed to lift some of the paralysis and people shifted about in their chairs and began to breathe again. The senior staff nurse spoke up:

'Well I feel as if I don't cope . . . as if I can't cope. It's ridiculous, I am in charge of this ward and I shouldn't be if I can't manage the violence. I had to ask for extra male cover for Heaven's sake!'

This meeting helped her to think about this; how much was realistic self-appraisal, how much was it reasonable for her to expect herself to cope with, how much others could reasonably demand of her, and how much of the personal dissatisfaction she felt was due to the unreasonable expectations of others with which she had become suffused.

The meeting also recognised that one of the reasons why she may have been feeling so bad was because the consultant had made such unfair remarks during the handover meeting at the beginning of the day. He had said that the absent charge nurse would have confronted the violent male patient. In making this remark he had invited an unfavourable comparison to be made between the young staff nurse and the older, more experienced and senior charge nurse. He implied that the staff nurse was weak, inefficient and unworthy of the position of trust and responsibility that she occupied. He failed entirely to acknowledge the difference in size and gender of the two staff members and that the patient concerned was quite large and had been very violent. In other words, an ordinary, important, everyday reality had been completely ignored – that it could be exceedingly dangerous for this slightly

built young woman to confront the large, older, violent man. Normal considerations of safety and concern were set aside and the staff nurse was made to feel that
she should have been able to cope with him alone.

The staff involved in the meeting worked hard and enabled the young staff nurse
to relinquish some of the blame that she had inappropriately been made to feel and
had subsequently apportioned herself. This particular meeting was exceptionally
healthy. It did not fall into the trap of scapegoating the consultant, it acknowledged
his gross insensitivity, lack of understanding and support, but it also recognised
some of the other issues which influenced the cycle of events. There was an early
glimmer of recognition that they were witnesses to and part of an interactive
phenomenon. There was some talk of the community meeting and a vague notion
that the patients might be feeling diminished too, like the staff nurse.

There was a notion that the patients' concern for the washing that was stuck in
the machine might also have symbolically represented some aspect of themselves
which was felt to be missing or unavailable. This theme of feeling that something
was somehow missing or unavailable was given added depth when it was
acknowledged that many of the student nurses who had staffed the ward for four
months or more were to leave at the end of the week.

The senior staff nurse thanked the students for their help and noted that they
would be missed because of the diligence, imagination and the high level of
responsibility that they brought to their work, as well as for the personal qualities
that each owned individually. The meeting ended on this note and some people
made their way out of the room whilst others stayed and chatted, or checked their
diaries, and so on. As the meeting broke up in this way several fluid groups formed
which shared a few comments, parted and reformed as other new groups, whence
the process was repeated and repeated again. These configurations may be termed
'naturally occurring groups'.

THE 'AFTER' GROUPS: NATURALLY OCCURING GROUPS

Much of the talk in these groups was about the meeting that had just ended. Within
the space of a few moments one nurse had been a member of several of them.
During the meeting he had been open and honest in expressing his views and the
understanding he had of the meanings that recent events had for the emotional life
of the ward. It was he who had expressed criticism of the remarks made by the
consultant earlier that day, and it was he too who had suggested that much of what
had happened and the feelings related to these events, may have been linked. He
had taken a view of the ward and its composite groups as an interrelating system of
hierarchies. He had been careful to present his opinions in a non-judgemental way
and to propose that each member of staff had been affected in his or her responses
by underlying, often unconscious group influences which played a role in
determining how each would react. It came as a suprise to him therefore, at least
initially, to hear some of the comments that were being made about the meeting
and his part in it.

In the first two fluid and short-lived groupings, which consisted of some staff nurses and third-year students, he was told that there was general agreement with what *he* had said about the consultant's remarks. His response had been to think that this was a little odd; he had by no means been the only person to express such views during the meeting. He thought it even more strange when he was told that he had 'stirred things up' and that those who were 'responsible for the status quo' would not like it.

In the third grouping he joined he was told that the student nurses who were leaving were valued because of their commitment to the ward and because of their ability to use their initiative in an appropriate and responsible way. It seemed that they were the best students to have passed through the ward in quite a long time. This grouping expressed the opinion that this was due to some recent changes which had been made in the way the ward was managed. Apparently the senior staff had been able to delegate more responsibility to their juniors who had been able to respond by becoming more responsible themselves. Among those who were leaving were students from the General Hospital who had been undertaking a placement in a psychiatric hospital as part of their training. For many of them this was the best placement they had known. They told the male nurse that they thought this was because they had been treated as individuals and that they felt as though the other staff were interested in them as people, rather than as bodies to make up the numbers. In addition they had been encouraged to acknowledge any difficulties that they encountered and this freedom made them feel respected and helped them own up to anxieties and uncertainties as they occurred, without feeling foolish. As a result they had enjoyed a satisfactory learning experience which helped them to feel more confident in using their own judgement, along with a willingness to accept when they were uncertain and to know when to seek help (Wright 1985).

There is a clear discrepancy between the views expressed by the first two groups and the third group. The first two groups had implied criticism of the senior staff as being mainly concerned with continuing the status quo, whilst the third group had suggested that the senior staff were flexible and able to change the way that they worked in order to improve the quality of care their staff provided.

This can be understood as a see-saw phenomenon, in which the group gradually comes to the realisation that the senior staff have qualities of both flexibility and rigidity. It is also evidence of other phenomena that can be seen in groups, especially in those which are based in institutions. These are the processes we first discussed in chapter 1 as splitting and projective identification and which we looked at later in chapter 7 as splitting, projective identification, mutual projection and scapegoating.

In this instance the first spontaneous grouping was engaged in an upward splitting manoeuvre, wherein the uncaring, inflexible aspects of the group's members were split off and projected into the senior staff. The group told the male nurse that he had stirred things up and that those responsible for the ward would not like him upsetting the status quo. The suggestion that this was a splitting manoeuvre is supported by the view of the third grouping which, in contrast, saw the senior staff as being supportive, flexible and willing to listen.

If we examine all of the information that we have gathered so far from the handover meeting, the community meeting, the staff meeting and the after-groups, we shall see how strands of the same processes weave in and out of them all. In this way we shall come to a better understanding of how naturally occuring groups fit into the patterns of communication (both conscious and unconscious) on any ward and in any institution (Menzies, 1976) and we shall see how these meetings are linked to each other.

Interwoven Communications

The first examples of splitting and projective identification that we saw took place during the handover meeting when the consultant criticised the staff nurse. He compared her unfavourably with the absent charge nurse and left others to infer that he believed her to be inadequate for the job.

If we consider where the real authority on the ward lies we see that it rests in the hands of the consultant doctors and the sister or charge nurse. There is usually an investment in keeping things the same in any institution and this may be particularly so when there is a perceived attempt to wrest power and authority from those who have it. Whether or not this staff nurse wished to win some power and authority from her senior colleagues is not material, there can be a perceived threat in circumstances where there is no threat at all. In this case the staff nurse was identified with the staff nurse group and it was the two naturally occurring groups composed of staff nurses who expressed dissatisfaction with the 'powers that be'. The senior staff on the ward would have known about any dissatisfactions before this particular day began; it was a continuing niggle for the staff nurses.

If we think about it, this may have been one reason why the consultant behaved as he did. In order to protect the domain of the senior staff, of which sub-group he was a member, he identified the charge nurse as being able to manage and the staff nurse as being unable. This was a downward split. There were other elements to this example, as we shall see.

The consultant missed the presence of his charge nurse colleague. So much is evident from his remarks. He may also have been identifying one of the reasons why the patient had become violent, although apparently he was not conscious of doing so. He linked the patient's behaviour to the absence of the charge nurse, but he had been unable to go further than this to understand that the violence had been an expression of anxiety to do with loss.

The impulsive, somewhat sulky behaviour which the patient displayed was very reminiscent of the 'protest' stage one sees in children who are parted from their parents for a time (Bowlby, 1974). Furthermore, the charge nurse was clearly seen to have an ability to manage or contain potentially violent patients. As we have seen, the consultant regretted his absence because of this specific ability, which he believed that the staff nurse did not possess. This enables us to make the assumption, with a reasonable degree of certainty, that there was a continuing process which identified the junior nurse group as a whole and the senior staff nurse in particular, with an inability or deficiency in this area. This again is evidence of a downward split.

To recapitulate, we have an upward split in which some of the junior nurses regard the senior staff as being rigid and inflexibly unable to share power or responsibility, and a downward split, in which the senior staff see the junior nurses as being incapable of successfully managing the authority and responsibility they seek. This sort of upward/downward split is a common feature of many organisations (Jacques, 1955). The material from the community meeting would tend to support this contention whilst also suggesting that the patients too had been affected by these unconsciously motivated and unconsciously enacted processes.

At the start of the meeting the patients had complained about the washing machine being broken. They also said that the staff were responsible for the machine and that two or three patients had clothes in it as they had been sharing a wash. If the staff are held to be responsible for the machine, then by a straight forward and logical extension, they can also be thought to be responsible for the washing that gets stuck in it when it breaks down. In this way there is a covert statement that the staff have something which belongs to the patients. Apparently what the staff have is the patients' clothing as it is locked in the machine. However, it would seem from the highly-charged emotional atmosphere that the machine and the clothes have some other significance.

It may be thought that their only other significance is to provide a way of avoiding dealing with the aggressive male patient, but they can also be seen as a reason for the patients' inability to deal with him.

It is easy to accept that the patients use the machine as an avoidance of other pressing problems. There is an easily defined link between the washing machine and the violence that the patients wished to avoid tackling. It became a symbol for the violence and the patients' responses to it. Instead of talking about violence, they talked about the machine, so the broken machine was used as a symbol for other things that the violent patient had damaged and for the harm that he had done to his relationships with others on the ward.

Furthermore, the clothing may be seen as symbolic of the adult, coping part of the patients which was placed in the staff (they were seen as being responsible for the washing that was stuck in the machine), particularly those staff who were seen as strong and capable. Thus, the inaccessible clothing represented those strengths which had been invested in the absent charge nurse, which had become inaccessible too. Consequently we can see that the patients used the broken washing machine not only to avoid talking about the violence, but also to illustrate why they felt they could not; all of their coping, assertive strengths had been invested in the charge nurse and were as absent as he was.

The thread of projected feelings and abilities, anxiety, dissatisfaction, depletion and upward/downward splitting is woven into the whole fabric of this ward. There is evidence of it in the handover meeting with the consultant denigrating the coping abilities of the staff nurse, in the community meeting it can be seen in the material about the washing machine, it was openly recognised in the staff meeting and it influenced the staff, their feelings and their conversation during the naturally occurring groups.

This ward was not unique in being vulnerable to these processes or phenomena; they happen in just about every ward, hostel or organisation in the country. Where they are not recognised, or go unchecked, they can have a profoundly detrimental effect on the well-being of many members of the organisation. If, for example, the staff group had not been able to recognise something of what was happening, then the senior staff nurse would have been left feeling inadequate to manage and depleted of many of her assertive abilities. Any organisation which continues to allow its staff to feel undermined in this way will find that its junior staff move on quickly, thus establishing a high turnover rate, the causes of which lie in the unconscious, splitting processes that we have followed in this chapter.

The first lesson that we should learn from this is that it is useful to pay attention to all communicatons, formal and informal, that take place on the wards and in hostels and clinics day by day, for they tell us a great deal about what the underlying concerns of those associated with them are. The second lesson is that, because it is difficult to understand symbolic communication, some attention should be paid to the quality of relationships between the various groups and individuals on the ward.

Certain types of management structure actively promote some of the potentially destructive processes discussed in this chapter, whilst others are positively enabling and therapeutic. In the next chapter we shall examine some styles of management, with particular attention being given to a systems perspective, and we shall describe some of the responses, or patterns of communication, associated with the various styles.

References

Bowlby J (1974) *Attachment*. London: The Hogarth Press and the Institute of Psycho-Analysis.

Jacques E (1955) Social systems as a defence against persecutory and depressive anxiety. In: *New Directions in Psycho-Analysis*. London: Tavistock Press.

Main T F (1946) The hospital as a therapeutic institution: *Bulletin of the Menninger Clinic*, **10 (3)**: 66–70.

Menzies I (1976) *The Functioning of Social Systems Against Anxiety*. London: The Tavistock Press.

Wright H (1985) One morning in a psychiatric admission unit. *Group Analysis*. **XVIII/I**.

15

Productive Management

When we discussed the importance of supervision and training in chapter 13, we suggested that managers should themselves possess some knowledge of group processes and have some experience of working with groups (see p. 167). There are many reasons for making this assertion. In chapter 13 it was made because managers need to have some idea of what skills group workers require before appointing staff to work in groups. When we consider that managers hold responsibility for running units, wards, hostels and departments which are definable as medium to large groups and that each of these groups is comprised of small groups, the need for them to have group skills becomes much more clear.

The understanding that we have of group processes and their relationship to the unconscious will be examined here from the point of view of the organisational structures that may be identified with wards, hostels and other institutions. Because hospital wards have a much more readily identified relationship with other parts of the institution and the world outside, we shall base our examples on the types of management structure that will be found in them. However, the descriptions provided are equally relevant to other institutions.

The ideas represented in this chapter are already familiar to us; they are based upon the structural and systems perspectives that we discussed in chapter 3 when we looked at the family as a group. The main difference is that here we shall be looking at the ward as a group.

THE WARD AS A GROUP: A STUCTURAL PERSPECTIVE

There is a great deal of truth in the old adage, 'Look after the pennies and the pounds will take care of themselves.' If we watch the basics, then the complex becomes much more available and much more manageable (see p. 101). In group work the basics are the boundaries of the group, which we have examined in detail in parts II and III of this book. If we pay attention to the boundaries of the ward (as a group), then it becomes much more possible to manage it as a healthy organism.

There are many types of boundary structure which wards may adopt, but we shall divide them into three main categories for the sake of clarity. These are illustrated in figure 15.1.

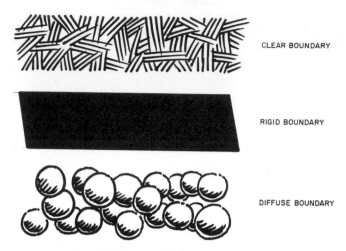

Fig. 15.1 Types of boundary structure

All wards have an individual identity which is given to it by those associated with it and by its relationship with the institution to which it belongs. In turn, the identity of the institution will be influenced by the wards which form it. It would be extremely simplistic to suggest that all wards fall into one of the three boundary types shown above, but if we regard the three types of structure as stages which overlap along a continuum, then we can see how it becomes possible to use them as helpful guidelines when thinking about boundaries (figure 15.2).

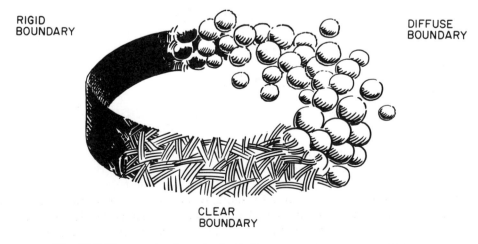

Fig. 15.2 Diagram to show the boundary types merging and blending

Boundaries exist between whole systems, such as one ward and another or one unit and another, and between sub-systems, such as identifiable groups within the wards. There are two easily identified main sub-groups on all wards – the staff sub-group and the patient sub-group. These are further divisible into a sub-group, or sub-system, of nurses and another sub-system of doctors and paramedical staff. There are other sub-divisions that we could follow, for instance the paramedics could be divided into sub-groups of psychologists, physiotherapists, psychotherapists, and so on. For our purposes it is sufficient to stay with three major sub-groupings: patients, junior nurses and senior staff. Within each of these sub-groupings there are many others possible, but to establish them all would serve only to complicate matters and confuse our purpose.

We shall take the three main types of boundary that we have described and apply them to the ward as they relate to the three main sub-groups we have chosen. Using this as our basis we shall discuss their characteristics and their effects upon the ward.

CHARACTERISTICS OF RIGID BOUNDARIES

These are presented graphically in figure 15.3.

Fig. 15.3 Rigid boundaries

It is important to remember that it is unlikely that any unit or ward will conform exactly to all of the descriptions given below. They are included to identify certain characteristics which may be found in wards which comply with the general classification of wards with rigid boundaries. There are many influences which will affect the balance of communication and the emotional climate of the ward, for instance, the addition of a particularly clear-sighted and diplomatic staff member to the staff group may enable an atmosphere of tolerance. This in turn may allow communications between sub-groups to flow more freely. This clarifying consideration is applicable to all three types of boundary; they are not absolutes, merely guidelines. Bearing this in mind it is possible to enumerate the characteristics of groups with rigid boundaries in the following way:

1. As we can see from figure 15.3, the sub-groups which occupy higher positions in the hierarchy of the ward intrude into those lower down.

2. In addition, lower-order sub-groups experience difficulty in communicating with those occupying higher hierarchical positions.

3. This means that there is little real communication across boundaries and between sub-groups of the main group.

4. Consequently, there is little real resolution of the conflicts which may arise between each of the sub-groups. Higher levels in the hierarchy will instruct those lower down, and these will be more likely to resort to subversion, or rebellion rather than discussion as this is found to be fruitless.

5. There is mistrust between each of the sub-groups as personal rights are challenged and held in contempt.

6. Because of the lack of communication, and the consequent lack of real resolution of conflicts between sub-groups, which in turn lead to denial of personal and group rights or responsibilities, there is considerable intrusion across boundaries. The higher-lever sub-groups will communicate to those lower down through instruction and edict, whilst those lower down may sometimes intrude into those higher up through verbal or physical aggression.

7. Responsibilities will be described, but in actuality will be diminished through a failure to provide the authority or resources necessary to their fulfilment.

8. The physical aspect of the boundaries represents the rigid nature of the structure. This is shown by those in higher hierarchical positions becoming inaccessible and remote, with those in lower positions having no access to them.

9. Management is based on the premise that all authority should be centralised in the focused grip of the person most senior in the hierarchy. It is biased towards autocracy and is suspicious of the legitimate aims of those lower down the hierarchy. The hierarchy is steepened.

10. Authority does not exist in any real form, that is, it is not based upon earned respect, but upon a 'discipline' which values blind obedience and scorns human qualities. The impetus is towards stasis through the disintegration of the group into opposed factions and the consequent disintegration of the internal structures of the individual via the processes of splitting and projective identification.

THE EFFECTS OF RIGID BOUNDARIES ON THE WARD

It should be said that it is unlikely that any staff group will make a conscious decision to operate a management structure that is based on a system of rigid boundaries. It is much more likely and more usual to find that such structures grow spontaneously in response to unconscious, individual and group processes, as we saw in the previous chapter.

The ward that we used as our example in Chapter 14 could be described as having features of both clear and rigid boundaries. If we were to place it along the continuum, it would straddle the point at which these two types of boundary meet. It could be seen to have features of rigid boundaries as clearly members of the three sub-groups (senior staff, junior nurses and patients) were suspicious of each other. Its clear boundaries were represented by a willingness to communicate, to delegate, and the intention to treat the student nurses as individuals. All wards are living organisms and this ward was in a state of flux which was provoked by the impact of a number of factors, including the particularly able group of students. Consequently the quality of the boundaries which operate at any given moment will be affected by a variety of changing influences. These include the personal characteristics of individual members of all the sub-groups, breaks and holidays, staff morale, the levels of trust and cohesiveness throughout the ward, and so on.

The ward that operates a system of rigid boundaries would have a staff group that fails to communicate. There would be meetings, but these would tend to be information-based, the talk would be about 'facts' and diagnoses would be 'reified', that is, they would be treated as if they were real, as if they really did describe the people to whom they were allocated. Consequently, the person of the patient would remain unknown, his emotional life would be regarded only as it related to the diagnosis, and all his moods and his behaviour would be considered in terms of the diagnosis. There would be little or no discussion of relationships and these again would be qualified by the diagnosis, as in such remarks as: 'That's typical of the manic depressive . . . ', or 'Yes, that's classic schizoid behaviour . . . ' These statements are similar to and reminiscent of the way in which patients are sometimes talked of in general hospitals. The purpose is the same; it is to see the individual as a collection of parts, rather than as a whole human being, in order that we might not be touched by his humanity and face echoes of his distress in ourselves. In addition there would be identifications made or labels given such as 'troublemaker' or 'professional patient'; such descriptions would be seen as the sum of the patient, or the staff member.

The meetings on these wards would allow no debate and most of the staff would be silent, with most of the discussion (such as it is) being undertaken by the senior staff. Patients would often be expected to attend part of these meetings to give an account of themselves and it would be unusual for any member of staff to think that this might be unfair and even alarming to them. If they did they would find it nearly impossible to voice such humane concerns and would be likely to find themselves branded as naive at best, or as troublemakers at worst.

There would be an apparent understanding of roles, but this would be accompanied by feelings of confusion and worthlessness in the staff, particularly the junior nurses, who would not feel that their contributions were either valued or therapeutic. If the staff were to feel like this then the same would apply to the patients, but for them it would be worse as they would be the final recipients of downward projections of unworthiness and inability.

Staff and patients would not mingle freely and it would be likely that the office would be the nurses' base, from which they would make occasional forays onto the ward. When on the ward nurses would tend to remain in groups, as would the patients. Privacy would not be respected and the staff would retain the right to pry in the name of treatment.

Other ancillary groups of staff, for example the porters, cleaners and maintenance staff, would see parts of the ward as their 'territory' and would act as if they should always have a right of access to them, despite any considerations which might suggest otherwise (such as group meetings and individual sessions with nurses). Conversely, the authority of the medical staff and the privacy of the medical interview would be fiercely defended. The relatives of patients on the ward would be excluded except at well-defined and arbitrarily decided times.

There may be an atmosphere of discontent, or even hostility, with staff and patients being suspicious of each other, and junior and senior staff being wary of and denigrated by each other. Alternatively, senior staff may be unrealistically idealised by their juniors. Denigration and idealisation are opposite sides of the same coin, whose value is measured in terms of the opportunities for splitting and projection. In denigration the senior staff are identified with the failings of their juniors, whilst in idealisation they are recipients for the positive qualities which it is unsafe for the junior staff to retain.

Those highest in the hierarchy would insist on making the smallest decisions for staff and patients alike, whilst those lower down would feel unable to make any decisions for themselves. This would lead to patients asking for permission to do anything and everything; even to go to the hospital shop.

There would be evidence of an upward/downward split with the various hierarchical levels voicing criticisms like:

● 'These students are useless, they can't do anything sensibly and won't think for themselves . . . I have to do everything for them . . . '

● 'Sister is hopelessly out of touch, she doesn't know and can't understand what is happening . . . we know far better what needs to be done'

This will lead to a prevalence of 'us' and 'them' views of reality becoming established.

Such wards are obviously unhappy and unhealthy places, but their unconscious purpose is to avoid the conflicts and anxieties that are provoked by the resonances between our own feelings and those of our patients. It is not only wards with rigid boundaries that operate in this defensive way, those with diffuse boundaries also use techniques of avoidance to protect against painful emotional contact.

CHARACTERISTICS OF WARDS WITH DIFFUSE BOUNDARIES

1. Figure 15.4 shows that communication would be muddled and confused. The source from which any communication emanates would be unclear, the direction uncertain and any positive outcome would be improbable.

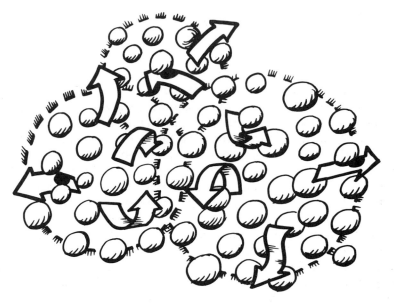

Fig. 15.4 Diffuse boundaries

2. Conflicts between individuals and sub-groups would be denied and therefore would be left unresolved. Differences between groups and between individuals would be unacknowledged, betraying a defensive fantasy or unconscious wish to believe that everyone is the same and therefore absolutely equal.

3. There would be no such thing as individual rights, the group would behave as if it were an absolute, single entity.

4. There would be a massive intrusion across boundaries as boundaries are not recognised.

5. There could be no clear identification of responsibility or where responsibility lies. It would be placed rather vaguely in 'the group'.

6. Authority would be confused with authoritarianism and such notions as: 'Authority is a denial of individual freedom' would gain general credence. Consequently it would be unlikely to find any healthy confrontations taking place. Thus the ward would lose its therapeutic value.

7. Management would be by demand and by mistake. In such systems it becomes very difficult to identify lines of responsibility and authority. Again, the impetus is towards stasis through the denial of the differences between oneself and others, and it may be seen as a defence against anxieties which would be provoked by having genuinely to face oneself and others. In other words, the form of structure is unconsciously adopted in order to prevent any enquiry which would provoke dis-ease in the staff through their having to encounter discomforting echoes in themselves of their patients' emotional pain.

THE EFFECT OF DIFFUSE BOUNDARIES ON THE WARD

We would see no distinctions made between different groups – staff and patients would mingle freely in each area. There would be no such thing as privacy, every area and every thing would be shared inappropriately. This would disregard the human need for personal space and ownership. The need for any change – whether personal or a change in the stucture of the ward – would be denied and opportunities for health-promoting confrontation would be lost.

There would be no definition of roles and a concommitant denial of worthlessness. Skills and experience would not be valued and may even be denigrated as 'elitist' because those with skills could be arbiters of the very change which is so rigorously prevented. Consequently everyone would be thought capable of doing anything, without training.

There would be an increased tolerance of apparently bizarre behaviour, which would be directly related to the dissolution of the boundary stuctures of the inner world of the individual. Such dissolution is promoted by intrusions across personal boundaries endemic to such wards. Distinctions between self and other, or inner world and external reality are continuously eroded. This would be visible in many ways, including the openness of the ward; visits from outsiders would be tolerated at almost any time. Even those with no legitimate reason for being on the ward may be neither questioned nor excluded (as has happened on more than one ward). As no distinction is made between inside and outside by the staff, it becomes more difficult for patients to maintain fragile personal boundaries between the inner world and outside reality. So fantasies may be enacted in reality without any notice being taken of them.

Meetings would frequently run over time and could be cancelled for one reason or another. No one would question this, nor would the absence of ward members from meetings be questioned. If any questions were to be asked the answers would most likely be lost somewhere in the muddle.

Once again it is worthwhile remembering that the properties that we have described as defining rigid and diffuse boundary structures are given only as guidelines, not as absolutes. Each of the characteristics oulined is real in the sense that they have actually been seen and identified on a number of wards and in a variety of types of institution. Those listed under the heading of 'rigid boundaries' are most commonly seen in wards with this type of boundary structure, and those identified with 'diffuse boundaries' are often seen in wards with diffuse boundaries. However, some wards which are defined as having rigid boundaries will often display one or more of the attributes usually discovered in diffuse boundary structures and vice versa. Nevertheless, the general outline provided in this chapter will be of assistance in making preliminary and informative observations about the nature of the system functioning on any given ward and will offer useful indicators of the prevailing unconscious anxieties and the defensive mechanisms being operated against them.

The first two boundary structures so far identified may be regarded as being dysfunctional as they militate against personal growth and the opportuntiy to deal effectively with interpersonal relationships. Whilst this is true as a general statement, or as an ideal, it must be remembered that such structures grow out of the need of the staff to find a way of coping with people and problems which are extremely distressing. It would be wrong to suggest that all wards should dismantle their particular (dysfuntional) structures overnight if this were to leave the staff unsupported and vulnerable. It is necessary to establish other support networks before they can successfully and humanely be replaced. If they are to be replaced, then how would we describe a better structure, and what would its characteristics be?

CHARACTERISTICS OF WARDS WITH CLEAR BOUNDARIES

Figure 15.5 shows the properties of wards with clear boundaries.

Fig. 15.5 Clear boundaries

1. There is open and responsive communication across boundaries and between sub-groups within the main group.

2.   Because communication is open it becomes more likely that conflicts between individuals and between sub-groups will be resolved appropriately, fairly and usually amicably.

3.   The rights of groups, sub-groups and individuals are acknowledged, respected and fostered.

4.   This leads to boundaries remaining intact with little or no intrusion across them, for this would be unnecessary.

5.   The responsibilities of each group, sub-group and individual are openly acknowledged and respected.

6.   Each group and sub-group is accorded the authority and given the information necessary to fulfil the responsibilities appropriately delegated to it (Menzies 1988).

7.   Physical boundaries, such as the entrance to the ward or to individual rooms, are respected by outsiders. Visitors to the ward have to seek the permission of the staff before entering the ward and the staff ask for permission before walking into a patient's bedroom. Appropriate access is usually freely given.

8.   Management is based upon an acknowledgement of the importance and value of the characteristics listed above and upon a recognition of the needs of the individual to privacy, respect and some personal space. This leads to the establishment of responsive hierarchies which are biased toward democracy and are sympathetic to the legitimate aims of those placed lower in the hierarchy. The impetus is towards healthy growth through the integration of the individual within a healthy society, which in turn enables the integration of internal structures within the individual. The hierarchy is clear and is flattened to an appropriate degree.

THE EFFECT OF CLEAR BOUNDARIES ON THE WARD

We would see a staff group who talk together in a way which values and is respectful of each member and his opinions, views and feelings. We would find that each member of the team has a clear understanding of his role and is able to act sensibly upon the responsibilities invested in him. He would be assisted in this by being delegated the appropriate degree of authority necessary to fulfil these responsibilities. The same would be true of the patient group. Their rights and responsibilities would also be recognised and they too would possess an appropriate level of authority. Staff and patients would be united in approaching the main tasks which define membership of the ward. In general terms these may be described as dealing with the illnesses which cause admission to the wards of general hospitals and dealing with the emotional and relationship difficulties which lead to admission to psychiatric hospitals or specialist hostels.

In both examples staff and patients alike would be regarded as whole persons. In other words, their physical, emotional and spiritual selves would be acknowledged, respected and valued.

We would notice that staff and patients intermingle in a variety of 'naturally occurring' and formal groups in the ward throughout the day, and that, particularly in the case of psychiatric wards and units, they would be indistinguishable one from the other. Badges of rank and uniforms would not be obvious or apparent. They would not be required as the members of the ward would be known to one another and visitors to the ward would be introduced in an ordinary way, just as colleagues in an office would be introduced to visitors. Some areas of the ward would be shared, including the office, but privacy would be respected.

Visiting hours would be arranged to suit local needs, such as the availability of public transport, the needs of the patients and the ward's treatment programmes. It would be possible to make special arrangements and this flexibility would take into account the balance that is required between the patient's need for treatment and his continuing need for satisfactory continuing contact with family and friends. Children, for example, need more frequent visits than adults. When a parent is a patient in hospital then his or her children may need very regular contact if they are not to suffer from the effects of an enforced separation later in life. So many of our adult patients have experienced considerable periods of separation as children when a parent was hospitalised for a long time. We should do all that we can to ensure that the difficulties that accrue from this sort of loss do not continue into subsequent generations.

Visitors to the ward, including maintenance staff, porters and patients' visitors, would arrange their visits by negotiation with the ward staff and the patients residing on the ward. They would call at the front door (i.e. the ward office) before entering the ward proper, or patients would meet their visitors.

In these days of increasing concern for the safety of staff and patients such measures can be seen as sensible and appropriate as they assist in maintaining a reasonable level of security. As individuals we are increasingly aware of the danger from intrusion by outsiders. Even when hospital employees gain entrance to a ward when this has not been negotiated and agreed, there is a sense of intrusion which we may disregard or push to the back of the mind. Yet it is still experienced and may touch us in other ways, perhaps as a feeling of vague unease or discomfort, or as a feeling of uncertainty, or as an increasing lack of self-confidence, or a diminishing sense of personal worth. It is essential to our emotional well-being that ordinary boundaries such as these are properly managed (Menzies, 1988).

It may be helpful to consider that we would be irritated or offended if the milkman, the postman or the plumber walked into our homes without seeking permission first. It would also be frightening and extremely disconcerting for our children suddenly to find strangers walking into their bedrooms. The equivalent of this sort of thing does happen to our patients, and although it may not be intended it is demeaning and denigrating. In a ward which operates a system of clear boundaries this would not be likely to happen, but if it did the patients would feel free to confront the staff about it, and they could expect to be heard. We would see also that staff and patients alike would confront each other about their feelings and responsibilities over a wide sphere of interests and issues. In addition junior staff would feel acknowledged by senior staff and, whilst rank or office would be respected, the qualities of the individual would form the basis to the respect he earns.

If we were to sample the atmosphere of the ward, then we would find that it is somehow ordinary, whilst being healthy and exciting. There would be an air of hopefulness and an acceptance of emotional pain. In some ways it would seem more like life at large than life in hospital. This would be an advantage as the problems that life presents to the individual continue to be accessible in the ward.

Before this chapter is concluded it is worth remembering that even wards which have clear boundaries are subjected to a number of influences that have an impact upon them. Holidays, admissions, discharges, staff departures and arrivals, the 'age' of the patient group, all affect the boundaries of the ward. Any changes may tilt the structure towards a rigid or a diffuse system. In general, wards with clear boundaries will be able to tolerate and adjust to such fluctuations appropriately without swinging too far away from the clear position, before returning to open and honest ways of communicating. There is always a temptation to suppose that the responsibility for rigid or diffuse management systems rests entirely with the senior staff. It is true that they contribute to the establishment of such structures, but it is not true to say that they are to blame. Sometimes senior staff find that there are extremely powerful resistances to their determined efforts to pass authority and responsibility down the hierarchy. Once again, this makes the point that organisations are interactive, living organisms whose management structures often are not based on any plan or design, but are unconsciously achieved compromises aimed at avoiding anxiety.

In the next chapter we shall develop our understanding of what constitutes productive management by examining the therapeutic community, which may be regarded as an evolutionary, or higher form of the ward with a clear boundary structure. We shall examine the basic concepts which originally defined therapeutic communities and relate these to established communities operating today. It is important to bear in mind that all of the principles of productive management and some of those relating to therapeutic communities are as applicable to general hospitals as to the world of psychiatry.

Reference

Menzies Lyth I E P (1988) *The Dynamics of the Social: Selected Essays*. London: Free Association Books.

16

Therapeutic Communities

When attention is paid to the management of boundaries, so that the ward begins to operate a higher level of communication, then we often see an improvement in the atmosphere of the ward and in the funtioning of individuals within it. We know that physically ill people feel better and recover more quickly if their emotional, as well as their physical needs are attended to. It is something we have known since at least the beginning of this century and, if we pause to reflect, we realise that it is something that we have always known as a self-evident truth.

Because of the inexaustible demand for nurses to serve in military hospitals during World War I many local, general and children's hospitals were short of staff. The obvious answer was to welcome mothers and other relatives to undertake nursing care of the patients. Where this was done it was found that recovery was more rapid and, in many cases, more complete. However, at the end of the war the country returned to the established practice of excluding family and friends from hospital, except at carefully defined times. Bearing in mind that recovery rates had improved radically in these hospitals during the war years, the decision to exclude relatives could not have been made for the benefit of the patients. Yet this is what patients and their relatives were told, and in some areas are still being told.

The failure of some hospitals to respond in an open and flexible way to the needs of individual patients and their families is clearly anti-therapeutic. This is true of both psychiatric and general hospitals. Both can, and should, operate in ways which support the total well-being of their patients, the emotional as well as the physical. Some of the ideas which follow could usefully be applied to many settings which provide residential care, e.g. homes for the elderly, general hospital wards, children's homes, residential schools, and so forth. It would make a great deal of sense, for example, for communities to have regular meetings together to discuss the wishes of the residents, and for the residents of a variety of homes to be able to voice their hopes, fears, desires and criticisms of each other and of the staff. Would it not be sensible for the wards of hospitals to seek the views of patients and their relatives about matters which concern them and upon which they could appropriately express an opinion?

When we discuss therapeutic communities, we shall be thinking particularly of settings where a particular form of treatment is practised. However, it would be useful to bear in mind that our discussion will help us to recognise other types of community which are therapeutic rather than anti–therapeutic, and why.

CHARACTERISTICS OF THERAPEUTIC COMMUNITIES

Since Main first coined the term in 1946, there have been many attempts at describing the ingredients which go into the making of a therapeutic community. Rapoport (1960) in his review of the work at The Henderson listed four qualities:

1. *Communalism*   This establishes the view that everything that happens within the community is to be shared openly.

2. *Democratisation*   This refers to the notion that all members of the community should share equally in the decision-making process and in the use of power.

3. *Permissiveness*   This recognises the view that the community should be able to accept and to tolerate the behaviour of its members which may be abnormal or even bizarre at times, whilst remaining free to comment upon personal responses to it.

4. *Reality confrontation*   Each member of the community would be faced with his behaviour and the consequences of it by having it reflected back to him each and every day, throughout the day.

Since then others have added to the debate, including Clarke (1965) who describes a number of properties in his review of the work done at Fulbourne Hospital.

1. *Size*   It should be small enough for people to know each other reasonably well.

2. *Meetings*   The community should meet regularly, even daily, and the meeting should include all associated with the community, including domestics and so on.

3. *Philosophy*   The underlying philosophy is a belief in psychodynamic principles.

4. *Social analysis*   Events in the unit are discussed in the meetings of the community so that they might be understood.

5. *Freeing of communications*   The flow of communication between various levels in the hierarchy is improved.

6. *Flattening of the authority pyramid*   The hierarchical structure is lessened and in this way the various levels in the hierarchy have improved access to one another and it becomes more possible to include an emotional element in the contacts between each level.

7. *Learning experiences*   Patients are provided with a secure (contained) environment in which it is safe to experiment with new ways of managing their difficulties.

8. *Role examination* Patients and particularly staff regularly examine their performance in their work and this enables them to change to more effective ways of working.

There is much in the above which is valuable, but as with all good ideas there is always the possibility of abuse. In fact many institutions which identify themselves as therapeutic communities, or as operating on therapeutic community principles, fall far short of the mark. This is often to do with a misguided idealism, a misunderstanding of the meaning of certain of the terms, or a failure to pay sufficient attention to the basics.

How do characteristics of productive management and therapeutic communities compare with each other? Is there any comparison between their guiding principles and those established as necessary to the development of the individual as a secure and stable person who is able to establish and maintain mutually satisfying, caring relationships with others? Let us take a look at them, using our definition of productive management as the basis for comparisons.

For the sake of clarity the elements which define productive management will be printed in *italics*, whilst the portion of the text which refers to the definition of the therapeutic community will be printed in ordinary type face.

Comparisons

1. *There is open and responsive communication across boundaries and between sub-groups within the main group.*

This is similar to 'freeing of communications', in which attention is given to facilitating the passing of information between levels in the hierarchy of the therapeutic community (figure 16.1). It is also similar to the maternal relationship wherein the mother attends to the infant's needs by being prepared to receive all of

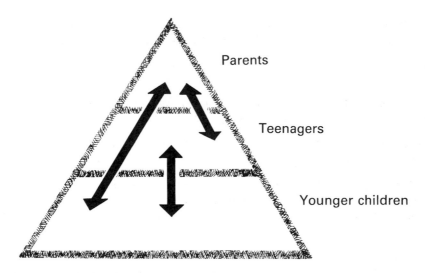

Fig. 16.1 An open, responsive hierarchy

his communications and to the pattern of relationships that would be found within a 'healthy' family as described in chapter 3.

2. *Because communication is open it becomes more likely that conflicts between individuals and between sub-groups will be resolved appropriately, fairly and usually amicably.*

This compares with the way in which reality confrontation is described and relates to the prototype for an effective resolution of conflicts which most families manage, most of the time. In some communities this principle unfortunately has been misunderstood and has been used as an excuse for verbal aggression. For example, in one community a patient had been talking about his feelings of resentment towards one of the charge nurses. This was perfectly reasonable, it is the sort of contact that one might expect in everyday life and which one would certainly strive to achieve in a therapeutic community. Unfortunately the charge nurse responded by angrily suggesting that the patient concerned only felt able to voice his feelings with others present and was not man enough to tackle him face to face in a 'fair' fight. Obviously this has nothing to do with what Rapaport meant when he wrote about reality confrontation; clearly it is bullying, and is likely to prevent an honest willingness to openly face relationship difficulties. It is a feature of communities with 'steepened' hierarchies (figure 16.2).

Fig. 16.2 A steepened, insensitive and intrusive hierarchy

3. *The rights of groups, of sub-groups and of individuals are acknowledged, respected and fostered.*

The intention of any community would be to establish and maintain the rights and freedoms of individuals, but the views which are held about these may differ greatly. If we consider the sort of community that is sometimes established for the treatment of drug addiction (with the deliberate reduction of its newest members to a condition of dependence, a system of rewards for good behaviour, the limitations placed upon personal liberty and so on) we might think that rights are contravened. In some cases this may be so, but if we further consider that each member would have been told about the regime before agreeing to admission, then we would get a different picture. Certain rights have been rescinded willingly in order to gain entrance to the community and to the help needed. If we place alongside this the knowledge that some addicts are completely unable to resist temptation whilst still chemically addicted, then we can see that such communities may be operating a system which prevents certain groups of individuals from destroying the help which is offered. In these terms, the right to treatment is protected by appropriately withdrawing other rights for specified reasons, with the agreement of all participants.

Democratisation might be seen as protecting and respecting the rights of individuals, and where it is properly managed it does. Yet it is sometimes abused and misunderstood to mean that the whole community has the right to make decisions which would more correctly be the responsibility of the staff.

The senior staff of the community are charged by a higher-order system, for example the NHS, with running the community. They are allocated funds for the payment of staff, for maintenance, domestic and catering requirements, planned developments, and so forth. The senior staff allocate some of these funds to middle-line staff to manage and it is their responsibility to allocate money to the clinical areas that they manage. In a 'total' therapeutic community – that is, one which intends to use every aspect of community living as a focus for treatment – budgets will be managed by patients working closely with clinical staff.

Patients will be democratically elected to positions of responsibility for a number of budgets, say a cleaning budget, a cooking budget, a decorating budget, etc; in fact, every aspect of the everyday financial life of the community. Hence, patients would be responsible for buying, preparing and presenting the food for the whole community, for buying cooking and cleaning materials, toilet rolls, paints and wallpaper, and so on. This is helpful as it provides an opportunity for people to examine the way that they conduct real relationships and manage real responsibilities in an atmosphere of tolerant enquiry.

They would not be responsible for future developments nor for staff pay as this would be entirely innappropriate. However, some communities do try to operate by sharing responsibility for selection and disciplining of staff with the patient group. This breaches many of the boundary structures which would otherwise provide the containment that people need in order to face up to their problems. Furthermore, there would be unconscious motivation to select staff members in the same ways in which friends are selected, with the concomitant risks that the staff members chosen would be more likely to support patients in their existing views of the world and that opportunities for change would be subsequently limited.

It is not helpful to avoid the differences between the staff and the patients. The most obvious of these is that the patients are there for treatment and the staff are not. This statement is not made to establish a difference of value and it is not meant to convey the notion that staff are inherently healthy people who will never need treatment. It is acknowledged in order that we might consider why these failures of definition and boundary occur.

This blurring of roles between patients and staff is similar to the blurring of staff roles that has been recommended by some well-known advocates of therapeutic communities. This is a feature of diffuse boundary structures wherein muddle, confusion and uncertain role-identity are used as a defence against the anxiety which is produced by conflict. If we are all the same then we do not have to experience differences, nor the envy, jealousy and hostility that ordinary differences reveal. These are the sorts of issue which are dealt with by any family day by day, the parents appropriately and sensibly recognising the differences of age and responsibility that exist between their children, or the jealousy that is sometimes felt by any child. Mostly these issues will be managed openly and fairly in a way which helps the child effectively to resolve many of his conflicts.

When a community seeks to avoid such areas of conflict it is a denial of proper authority and prevents helpful confrontation. Or as Dr Tom Main puts it (1983):

● Is it not an example of the defence of appeasement against persecutory anxiety, the fear of being attacked for being active and clear? . . . Better if the staff fears about pursuing a role which is essential but unpopular are brought to light, discussed openly and studied in depth by all as human equals.

If this were done as Dr Main suggests then we would find that:

4. *This leads to boundaries remaining intact with little or no intrusion across them, for this would be unnecessary.*

Once again the intention in many communities would be to promote healthy structures, but the notion of Communalisation (Rapoport 1960) as it is described by Clarke (1965) would seem to encourage a chaotic breaching of boundaries:

● 'Communalisation: Equality and sharing were valuable; everyone should express their thoughts and share them with others.'

Unfortunately these words have been open to misinterpretation and have been understood to mean that everyone should speak to everyone else about everything, all of the time. No one would feel that he could or should speak with, say a hundred people about his thoughts and feelings. In everyday life we might share personal and intimate details with some close friends, but rarely with more than two or three, perhaps four at most.

Sometimes communities fail to recognise the importance of personal and sub-system boundaries in their headlong pursuit of the truth and of therapy at all costs. Sharing is important, so is equality, but they must be governed by what is sensible and appropriate. It is the responsibility of the staff to help their patients, many of whom may have a weak sense of identity, by maintaining system and personal structures for them. We should not encourage the further dissolution of internal structures by encouraging an indiscriminate spilling over of one into another and each into each. As the mother helps her child towards a sound sense of self by managing the boundaries between self and other for him, so should we as staff help our patients by managing an appropriate level of intimacy and self-revelation.

These issues are complex, and it is generally true that most of us prosper in circumstances which provide well-maintained boundary structures. When the hierarchy is clear and responsive, it becomes possible to work with groups of people who need a more intensive approach which is designed to maximise the potential for change offered by the community. Everything is seen as communication, every act, omission, comment or gesture; and all communication is available to a quality of enquiry which leads to a psychological understanding of why. If this depth of involvement is to be required of patients and staff within the community, then it is imperative that roles and responsibilities are clear and well defined.

5. *The responsibilities of each group, sub-group and individual are openly acknowledged and respected.*

If we were to take the concept of democratisation and misapply it, as sometimes happens, then we would see that it runs counter to point 5. If we understand democratisation to mean that everyone's opinion is as good as everyone else's about everything (which is how it has been described) then there is a denial that some areas are the particular responsibility of one particular group or another. There may be a denial that some people have training and ability, some have ability and no training, some have training and no ability and so on. Once again, all differences which might reveal envious, jealous or other hostile feelings are avoided along with other conflictual issues and consequently cannot be dealt with by the community.

In the therapeutic community democratisation should be encouraged and fostered appropriately. For example, it would be appropriate for the community to vote upon who amongst the patient group should represent the patients' viewpoint at management meetings, but it would be inappropriate for the patient representative to have a vote at the management meeting. The staff are charged with the responsibility of management and it is they who will be censured for mismanagement, not the patients. Just as there should be 'no taxation without representation', there should be no representation without obligation.

6. *Each group and sub-group is accorded the authority and given the information necessary to fulfil the responsibilities appropriately delegated to it.*

This is what is meant by 'flattening of the authority pyramid', and is something which will happen anyway if the other conditions of productive management are met.

Sometimes it is misunderstood to mean that everyone has equal authority, which is why the description in point 6 is clarified by acknowledging that appropriate authority is delegated. Once again there is a risk that misinterpretation could lead to the dissolution of boundaries and chaos in the community as a defence against the anxieties that conflicts to do with authority would otherwise disclose (figure 16.3).

7. *Physical boundaries, such as the entrance to the ward or to individual rooms, are respected by outsiders. So, visitors to the ward would seek the permission of the staff before entering the ward, and the staff would ask for permission before walking into a patient's bedroom. Appropriate access is usually freely given.*

In most reasonably well-managed communities there would be an adherence to these principles, but because flexibility is sometimes confused with unquestioning tolerance it is sometimes understood to mean that anything goes.

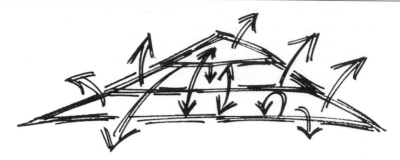

Fig. 16.3 An overflattened, chaotic hierarchy

There is one well-known community which is housed in the ward of a psychiatric hospital and is used as a shortcut to other areas of the hospital by the residents of other wards. This is an example of ineffective (anti-therapeutic) boundary management, which leads to an identification with poor role-models (i.e. the staff who fail to manage boundaries) and to a sense of uncertainty and insecurity. Isabel Menzies Lyth (1988) writes about this in the following way:

● An aspect of healthy development in the individual is the establishment of a firm boundary for the self and others across which realistic and effective relationships and transactions can take place and a sense of one's own identity be established.

8. *Management is based upon an acknowledgement of the importance and value of the characteristics listed above and upon a recognition of the needs of the individual to privacy, respect and some personal space. This leads to the establishment of responsive hierarchies which are biased towards democracy and are sympathetic to the legitimate aims of those placed lower in the hierarchy. The impetus is towards healthy growth through the integration of the individual within a healthy society, which in turn enables the integration of the internal structures within the individual. The hierarchy is clear and is flattened to an appropriate degree.*

This last quality of productive management systems serves also to illuminate the aims of therapeutic communities. The intention is to provide an atmosphere of tolerance within an environment that is established upon a respect for the individual and a willingness to recognise and to work with his feelings as they are revealed in the relationships he develops within the communtity. This means that many different points of view would be accepted and each, whether it is expressed by a member of staff or by a member of the patient group, would become available for thoughtful enquiry.

We have taken quite a long look at the characteristics which define therapeutic communities and examined them alongside the qualities which enable productive management, whilst identifying a number of properties which are sometimes poorly understood and consequently misapplied. One further comment needs to be made. There are many points of contact between the characteristics of productive management and of therapeutic communities, but whilst it is not possible to apply all the qualities which define therapeutic communities to all residential situations, it is possible, and desirable, to apply all the features identified with productive management to a wide variety of management situations, including residential communities. Our aim in discussing therapeutic communities in this way has been to demystify them and to clarify some of the basic concepts in a way that will limit the misuse to which sound concepts may sometimes be put by inexperienced practitioners.

We need now to sample the everyday life of a therapeutic community to ascertain how these concepts may be applied. What provisions are made within these communities which allow a continuing examination of the behaviour, feelings and relationships of all its members? To address these considerations we shall present a typical day from the life of a community and relate it to other events which occur throughout the week, each week. The community described is based upon the community at the Cassel Hospital which was initially established as a therapeutic community by Dr Tom Main, in association with others, after World War II. It is a living organism, so the details of daily organisation may change, but the guiding principles will remain the same.

THE COMMUNITY OF THE CASSEL HOSPITAL

An Introduction to the Background

The Cassel Hospital is a small community housed in a beautiful old Regency building on Ham Common, near Richmond, Surrey. On average there are about 45 patients in residence at any one time, allowing for the overlapping of admissions and discharges. The average length of stay is between six months and a year, although this varies with some perhaps leaving after six months and others staying for about two years. This variation is related to individual need and external considerations, such as employment opportunities, and so on. The hospital admits whole families, single adults and some adolescents without their parents. There is flexibility in the approach to the treatment of any individual or family. For instance, a single adult may be offered regular treatment sessions with his or her family, even when the individual is the only member of the family to be residing at the hospital. Or the parents of an adolescent member of the community may be offered regular sessions of their own as a couple, or membership of a group which meets regularly. Similarly, each member of a family residing on the Families Unit may be offered individual psychotherapy and frequent meetings as a family together.

Much or most of the work in the therapeutic community is undertaken by a small group of nurses, each of whom is identified as the key nurse to a small (8–9) group of patients. Normally there will be an identified second nurse who takes on the responsibilities of the key nurse if she is absent for any reason. There is regular contact between the nurses and the doctors and other psychotherapists each day, as we shall see, together with daily contact between nurses, patients and therapists in regular meetings. The nurses and patients share much of the work that is an essential part of everyday life and spend a great deal of time together.

The nurses cover the hospital twenty-four hours a day throughout the year. The clinical nursing establishment is quite low, perhaps only twelve in number and the system operates in this way:

● One of the nurses will be allocated to night duty and she will start at 6.30 p.m., when she will take a handover from the duty nurse who will leave at 7 p.m. to be 'on call' at home to provide a first line of support for her colleague and in case of emergency.

● The night nurse will join the community to participate in community events, starting with supper at 7 p.m., until 11 p.m., when she will go to bed in the nurses' bedroom. She is effectively 'on call' within the hospital to the community via a night orderly, who will wake her if there is a need.

● The night nurse gets up at 7 a.m. and is again generally available to the community and breakfasts with patients.

● The bulk of the nursing group arrive for a morning handover from the night nurse at 8.45 a.m., and the night nurse remains on duty with a special responsibility to the whole community until 1 p.m.

● At 1 p.m. the 'duty nurse' arrives and is on duty until 7 p.m., after she has handed over to the next night nurse. The system continues to follow this pattern throughout the year, with a minor variation at weekends. The hospital works on the basis of a five-day week from, 9 a.m. to 5 pm. Patients are encouraged to take leave to go home or visit friends at weekends, but there is always a nurse on duty. Each of the members of the clinical nurse group undertakes these duties equally.

As we proceed there are one or two points which should be mentioned here. The notion of a key nurse is a familiar one, as is that of a secondary nurse to the key worker. It is important that there is continuity of care and involvement with one or two people if problems rooted in development are to be tackled. This system of cover allows for this and for a more general continuity of care for each within the community. It would be less burdensome for the nurses, if there was a regular night staff, but there would be inevitable differences of approach which could not be successfully addressed because of the necessary limitations of contact between night and day staff.

Also, there is only one nurse on night duty for a community of over forty people, each of whom may be quite emotionally troubled. How can this work? At the Cassel the patients are regarded as a resource to the community in much the same way that nurses are. Despite the emotional problems that bring people to the hospital as patients they have great strengths and abilities which are valued, respected and nutured during their stay. It is not unusual to find that a group of patients is willing, and able, to organise a rota of support for another who is experiencing considerable difficulty. Of course, this can be abused by some, but such misuse will quickly be identified and confronted by patients and staff together, to the benefit of the patient involved.

Furthermore, the one nurse on night duty goes to bed at 11 p.m. How is this possible? The intention at the Cassel is to provide as close an approximation to everyday life as is possible. People retire to bed in the outside world and this is encouraged in the hospital too. Also, there is a recognition that membership of the community means work, and to work effectively requires sufficient rest. Consequently the nursing task becomes that of nursing the community to bed. The nurse does this by facilitating comfortable social contacts between people, by being interested in and concerned for each member of the community, and by recognising that she is not the answer to everyone's problems. Some things should be left until morning. In this sense she is like the mother who contains her distressed infant by helping him to feel included and wanted and by knowing that tomorrow is another day.

There are occasions when the community spends a disturbed night and there are many reasons why this happens. Sometimes it may be because a particularly disturbed patient has not had sufficient time to have been able to make a good enough relationship with his nurse or the rest of the community, or it may be related to breaks and separations from therapists, nurses and fellow patients because of holidays, leavings and so on. Often it has to do with an anxious nurse being unable to manage her own anxiety well enough to be able to manage the community. Or it may be to do with an unconscious feeling that nurses sometimes have that they should be doing something. When this happens, someone in the community will usually oblige by desperately needing help.

In transactional analysis terms, the rescuer needs a victim. In psychodynamic terms it is a process of projective identification; the nurse evokes anxiety in the patient through her behaviour and the patient responds anxiously with disturbed behaviour which the nurse can manage. Consequently, the nurse is able to feel that she can cope and her anxiety is reduced. This sort of interaction has long been recognised, particularly at the Cassel, and is worked with openly. It happens on all wards in all hospitals, but most often it goes unnoticed and a valuable opportunity for learning, for both the patient and the nurse, is missed.

Daily Events

The community's day begins in the dining room at eight o'clock where the night nurse and patients breakfast together. This meal is prepared by the hospital's catering staff, but staples, such as bread and cereals are bought from a budget which is managed by one of the patients. Some of the day nurses might arrive early to have a cup of tea in the relaxed atmosphere before the round of meetings and other activities begin. Some of the mothers with young children will breakfast on the Families Unit, but this is a personal choice, as is attendance at breakfast at all, except for the nurse. This is in recognition of the needs of small children for clear boundaries; small children need to be able to identify with one or two constant figures and for some involvement with twenty or more people, particularly at the beginning of the day when they are negotiating the move from the inner world of sleep to external reality, can be unnecessarily problematic and unsettling. There is no requirement that patients should attend breakfast, but there is an interest in whether they do or not, which may form the basis of useful enquiry. If we remember the importance of the early feeding relationship (see chapter 1) then we shall begin to understand why mealtimes should be considered important.

Whilst the nurses are holding their handover meeting the patients will be engaged in the usual sort of things that people do when preparing for the day; washing and dressing, making beds, getting the children off to school, or the wage-earner out to work. When families are admitted there is an acknowledgement that employment has to be protected, bills have to be paid and the rent or mortgage paid. Consequently there is a reasonable amount of flexibility which allows continuity of employment whilst offering various forms of treatment at times that the wage-earner can manage. For example, the Families Unit will hold at least one meeting in the evening each week so that those who work outside the community can attend.

Work Groups

At 9 o'clock perhaps later for the Families Unit, in recognition of the need for a breather after the morning rush to get children and workers off, nurses will join with their own groups of patients to clean and tidy those parts of the building that are used by patients. Any areas which are used exclusively by staff will be cleaned by domestic staff.

Each of the units has a cleaning budget which is managed by a patient who is responsible for buying equipment (e.g. brushes and mops) and items such as bleach, cleaning fluids, toilet rolls and so on, whilst also balancing the budget.

Patients and nurses together roll up their sleeves and get on with the job of cleaning each area. Often one or more patients will fail to attend to share in these tasks and sometimes this will be because other commitments prevent them from doing so. For example, one may stay in bed regularly, another might have a psychotherapy session at this time. If this is the case then each circumstance will be investigated by staff and patients together. It is important to discover why the therapist concerned is offering sessions at a time when he knows that his patient is required to help with the cleaning and why the patient has not negotiated another time, or why one patient feels he can stay in bed and let the others do the work. It is also important that the others in his cleaning group have the chance to give voice to how they feel about it. For example, the other patients may feel that the everyday tasks they undertake are not valued, with the consequence that they feel denigrated; or they may feel that there is a covert statement that the 'real' treatment is psychotherapy and that the therapeutic community is regarded by the therapist as merely custodial care.

It is important to be able to pick the bones out of these conflicts. It may be that there simply was no other time possible for the session, but then the cleaning group should have been told of this. In this case it opens up the possibility that the denigration felt by the patient group may have had more to do with experiences which belong within the family of origin than to the current setting. If this is the case, then something which influences the quality of relationships between individual patients and others, and which hitherto had been concealed, is now available for work in a situation that allows rights and wrongs to be debated. If the therapist had not negotiated with the cleaning group, then there is room for this small wrong to be acknowledged, which in turn allows patients to experience what may be a difference between the way the current situation is handled and the way it was dealt with in the family of origin. Through these opportunities to recognise and resolve areas of conflict it becomes possible to work through difficulties which belong to disturbances in the emotional development of the individual.

Unit Meetings

These are held daily from Monday to Friday at about 9.30 a.m. immediately after the work groups. Everyone is expected to attend, including the doctors, if their other duties permit. The events of the last twenty-four hours will be openly discussed, including any disturbances, continuing lack of involvement on the part of any patient and other, more positive occurrences such as the success of an individual in overcoming a particular problem for the first time, or an enjoyable outing. Whilst the community will face most problematic situations as they arise at the time they occur and continue to work with them outside of the unit meetings, these meetings will also pay attention to ongoing difficulties and all involved in them will be encouraged to express their views and feelings openly. In this way the hard work of facing conflicts and of confronting difficulties is supported by all of the members of the unit together.

Staff Meetings

These follow on from the unit meetings at 10 o'clock (again it will probably be later for the Families Unit, but all meetings have a set time. See chapter 10, the 'Time boundary'). All of the nurses, doctors, social workers and therapists will attend these meetings. It is a chance for all concerned with the treatment of the patients to share information about patients individually and to form a more clear picture of the work that is being undertaken with each. It is a chance to clarify ideas and to receive helpful suggestions on the management of individuals and of groups. It is also an opportunity to voice differences of opinion, of style and of personality with colleagues, with the help of the staff group to understand how they arise and how they might be related to the patients (Main, 1957).

Whilst the staff are meeting, the patient group will be engaged in a variety of activities. Some will be on their way to part-time work or to study, others will be chatting over a hot drink, some will be playing with the children, tidying their own rooms, or shopping. There is no artificial limit imposed upon the things that patients might do, but all that they do will become the focus of thoughtful consideration.

The staff meeting will last until 10.45 a.m., when the staff will go off to have coffee together or with the patients. From 11 o'clock the patients will either have free time, or be involved in psychotherapy sessions, family therapy, community or other group meetings.

Group Meetings

The nurses will run a number of different group meetings throughout the week; some will focus on the interpersonal relationships between members of the same work group (the patients who relate to each key nurse make up the work groups), others may offer the opportunity to practise interview techniques, or the chance to work on specific fears and anxieties. Many will involve leisure activities, such as music or drama, painting, gardening, and so on. There is usually someone involved in decorating one or another of the patients' bedrooms. The main aim of the leisure groups will be to enjoy a pleasurable activity in the company of others, but the same attitude of interested concern and open enquiry that applies in other spheres will be present here. It matters that someone is not able to enjoy himself, or can't get herself to the music group that she is so keen on. It matters that one or another has been let down by a partner in the duet that was being planned as a suprise for someone's birthday celebration, and in paying attention to these issues it is possible to reveal and work with major difficulties in a patient's life.

Community Meetings

All of the patients who make up the community and those staff members who are directly involved with the patients attend these meetings which are held at least once each week. There is some variation in the frequency of these meetings. For many months or even years they will be held once weekly, then it may seem more proper to hold them more often, perhaps twice or three times each week. It is probably best to hold them several times a week as there are many points of contact between the members of each of the units which make up the community, and the community meeting is the only time when the whole community can get together to deal with community issues. Their purpose is to deal with community concerns, for example, the adolescent patients might have been playing records too loud and too late for the taste of the parents on the Families Unit. Teenagers need to let off steam and to have fun, but parents need to get some sleep and to ensure that their children are not woken throughout the night. These conflicting needs can be faced in the community meetings and dealt with openly with the support of the other, less biased patients.

Mealtimes

The mid-day meal is prepared by kitchen staff, who will also wash up for the staff, whilst there is a rota of patients to wash their crockery and so on. Nurses will often share in the washing-up with patients but this is limited by the time available as the nurses have a nursing handover meeting immediately after lunch. Nurses and patients will dine together. Again it is a relaxed social event during an intensive day. The inherent therapeutic value of mealtimes should not be underestimated; it is the quality of the feeding relationship that the baby has with his mother, as well as the gratifying of his hunger, that enables him to feel contained or held. In addition, it is helpful to see who sits with whom, who is avoided and perhaps why – unsavoury eating habits can be very off-putting! – who is regularly absent, who is greedy, who doesn't eat and who eats very little. These are all things which can help us to understand our patients and their difficulties better, and which may be clues to underlying problems of great magnitude.

The evening meal will be prepared by patients, again on a rota basis, and each week's menu will be planned within budget limits with the catering officer. It is possible to negotiate spending less on one or two meals in order to be able to spend more on another meal for a special occasion. Nurses will help in the preparation of these meals and again, this is an opportunity to identify and begin to work with a range of issues which will surface over time when attention is paid to the ordinary in everyday life.

The Afternoon and Evening

During the afternoon some patients will have part-time work. This is encouraged so that difficulties with work and with employers can be recognised and dealt with during an individual's stay in the community. Some will have sessions with their psychotherapists and others will go out with the children for the afternoon. Some parents will have to collect their children from school and several people will be preparing the evening meal in the patients' kitchen.

In the evening people are free to do what they wish, but there is an expectation that they will tell the nurse where they will be if they are leaving the building. Some go to the pub, some to the cinema or to friends, others stay in to read, or chat or watch television. Whatever anyone does will remain the focus of attention. Perhaps one patient drinks too much, or another goes out every evening. Could these be examples of something being avoided within the individual and the community?

The Cassel Hospital is one type of community and there are many others, but it offers a very clear picture of the properties of a therapeutic community in action and a good model to follow. One final point: therapeutic communities are living organisms and they should be affected by and responsive to the people involved with them. There is no perfect prototype which should blindly be established or rigidly adhered to. To do so would be to run counter to the essence of what is therapeutic in them. We could do worse than measure our wards and communities against the guidelines for productive management established in the last chapter and discussed earlier in this. If something doesn't work, then we should talk about it openly, staff and patients together, to find out why. There is great potential for growth inherent in all groups if we have the courage and wisdom to face and overcome our own anxieties and avail ourselves of their rich splendour.

Working with groups does take courage, which is why the next brief chapter on beginning in groups is offered before this book is concluded.

References

Clark D H (1965) The therapeutic community–concept, practice and future. *British Journal of Psychiatry*, **111**: 947–954.

Main T F (1946) The hospital as a therapeutic institution. *Bulletin of the Menninger Clinic*, **10 (3)**: 66–70.

Main T F (1957) The ailment. *British Journal of Medical Psychology*, **30**: 29–45.

Main T F (1983) The concept of the therapeutic community: variations and vicissitudes. In: *The Evolution of Group Analysis*, ed Malcom Pines. London: Routledge and Kegan Paul.

Menzies Lyth I (1988) The development of the self in children in institutions. In: *The Dynamics of the Social: Selected Essays*. London: Free Association Books.

Rapoport R (1960) *Community as Doctor* London: Tavistock Press.

17

Beginning to Work

in Groups

It has been the intention throughout this book to give a sound introduction to the practice of group work so that those who are experienced and those who are beginning may develop their knowledge and understanding of the life of groups and the dynamics which underpin all that happens in them. Considerable attention has been given to the importance of the early emotional development of the individual and its relevance to the quality of relationships established throughout his life. This has been done in order to establish how problems evolve and why treatment in groups is effective.

We have acknowledged that groups are a part of everyday life, that everyone belongs to many, and that the same processes that govern treatment groups are present in all sorts of situations in which people gather together. This has made us aware that the wards of hospitals are groups, as are hostels, children's homes, homes for the elderly, schools, staff teams and so on, and consequently that a knowledge of what happens in groups and why is of great value to all who work in these situations, whether they are part of the management structure or the clinical team.

Even though we have all belonged to groups throughout our lives, many of us will experience a great deal of anxiety when beginning to work with groups with the intention of trying to understand processes and phenomena, and to use this understanding productively to the benefit of our clients and our colleagues. We should not suppress these anxieties. We should recognise them and use them to aid our understanding of ourselves and the circumstances of the group. When we cannot work out the meanings for ourselves we should seek the support of others who may be able to help us recognise what we cannot see on our own. Groups are not just useful for treatment, seminar groups are invaluable settings for teaching too.

The first thing to remember about beginning in groups is that the beginning was many years ago for all of us. We have already begun. This reassuring thought should not be misapplied. It is essential that we each work at our own level of competence. We can recognise this if we are able honestly to appraise our skills and abilities without pretension or unhelpful modesty. Those who are wise would not suppose that a basic professional training is sufficient to equip us to undertake all of the duties or treatments that are provided by members of our profession. Further training at a deeper level is usually necessary. Those who are sensible would be able to recognise their own limitations and would seek the support and advice of more experienced colleagues or further training before working at a more advanced level.

It would be presumptuous to prescribe the limits for levels of training; natural abilities and personal suitability as well as considerations to do with sensitivity and maturity have to be taken into account, as does the availability of training and supervision. But we might recommend some basic guidelines, a rule of thumb against which to measure the soundness of our aspirations and intentions.

SOME GUIDELINES

Anyone can work with groups whose purpose is to clarify interpersonal relationships, as long as we bear in mind that everyone is entitled to an opinion and has the right to express it, so long as it is done with respect, sensitivity and a quality of understanding which recognises that some comments can be hurtful. Such comments can be counterproductive and may only serve to alienate. It is helpful to remember the maxim 'Do unto others as you would be done by.' One should also keep to the task. When dealing with relationship issues it is not acceptable to offer psychological explanations of why a member of the group behaves in a certain way. It is much more helpful to acknowledge the feeling that another evokes in oneself through his attitudes or behaviour, or to speak of the echoes that sound within and which relate to experiences that are current for the group. For example:

● 'When you treat us as if we didn't matter, I find it saddening and frustrating, it makes me not want to have anything to do with you at the same time as feeling that you need someone.'

Or:

● 'What you did last night reminded me of when Joan was so hostile last week. Can you remember what that was like for you, Joan?'

If we wish to work in a more interpretive way, then it is advisable to seek further training. There are a number of very sound introductory courses offering experience through membership of a group and through teaching the basics of group work. This sort of course lasts for about a year of weekly groups, seminars and lectures. Here one should remember that it is an introduction which enables one to work at some depth but that more advanced work would require more advanced training. Such training will usually require that prospective students have undertaken an introductory course and will last for between two and four years. It is evident then that it would be foolhardy to suppose that it is possible to know all there is to know about groups from short training courses, weekend workshops and so on.

However, for most of us who need only to have a good background knowledge of groups so that we might fulfil other aspects of our professional roles more effectively (for example, managing a ward or a unit, residential homes, etc.) a one-year introductory course will normally suffice.

COMMON ANXIETIES

The first thing to remember is that the conductor is prey to the same sort of anxieties that the members of the group will face. These have been outlined in chapter 6, Group Development. If he has undertaken some further training, such as a one-year course (which offers membership of a group for the year) then he will have had the opportunity to recognise some of these within himself and to work through them in the group. Consequently, he will be better able to manage his own inevitable anxiety and to help the members of the group he is running with theirs. Some specific anxieties which have been acknowledged by those about to start work with groups for the first time have been included here so that we might benefit from the group processes of *universality* and *sharing* (see chapter 8, Therapeutic Properties of Groups).

The comments which follow are not placed in any order of priority – anxieties which were at the top of the list for some came further down in the list for others. The first three groups are of anxieties that were expressed by all those who were asked to participate in the exercise. Those which follow were offered by some but not all.

1. 'I don't know if I can do it, what if I fail to put it all together?'
   'Can I deliver?'

These anxieties are obviously to do with a professional ability to put theory into practice and also have to do with the universal concern faced by every member of the group about being able to cope in the group.

2. 'What if I make a fool of myself?'
   'What if I do something foolish?'
   'I keep thinking that I might be caught out.'

This is a perennial problem for all who take part in groups and has to do with how one is going to be received by the rest of the members. It is related to the conflict between Basic Trust v. Basic Mistrust described in chapter 6, and to elements within the inner world of the individual. Each of us has aspects which we may be vaguely aware of but which we conceal from ourselves as well as from others. This worry illustrates how the group experience resonates with the inner world and makes concealed material potentially more available. It indicates discomfort about pretending to be something we are not. In other words, most of us have aspects which we have failed to integrate with the personality that we present to the world, or which have been only partially assimilated, so that the personality we present cannot be the total of the sum of the person each of us is. Consequently we may feel that we have not taken into account, or openly acknowledged, something that we should have. Hence there is concern about being caught out or doing something foolish.

One should also consider that, whilst the group and the conductor may effectively deal with these issues later in the life of the group, it would be inappropriate to deal with them here. In this case it would be relevant to acknowledge the anxiety, but to decline to examine it in detail until the members have completed the more appropriate task of finding out about the group's trustworthiness.

3. 'I worry about being presented material that I couldn't make use of . . . '
   'What if someone brings something I can't handle?'

Obviously these are worries which every professional must face, but it is helpful to remember that the group is as nervous about these things as the conductor and it is very unlikely that profoundly difficult material will be brought at the beginning of the group. Furthermore, it is not the conductor's responsibility to handle all the material himself, his task is to look at how the group handles it and to offer his observations. Also it is not appropriate for the group to deal with profoundly difficult or personal issues at the very beginning. If they are brought, then it is quite possibly a response to, and a way of avoiding, early anxieties to do with trust. In this case the conductor can handle it simply by recognising the inappropriateness and the anxiety.

If such profound problems arise later in the life of the group, then it is likely that both the group and the conductor will have grown sufficiently to be able to manage them. Whether this is the case or not the conductor would be wise to be a member of a supervision group which will be able to offer support and advice.

4. 'What if others, I mean staff . . . colleagues, make fun of the group and through the group make fun of me?'

This is a thorny problem. If the conductor has negotiated with his colleagues well enough (see chapter 9, The Role of the Conductor, and chapter 10, Settings) then the problem should not arise. However, one must recognise that it can do, even with the best negotiated of settlements. Once again this is where one's own training and the support of a supervision group are invaluable, as they help one to withstand the destructive attacks which may quite unconsciously be perpetrated in order to maintain the status quo of the institution. This is a useful pointer; when working with groups it is essential to remember the place of the group in the institution and to bear in mind the unconscious resistances that there are to change and why (see chapter 14, Naturally Occurring Groups, and chapter 15, Productive Management). It is the conductor's responsibility to work with these higher-order systems and to respect their real concerns, whilst protecting the integrity of his group.

5. 'What if I don't understand what's going on?'
   'What if I miss something?'

One of the marvellous qualities of groups is that an issue will be worked and reworked throughout the life of the group at a deeper level each time, until it has been fully understood or worked through. Inevitably some things are missed, but the group will keep coming back to them until they are resolved, at least in part. Again, it is not just the conductor's responsibility, the group has some responsibility too and, as we have learned (chapter 8, Therapeutic Properties of groups), much that helps people to change is undertaken between group members.

It would be possible to continue with this list for a good while longer, but it would be foolish to try to address every worry that a new group conductor might face. The aim is much less daunting – it is to recognise that it is usual for most people to be nervous about starting out and to acknowledge two further points.

The first is that many of the anxieties that the new conductor will face are experienced by all group members and have been described and discussed throughout this book. Consequently, the new conductor will find much that will help him to understand his own anxieties if he reads each chapter with himself as well as his patients in mind.

The second is related to the first and it echoes with Foulkes' (1975) definition of group-analytic psychotherapy as 'a form of pschotherapy by the group, of the group, including its conductor.' Or, as one of the new group conductors, who took part in this survey put it:

● 'When I looked at my list of anxieties, I realised the worries that I had expressed were not just to do with how I might handle the group, they also were related to how I get on with other people anyway.'

Reference

Foulkes S H (1975) *Group Analytic Psychotherapy: Method and Principles*. London: Gordon and Breach.

Index

Alexander, F. 95, 99
alienation 93
altruism 93–4, 98
ambivalence, age of, 8–9, 69
amniotic fluid 3
Anthony, E.J. 65, 77, 80,88, 90, 91
assessment of patients for groups 131–45
    antipathy 133–4
    examples of notes 135–9
    interviews 133–4
    process 132–3
authority pyramid 207
Autonomy v. Shame and Doubt 69

baby, newly-born babies
    anxiety 5–7
    bladder control 8
    bowel control 8
    development 9–12
        theories 9–12
    effect on adult life 6–7
    feeding 8
    feelings 4–5
    first months of life 3–5
    frustration 5–7
    introjection process 41
    mother's role 5–7
    observations 5–8
    relationship with mother and guilt 53–4
    relationships 8–9
    rivalry and cooperation 9–12
    'rudimentary ego' 3–5
baby battering 21
bad practices 167–71
Basic Assumption 66, 68, 69, 71, 73, 74, 113, 169
Basic Mistrust 81, 219
Basic Trust 81, 219
Bettelheim, Bruno 94, 95
Bion, W.R. 12, 69, 75, 91, 119, 129, 132, 145
Bowlby, J 185, 187

Carkhuff, R.R. 90
Cassel Hospital 209–15
    community meetings 214
    daily events 211–15
    Family Unit 209, 211
    group meetings 213–14
    mealtimes 214–15
    nursing in 209
    staff meetings 213

    system 209–11
    unit meetings 213
    work groups 212
character traits 52–3
chain phenomena 79
child and mother 3–12
Clarke, D.H. 202, 206, 215
communalisation 202, 206
community meeting 180–2
    nurses' role in 181–2
Concept of Development Lines 9
conductor
    as administrator 101–09
        boundaries 103–05
        and drugs 105–06
        selection of groups 102
        setting of groups 102–03
        register 106
    analysis attitudes 113–14
    assessment of patients 132–3
    bad practices 167–71
    common anxieties 219–21
    communication in group 157–63
    cultural setting 120
    definition 101
    and emerging themes 149
    and ethnic groupings 120
    further training 219
    group sessions 152–7
    group stages 147–8
    interviews with patients 133–45
    institutional setting 121–2
    narrower setting 128
    and patients' notes 139
    paying attention 139–45
        interviews, examples of 140–4
    process material 148–9
    register 106–08
    referral 132
    role of 101–14
    the seminar 171–4
    as therapist 101, 108–14
        analysis attitudes 113
        conducting interviews 108–09
        following 110–12
        interpreting 112–13
        modelling 110
    unhelpful practices 167–71
    and see bad practices